THE GLOBAL UNIVERSITY

HISTORICAL STUDIES IN EDUCATION

Edited by William J. Reese and John L. Rury

William J. Reese, Carl F. Kaestle WARF Professor of Educational Policy Studies and History, the University of Wisconsin-Madison

John L. Rury, Professor of Education and (by courtesy) History, the University of Kansas

This series features new scholarship on the historical development of education, defined broadly, in the United States and elsewhere. Interdisciplinary in orientation and comprehensive in scope, it spans methodological boundaries and interpretive traditions. Imaginative and thoughtful history can contribute to the global conversation about educational change. Inspired history lends itself to continued hope for reform, and to realizing the potential for progress in all educational experiences.

Published by Palgrave Macmillan:

Democracy and Schooling in California: The Legacy of Helen Heffernan and Corinne Seeds
By Kathleen Weiler

The Global University: Past, Present, and Future Perspectives
Edited by Adam R. Nelson and Ian P. Wei

THE GLOBAL UNIVERSITY

Past, Present, and Future Perspectives

Edited by

Adam R. Nelson and Ian P. Wei

palgrave
macmillan

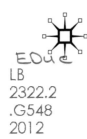

EDu e
LB
2322.2
.G548
2012

First published in 2012 by
PALGRAVE MACMILLAN®
in the United States—a division of St. Martin's Press LLC,
175 Fifth Avenue, New York, NY 10010.

Where this book is distributed in the UK, Europe and the rest of the world,
this is by Palgrave Macmillan, a division of Macmillan Publishers Limited,
registered in England, company number 785998, of Houndmills,
Basingstoke, Hampshire RG21 6XS.

Palgrave Macmillan is the global academic imprint of the above companies
and has companies and representatives throughout the world.

Palgrave® and Macmillan® are registered trademarks in the United States,
the United Kingdom, Europe and other countries.

ISBN: 978–0–230–39245–8

Library of Congress Cataloging-in-Publication Data

The global university : past, present, and future perspectives /
edited by Adam R. Nelson and Ian P. Wei.
    p. cm.—(Historical studies in education)
    ISBN 978–0–230–39245–8
    1. Education, Higher—Cross-cultural studies. 2. Universities and
colleges—Cross-cultural studies. 3. Education and globalization—
Cross-cultural studies. 4. Higher education and state—Cross-cultural
studies. 5. Education—Aims and objectives—Cross-cultural studies.
I. Nelson, Adam R. II. Wei, Ian P.

LB2322.2.G548 2012
378—dc23   2011040817

A catalogue record of the book is available from the British Library.

Design by Newgen Imaging Systems (P) Ltd., Chennai, India.

First edition: April 2012

10 9 8 7 6 5 4 3 2 1

Printed in the United States of America.

CONTENTS

Part III   Academic Roles and the Purposes of Universities

Part IV   Shifting Patterns of Graduate and Undergraduate Education

Part V   Universities and External Funding

Figures and Tables

Figures

Tables

FOREWORD

There can be little doubt that the age of the global university is upon us. As the contributors to this volume make clear, however, there is little consensus on what exactly the term may mean. In the pages that follow Adam Nelson's expansive introduction, they explore a wide range of issues in the development of universities around the world in addressing the question. Ultimately, it appears, the global university can take many forms as it responds to an array of social, economic, and political forces that stem from particular historical contexts. The chapters in this book demonstrate the salience of past circumstances by examining the development of higher education in a variety of settings.

As Professor Nelson notes, a great deal has been written about globalization in higher education in recent years. Much of this literature has been sociological or economic in orientation, focusing on isomorphic or market forces that appear to compel convergence in university policies, curricula, governance structures, and institutional goals. The chapters in this book acknowledge these trends but also point to the great variety that exists in institutional forms from one part of the world to another. Universities exist in specific places and are inevitably shaped by local traditions, political conflicts, resource limitations, and competitive pressures. Implicitly and explicitly, these chapters collectively challenge the idea that there is a single path for higher education in an age of global social and economic development. To a large extent this perspective flows from a historical interpretive vantage point.

In the course of this discussion, the book addresses a host of issues germane to universities today. One is the growing role of the state in fostering—or limiting—the development of institutions. Another is the neoliberal policy regime that appears ascendant in policy formation throughout much of the West. Universities in less developed countries clearly face a different set of issues than their counterparts in North America and Europe. Institutions in so-called emergent nations, especially on the Pacific Rim, may face different challenges.

The role of research and its support is widely variable, as are the conditions of faculty life, and by extension curricular development and teaching. Student goals and dispositions differ as well. Reviewing the great variety of perspectives on these questions across different parts of the world, with contributions from a truly global group of contributors, is a useful corrective to much of the extant literature on the global university, which has failed to capture the richness of this diversity.

With these contributions in view, we are pleased to include this volume in the series, *Historical Studies in Education*. Our hope is that other researchers will view this collection as a starting point for yet more investigation of the historical circumstances of higher education in particular places around the world. In the end, such work will be essential to understanding just what the "global university" represents as an institutional form and as a historic development.

WILLIAM J. REESE
AND
JOHN L. RURY

Acknowledgments

This volume would not have been possible without the generous help of several organizations, starting with the Worldwide Universities Network (WUN), a consortium of leading research universities around the world that have come together to facilitate cross-national research and teaching. WUN is the host of the "Ideas and Universities" Project out of which this volume grew. Established in 2006, the Ideas and Universities project brings together higher-education scholars and institutional leaders from the United States, United Kingdom, China, Australia, Norway, Canada, and other countries to discuss the roles that universities have played—and continue to play—in a global knowledge society. The aim of the project is to examine what it means to be a "world-class" university in the twenty-first century and to inform contemporary policy debates about the future of higher education.

Through conferences and virtual seminars, the project explores the ways in which ideas—broadly construed—have found expression in universities since the development of the earliest Western universities in the late twelfth century. The project considers ideas about how people learn, generate new theories, and organize knowledge into subjects and disciplines; it asks how the work of academics (or intellectuals) has changed over time and what relationship academics have, or should have, with the societies in which they live. The project also examines the governance of universities (their constitutional structures and decision-making processes), the internal organization of universities (departments, schools, faculties, etc.), and the curricula and pedagogies of universities, as well as the ever-changing relationship between teaching and research.

Since its establishment a half decade ago, the Ideas and Universities Project has organized four international conferences. The first conference, in April 2007, took place at Zhejiang University in Hangzhou, China; the second, in November 2007, was hosted by the University of Bristol in London; the third, in early February 2010, took place at the University of Wisconsin-Madison; the fourth, in November 2011, was held at the Hong Kong Institute of Education. By examining universities across periods and cultures, these events have sought a shared language (though not a shared theoretical framework) in which to discuss the purposes and values of universities. Indeed, the comparative and historical approach of the Ideas and Universities Project—the chance to study universities across Europe, North America, Australia, Africa, and Asia—has attracted worldwide attention, not only from students and scholars but also from university leaders who are looking for a greater range of possibilities to inform strategic planning.

This volume owes much to these ongoing discussions and to the institutions that made them possible. We would like to express our thanks for the support of the University of Bristol, the University of Illinois in Urbana-Champaign, and the University of Wisconsin-Madison's Division of International Studies and Center for Global Studies, as well as the Division's program in Global Studies in Higher Education. We would also like to thank the staff of the Department of Educational Policy Studies at the University of Wisconsin-Madison, which hosted the conference in which the chapters in this volume were initially presented. In addition, we would like to thank the faculty at the University of Wisconsin-Madison who helped with the conference, offering comments on the chapters and helping in myriad other ways. Heartfelt thanks go to Michael Apple, Mark Johnson, Venkat Mani, Kris Olds, Amy Stambach, and Jeremi Suri. We would also like to thank Isobel Howe, formerly at the University of Bristol, who served for many years as the ace administrator of the Ideas and Universities Project.

Finally, we would like to thank our friends at Palgrave Macmillan, including our series editors, William J. Reese and John L. Rury, and our book editors, Burke Gerstenschlager and Kaylan Connally, who managed all aspects of the publication process with skill and grace.

Introduction

Adam R. Nelson

Few subjects in the study of international higher education have attracted more attention in recent years than the idea of "the global university." Dozens of books and hundreds of scholarly articles have appeared on this subject, generating vigorous debate in policy circles as well as the popular media around the world. Observers ask: how are the forces of globalization reshaping the modern university—its purposes, priorities, and procedures? What exactly is a "global" university? What distinguishes its approach to teaching, to research, to knowledge? Whose interests does it serve, and how? Too often, a global, or world-class, university is defined simply as one that receives high marks in international rankings or league tables. But what do such rankings measure? Do they reveal anything essential about the core mission, or values, of the university, or do they merely construct, then reify, a marketable category: The Global University? This volume seeks to examine the substance of this idea, demonstrating not only how the category of "the global university" developed over time but also how it has come to influence higher education worldwide. According to most current ranking criteria, a world-class university is one that pursues readily quantifiable (and commercializable) research and emphasizes postgraduate and professional over undergraduate education, often through international partnerships and with the help of internationally mobile students and scholars. Underlying both the pursuit of research and the focus on postgraduate education is the presumption that a world-class university will contribute to economic development in an ever-more-competitive knowledge society. Through patents and other forms of intellectual property, as well as collaborations with business and industry, the new global university is assumed to promote a spirit of entrepreneurialism, advance private enterprise, and foster economic growth. In various ways, the global university resembles a multinational corporation. The question is, in what ways, if any, does it—or should it—differ?

The importance of this question has become clear in recent years. As the literature on globalization and higher education has proliferated, the links between universities and businesses—or business practices—have been subjected to close analysis. Much of this analysis came into focus in the late 1990s in Sheila Slaughter and Larry Leslie's volume *Academic Capitalism: Politics, Policies, and the Entrepreneurial University* (1999). A comparative study of academic labor in the United States, United Kingdom, Canada, and Australia, this influential book described the rapid corporatization of higher education in the late twentieth century. A year later, Simon Marginson's related work, *The Enterprise University: Power, Governance, and Reinvention in Australia* (2000), traced the dramatic evolution of the modern university "from academy to global business." Marginson noted, among other changes, the increasing emphasis on applied science leading to intellectual property, an emphasis that had come to dominate universities' strategic decision making. The next year, two more volumes added to the discussion: Burton Clark's work, *Creating Entrepreneurial Universities: Organizational Pathways of Transformation* (2001), which sought to reconcile the press toward entrepreneurialism with the university's "traditional" commitment to "the common good," and Gerard Delanty's *Challenging Knowledge: The University in the Knowledge Society* (2001), a sweeping intellectual history of university-based knowledge production. Delanty explored not only the functional appropriation of higher education by the modern capitalist state but also the co-optation of academic critique within the institutional framework of the (postmodern) university. Building on the work of Marilyn Strathern in *Audit Cultures: Anthropological Studies in Accountability, Ethics, and the Academy* (2000), Delanty showed how the rise of an accountability-oriented "new managerialism" in higher education not only compromised academic freedom but also left the very idea of the autonomous university "in ruins"—a reference to *The University in Ruins* (1996) by the late critical theorist Bill Readings.

These works set the stage for continued debate about "the global university." By the beginning of the new millennium, most scholars agreed that both the institutional and intellectual frameworks of higher education were changing—perhaps fundamentally. The modern university, it seemed, was indeed becoming more like a business. In *Universities and Globalization: Private Linkages, Public Trust* (2003), for example, Gilles Breton and Michel Lambert asked a series of key questions about the global economic forces behind the marketization of universities and the commercialization of knowledge. Among other policies, they stressed the General Agreement on Trade in Services (GATS), promulgated in 1995 by the World Trade Organization, which designated education as a "commodity" tradable on the global market, a designation with significant implications for universities in both developed and developing countries. Roberta Bassett took up this subject in *The WTO and the University: Globalization, GATS, and American Higher Education* (2006), and Jane Knight gave her own take on the issue in *Higher Education Crossing Borders: A Guide to the Implications of the General Agreement on Trade in Services (GATS) for Cross-Border Education* (2006), a discussion expanded in *Higher Education in Turmoil: The Changing World of Internationalization* (2008). Virtually everywhere, Bassett and Knight noted, higher education was being construed as a "private good," a consumption item bought and sold for personal benefit (and tallied on nations' balance sheets). At the same time, the "market" for higher education was changing, with for-profit and online universities competing with established institutions for students—themselves redefined as sources of profit. No longer reserved for an elite few, universities in the twenty-first century were becoming "knowledge spaces" (some called them "knowledge factories") for millions of aspiring youth. As globalization reframed traditional conceptions of the university, the literature on this subject began to evolve.

Several themes emerged. The first, derived from Slaughter and Leslie's analysis, concerned the changing nature of academic labor. A second, related theme concerned the international political economy of higher education, particularly the "privatization" of the university. The year 2004 seemed to bring the issues of privatization and marketization to a head. That year, former Harvard president Derek Bok published his book, *Universities in the Marketplace: The Commercialization of Higher Education* (2004), while historian Roger Geiger published *Knowledge and Money: Research Universities and the Paradox of the Marketplace* (2004). Both volumes investigated the new strategies that American universities were adopting to "make research pay." Both noted that, as early as 1980, the US Congress had passed the Bayh-Dole Act, which allowed universities to keep profits from patents on research conducted with public funds, and both observed that, over time, universities had established closer ties with industry. According to Bok, however, "closer ties between university science and industry create all sorts of risks for compromising the openness, objectivity, and independence of academic research."

Stories about businesses funding projects and then refusing to share discoveries (or even suppressing unfavorable results) spread as university-industry partnerships grew in size and scope. As Luc Weber, former rector of the University of Geneva, and James Duderstadt, former president of the University of Michigan, noted in *Reinventing the Research University* (2004), the quest for commercializable knowledge likely created as many problems as it solved. Given the costs of research—costs that mounted every year—many universities felt they had to rely on private support, but they found themselves struggling to defend core academic values. Weber and Duderstadt described the emerging "global" university as an entrepreneurial institution committed to both public and private ends; the challenge, they confessed, was finding a way to balance these often competing aims.

The literature on "privatization" is not, of course, limited to institutions that might consider themselves global; nonetheless, virtually everyone agrees that so-called global universities are likely to embrace—perhaps must embrace, in some way—the pursuit of private resources. This pursuit has attracted considerable attention among scholars. For example, in *Privatization and Public Universities* (2006), Douglas Priest and Edward St. John laid out the strategies that universities, mainly in the United States, have adopted to cope with declining public support. They noted universities' increasing pursuit of patents and royalties; their adoption of so-called incentive-based budgeting; their reliance on revenue-generating auxiliary functions, notably e-learning; their cultivation of corporate and philanthropic donors; their use of tuition and student-loan strategies that shift costs onto parents; their push for professional schools to create high-fee nondegree programs; their habit of describing students as "consumers" (or "clients"); and so on. This analysis continued the next year in Roger Geiger, Carol Colbeck, Roger Williams, and Christian Anderson's work, *The Future of the American Public Research University* (2007), with essays by Donald Heller (whose work also appeared in the volume by Priest and St. John) and D. Bruce Johnstone, who situated the lessons of public-university finance in a global context. With governments in Europe—especially in the United Kingdom—shifting costs to the private sector even as governments in Asia, especially in China, pursued historic increases in state higher-education spending, the outlook for "public" higher education, at least in the West, looked bleak. Philip Altbach and Jorge Balán echoed this view in *World-Class Worldwide: Transforming Research Universities in Asia and Latin America* (2007), which documented the strategies that China, Korea, India, Mexico, Argentina, Chile, and Brazil were using to build globally competitive research universities. In every case, they found, both public and private investment was required to create world-class institutions.

The question of public versus private support for higher education had likewise surfaced in *Creating Knowledge, Strengthening Nations: The Changing Role of Higher Education* (2005), edited by Glen Jones, Patricia McCarney, and Michael Skolnik. With an opening section on the local and regional geographies of the "knowledge economy"— including McCarney's chapter on the close relationship between cities, universities, and commerce—this volume stressed the interconnectedness of knowledge institutions and economic growth in modern states. For most of the twentieth century, the contributors observed, the link between research and prosperity had bolstered the case for increasing public spending on higher education, but in the twenty-first century (despite an emphasis on "the needs of the knowledge economy") the public share of higher-education spending is rapidly declining in many developed countries. While some heralded this shift toward "entrepreneurialism," others worried that, as public funds gave way to private investment, values such as free inquiry and equal access might suffer. This concern directly informed Marek Kwiek's work, *The University and the State: A Study into Global Transformations* (2006), which offered a sophisticated historical interpretation of the "public mission" of the European university. Describing globalization as "the fundamental factor behind the retreat of the welfare state," Kwiek weighed the demise of the historic pact between the university and the state against the prospect of a new civic role for European universities within a framework of international coordination and the pursuit of a ("postnational") European Higher-Education Area. The Bologna Process, launched in 1999 with 29 participating countries (now 47), has attracted worldwide attention for its efforts to promote regional integration in European higher education. This emphasis on regional oversight and the reorientation of the university's "public mission" in response to neoliberal privatization has become a prominent theme in the literature on global higher education.

Kwiek's emphasis on regionalization also pointed to another emerging theme in the literature, namely, the changing relationship between the university and citizenship in a "global" era. Throughout its modern history, the university has played a pivotal role in the construction of national citizens and the promotion of the idea of national service. Not only the undergraduate curriculum, with its emphasis on a national language as well as a national heritage, but also the certification functions of the university (e.g., in the faculties of law, medicine, and theology) have signaled the connections between higher education, citizenship, and service to the state. In a European context, universities often prepared students for national civil-service examinations. The university, largely through the development of the humanities and social sciences during the nineteenth and twentieth centuries, was presumed to cultivate a sense of national identity and the "common" (i.e., national) good. In a global age, however, the concept of citizenship has changed. It has become more fluid and diffuse, with ambiguous implications for the university's mission. Kwiek and others have noted how, as new debates unfold over the meaning of citizenship in Europe (or the European Community), the university's role is contested. For example, even as European higher-education leaders call for greater mobility among students and scholars—in part to promote a process of "Europeanization"—mobility policies have generated debate over "equal access" for citizens from Central and Eastern Europe. Thus, a regional (European) reform has created, or deepened, subregional inequities, with stark implications for economic development (not to mention a sense of equal participation or belonging in the European knowledge economy). Scholars of "the global university" are only beginning to understand the dynamics that shape the regional dimensions of higher-education policy. As with privatization and marketization, regionalization has become a major theme in the literature on the global university.

Of course, while some emphasize regional variation in higher-education policy, others emphasize the idea of global conformity in university policies and practices. The case for conformity—or institutional "convergence"—has surfaced in many works, most notably in the organizational theories of John W. Meyer and his colleagues. Among other publications, *Science in the Modern World Polity: Institutionalization and Globalization* (2003) advanced the idea that governments around the world often read from a common "script" when it comes to knowledge policies and institutional models. This idea has led to related works, including David John Frank and Jay Gabler's recent comparative study, *Reconstructing the University: Worldwide Shifts in Academia in the Twentieth Century* (2006), which applied the convergence theory to disciplinary evolution. Frank and Gabler tested the claim that in the modern university the "academic core," or basic teaching and research priorities, had been "compromised by external financial and political interests" (as might be predicted by world-culture theory as well as many theories of globalization). Mining data on faculty and student attitudes in universities around the world to assess the shift from pure to applied research and from the humanities to natural and social sciences in undergraduate and postgraduate course selections, Frank and Gabler ascribed the rise of applied science not to external financial pressures but rather to underlying disciplinary changes and "globally institutionalized understandings of reality." Noting the intellectual ascendance of positivism across a wide array of disciplines, both in the modern university and in the modern state, they embraced a neoinstitutionalist perspective and attributed the reorientation of the modern university to the (ostensibly "free" and "rational") choices of academics themselves. In short, Frank and Gabler linked the institutional and intellectual convergence associated with globalization to internal rather than external factors. Their work, and others like it, set the stage for continuing debate over the idea of "institutional isomorphism" in global higher education.

Not everyone accepts the idea of institutional isomorphism. The same year that Frank and Gabler published their book (with a foreword by Meyer), two very different interpretations appeared. One came from Guy Neave in *Knowledge, Power, and Dissent: Critical Perspectives on Higher Education and Research in a Knowledge Society* (2007), which challenged the world-culture theorists by drawing attention to peripheral voices—from India, Brazil, Panama, Nigeria, Tanzania, and other countries—and stressing the global diversity of views on the university's role in society. Another came from Robert Rhoads and Carlos Torres, whose edited volume, *The University, State, and Market: The Political Economy of Globalization in the Americas* (2007), also stressed diversity. While not contesting the notion of "convergence" per se, Rhoads and Torres appraised its consequences. With a regional focus on Central and South America, they assessed the rapid privatization of the higher-education sector in the United States, Mexico, Argentina, Brazil, and the Caribbean. Chapters on the demise of undergraduate instruction, the demands for graduate-student unions, and the delegitimation of state support for public higher education revealed the difficulties facing national universities across the region. In response to these difficulties, the contributors— including Atilio Alberto Boron, Boaventura de Sousa Santos, Sheila Slaughter, and others—called for a new social movement to "democratize" knowledge and reclaim an "emancipatory" role for universities. In a sense, they called for precisely the sort of contest over "globally institutionalized understandings of reality" that Frank and Gabler had studied, but with a radically different political and theoretical orientation. Though positioned at opposite ends of an intellectual spectrum, Frank and Gabler on the one hand and Rhoads and Torres on the other shared one thing in common: a sense that, ultimately, the debate over globalization in higher education was a debate over ideas (or ideology) and the university's capacity to mobilize ideas on behalf of social ends; it was a debate, in other words, over intellectual and institutional agency.

Whether this debate over ideas and agency will lead to institutional convergence or divergence remains an open question in the literature. Neoinstitutionalists like Meyer (and Frank and Gabler) often point to science—or "scientization"—as their paradigmatic example of institutional convergence, but historians and sociologists of science routinely note that science has taken different forms in different places over time. This diversity is certainly evident in an edited volume by Paula Stephan and Ronald Ehrenberg, *Science and the University* (2007), which combined the national idiosyncrasies of research funding with the international politics of scientific labor markets, in particular the role of foreign students in American doctoral programs. Topics ranged from "Commercialization and the Scientific Research Process" to "University Science Research Funding: Privatizing Policy and Practice" to "How Does the Government (Want to) Fund Science? Politics, Lobbying, and Academic Earmarks" (a continuation of a discussion introduced by James Savage in *Funding Science in America: Congress, Universities, and the Politics of the Academic Pork Barrel* [2000]). On the globalization of scientific labor, contributors explored such topics as "Foreign Scholars in U.S. Science: Contributions and Costs," "Where Do New U.S.-Trained Science and Engineering PhD's Come From?" and, most provocatively, "Do Foreign Students Crowd Out Native Students From Graduate Programs?" As these titles made clear, global competition for scientific talent—and output—shapes the ways universities balance their service to local, national, and international constituencies, and different universities strike very different balances depending on state-level constraints. (A year after this volume was published, the issue of foreign-student access to American universities attracted further attention owing to the terrorist attacks of September 2001. When the United States cut its supply of visas, thus hindering research, some feared the country might never regain its dominance in postgraduate training in the natural sciences.)

The globalization of scientific labor—indeed, the globalization of academic labor in general—remains a key theme in the literature on "the global university." For example, in *The Exchange University: The Corporatization of Academic Culture* (2008), Adrienne Chan and Donald Fisher situated the structures of academic employment in the context of neoliberal marketization. With an opening chapter by Sheila Slaughter and Gary Rhoades on recent developments in academic capitalism, *The Exchange University* examined the increasing use of "contingent" (adjunct) faculty and the implications of such policies for gender equity and the erosion of scholarly autonomy (in this regard, the volume built on work that Jan Currie, Bev Thiele, and Patricia Harris had begun in *Gendered Universities in Globalized Economies: Power, Careers, and Sacrifices* (2002).) The stratification of academic labor similarly concerned Marc Bousquet in *How the University Works: Higher Education and the Low-Wage Nation* (2008); Frank Donoghue in *The Last Professors: The Corporate University and the Fate of the Humanities* (2008); and Catherine Chaput in *Inside the Teaching Machine: Rhetoric and Globalization in the U.S. Public Research University* (2008); as well as Joyce Canaan and Wesley Shumar in *Structure and Agency in the Neoliberal University* (2008). More than most, Canaan and Shumar broadened their analytical scope beyond the leading research universities of North America, Europe, Asia, and Australia to uncover the effects of globalization on academic labor in the developing world. Stressing the categories of gender, race, and ethnicity (including local indigenous populations), their volume revealed the human consequences of market-based initiatives that pushed for disinvestment in the higher-education sector and the deprofessionalization of scholarly work. A more radical elaboration of these ideas appeared a year later in the *Edu-Factory Collective's toward a Global Autonomous University: Cognitive Labor, the Production of Knowledge, and Exodus from the Education Factory* (2009), which saw the "ruins" of the modern university as an opportunity for progressive global reform.

The deprofessionalization—some have said the proletarianization—of academic labor continues to attract interest among scholars of globalization and higher education. Yet, where some fear the disintegration of academic life as university managers seek to "make research pay," others see extraordinary, perhaps unprecedented, opportunities for intellectual entrepreneurs. It seems, however, that opportunities may exist for some more than others. Take, for example, a recent volume edited by comparative literature scholar Brett de Bary, *Universities in Translation: The Mental Labor of Globalization* (2010). In a collection of essays spanning France, Germany, Scotland, Russia, China, Japan, South Korea, Singapore, Mexico, and the United States, de Bary and his colleagues connect the global politics of academic labor with the global politics of academic language. Part of a Hong Kong-based project known as Traces ("a multilingual book series of cultural theory and translation"), this volume features chapters translated from non-English languages—an effort to counter "both the monolingual restrictions of national publishing industries and the exclusions and asymmetries of the global English-language academic publishing system." The critique of English-language hegemony in the discourse surrounding "the global university" (a hegemony reinforced by rankings grounded in the Science Citations Index (SCI), the Social Science Citations Index (SSCI), and other indexes biased toward "international" English-language journals) has become a leitmotif in the literature. This critiques surfaces, for example, in the recent work of Ellen Hazelkorn, whose *Rankings and the Reshaping of Higher Education: The Battle for World-Class Excellence* (2011) reveals the competitive edge that English-medium universities enjoy in global rankings. Hazelkorn notes that, with universities constantly reconfiguring themselves to meet the shifting criteria of the rankings, the stratification of English- and non-English-language universities has become a source of increasing controversy.

In the global contest over ideas of the university, what is a "controversy" for some is simply "competition" for others. Some emphasize social justice; others, market forces. Scholars from different theoretical perspectives on the left and right disagree profoundly in their assessment of the effects of globalization on higher education. In some cases, the disagreements reveal clear ideological positions. For example, in *The Great Brain Race: How Universities Are Reshaping the World* (2010), journalist Ben Wildavsky, formerly of US *News and World Report*, lists five key aspects of globalization in higher education: the increasing mobility of students and scholars across borders, the emergence of foreign branch campuses, the race to build world-class research institutions focusing on science and technology, the proliferation of international college rankings, and the growth of for-profit education service providers that compete with traditional universities for students, faculty, and revenue. According to Wildavsky, higher education has become "a form of international trade," a competitive institutional marketplace pursuing what he calls "free trade in minds." Wildavsky illustrates how the process of globalization has gone hand in hand with the de facto privatization of universities, not least in the United States, where nearly every aspect of the modern university has been commodified. The enrollment of international students is now factored into a global "balance of trade" in tuition revenues; a similar calculus drives the recruitment of star faculty (and the intellectual property they generate). Despite the notion that knowledge is a public good, Wildavsky maintains that knowledge is also a private good and that cash-starved universities may need to abandon other values, such as academic freedom or nondiscrimination policies, to "fill the budget hole." While admitting that most shoppers in the global supermarket of universities come from affluent backgrounds, Wildavsky argues that, over time, international mobility will "undermine rather than reinforce elites based on inherited privilege and political pull."

Wildavsky's rhetoric may be more provocative—and ideologically transparent—than most, but his overall assessment is not unique. Most of his findings are echoed, for example, in Charles Clotfelter's recent edited volume, *American Universities in a Global Market* (2010). Revisiting such recurrent themes as the United States' declining influence in the global higher-education market, the gradual shift in doctoral enrollment away from American universities, the attempts by some institutions to extend their reach (as well as their revenues) by investing in branch campuses, and the United States' rather sluggish response to all of these developments, Clotfelter, like Wildavsky, urges American policymakers to see universities as "firms in a global market"—a fiercely competitive market in which only the fittest (i.e., the most privatized) institutions will survive. In making this argument, both Clotfelter and Wildavsky borrow a page from the neoinstitutionalist playbook of Meyer and others who believe that "knowledge institutions" around the world are converging toward a common model. This view is widespread. John Aubrey Douglass, C. Judson King, and Irwin Feller advanced the same line of reasoning in their recent work *Globalization's Muse: Universities and Higher Education Systems in a Changing World* (2009)—its title a reference to universities' starring role in nearly every discussion of the twenty-first-century knowledge society. With chapters on science and technology policy, higher-education finance at the national and supranational levels, and universities' role in human-capital development, Douglass et al. offered various cases from the United States, the United Kingdom, Sweden, Germany, China, India, Australia, and sub-Saharan Africa to suggest that universities everywhere seem to be moving in the same direction. In this context, they advised higher-education officials to adopt more comparative perspectives in their work and, in this way, to learn from one another's successes and failures.

By now the idea that universities operate as firms in a global market has become axiomatic for most scholars of higher education, even if some continue to challenge the normalization of this paradigm. In many ways, the modern research university has come to resemble a multinational corporation; the question remains, however, in what ways, if any, does it—or should it—differ? To address this question, the present volume takes a broad historical perspective. As its title suggests, it places the challenges facing today's universities in historical context. Looking back not just a decade or two, but a century or two (or ten), it reveals that, in many respects, the university, as an idea—and an ideal—has always been "international" (even if the international contexts in which the university operates have changed over time). Moreover, at least in the modern period, the university has long bridged "public" and "private," "intellectual" and "industrial" spheres. What can today's university administrators learn from the past? Today, of course, higher-education leaders are struck by the vast scale and rapid pace of global change, but as they respond to these changes, it behooves them to ask the questions pursued in this volume: What is "the global university"? Whose interests does it serve, and how? What distinguishes its approach to teaching, to research, to knowledge? This volume, like the conference from which it sprang, takes a wide-ranging approach to these questions. Chronologically, it extends from the medieval period to the early modern, modern, and postmodern periods. Geographically, it examines higher-education systems in China, South Korea, Singapore, Australia, Malaysia, Vietnam, Kenya, Tanzania, Uganda, Botswana, Ghana, Mauritius, France, Sweden, Norway, Denmark, Finland, Canada, the United States, and the United Kingdom. Thematically, it covers an extraordinary diversity of responses to globalization in higher education, revealing both convergence and divergence in national approaches. In the end, its contributors find, "the global university" is not one thing but many.

* * *

To highlight its cross-cutting themes, the volume's ten chapters have been divided into five parts. The first, "Regionalism(s) and Global Higher Education Reform," explores the rapid expansion of regional networks and partnerships in East Asia, Southeast Asia, and Europe. While the Bologna Process is the best-known example of regionalization in higher-education governance, both Ka Ho Mok and Anthony Welch reveal the ways in which Asian and Australian universities have sought to add value and secure competitive advantage through regional collaborations and new partnerships. The next section, "The Changing Dimensions of University Governance," looks more closely at the structures of academic labor and specifically the ways in which university scholars and administrators have either promoted or resisted the hierarchical rationalization of (formerly) "collegial" or "loosely coupled" organizations. Ivar Bleiklie and Rosemary Deem both see a shift in university governance from collegial to hierarchical models, but they differ significantly in their assessment of the effect of this reorientation on higher-education management. The third section, "Academic Roles and the Purposes of the University," brings the focus of the discussion to academics themselves. Ian Wei as well as Xu Xiaozhou and Xue Shan examine the changing nature of scholarly work and the degree to which academics may or may not share a sense of common values or mission. Without shared values, they ask, how can academics respond to the diverse "external" demands on the modern university?

The fourth section, "Shifting Patterns of Graduate and Undergraduate Education," looks at students—both graduate and undergraduate—especially those in research universities where teaching has become a secondary priority (often fulfilled by adjunct faculty). On the one hand, Chen Hongjie, Shen Wenqin, and Cai Leiluo note a shift from specialized to general education in an attempt to prepare elite undergraduates for a rapidly changing global "knowledge economy"; on the other hand, Glen Jones and Bryan Gopaul reveal a paradox at the graduate level whereby this knowledge economy renders certain doctoral students (chiefly those in applied sciences) highly marketable—and thus internationally mobile—even as it pushes others toward increasingly marginal academic employment. The fifth and final section, "Universities and External Funding," examines what may be the most pressing dilemma in modern higher education: the influence of external funding on university priorities and values. As John Taylor and Peter Maassen observe, external funding per se is not a new phenomenon; what matters is the connection between funding and governance and, specifically, the degree to which external partners share in decision making. External funding, they find, is most constructive when the resources it provides strengthen the university's self-governing academic core.

The authors of these chapters bring a breadth of scholarly expertise and a wealth of administrative experience to bear on questions of leadership and planning in the new "global university." For example, in the volume's opening chapter, "Global Aspirations and Strategizing for World-Class Status: New Modes of Higher-Education Governance and the Emergence of Regulatory Regionalism in East Asia," Ka Ho Mok, vice president of the Hong Kong Institute of Education, explores the increasing regionalization of higher-education management in East Asia. Noting the rise of "network governance," including "new forms of regional governance that transcend the territorial spaces of nation-states," Mok charts the diverse strategies that mainland China, Taiwan, Hong Kong, South Korea, Singapore, and Malaysia have used to achieve "world-class status" for their universities. Following the model of the European Union's Bologna Process, universities in East Asia have initiated regional connections and collaborations to leverage the growing strength of their research institutions. Significantly, most of these changes—including the increasing liberalization of private-sector universities, the encouragement of transnational higher-education partnerships (including offshore campuses), and so on—have been initiated by the state and its careful management of a process Mok calls "centralized decentralization." Mok writes: "these states have gradually converged around a similar pattern of reform: rendering more autonomy and flexibility to public universities in order to promote their vitality, efficiency, and competitiveness while at the same time wielding regulatory power more aggressively to guide strategic developments." Unlike those who see the inexorable "privatization" of universities, Mok traces recent changes in higher-education governance in both Asia and Europe and sees an important and enduring (though not unproblematic) role for the state, particularly in the cultivation of regional networks intended to advance institutional as well as national competitiveness.

In the volume's second chapter, "Contributing to the Southeast Asian Knowledge Economy? Australian Offshore Campuses in Malaysia and Vietnam," professor Anthony Welch of the University of Sydney looks in depth at one aspect of the "regionalization" that Mok outlines: the pursuit of cross-national university partnerships to build higher-education capacity and competitiveness in Southeast Asia. Specifically, Welch examines the rise in foreign direct investment (FDI) in higher-education services in Malaysia and Vietnam, focusing on two Australian universities' development of offshore ("branch") campuses in these countries. Using two cases, Monash University's campus in Malaysia and the Royal Melbourne Institute of Technology's campus in Vietnam, he situates the branch-campus phenomenon in the context of a "knowledge economy" in which states with limited higher-education capacity seek assistance from international providers even as they frame international higher-education partnerships as a form of "trade rather than aid." Neoliberal marketization (prompted by World Bank structural adjustment programs in the 1980s and 1990s) led both Malaysia and Vietnam to embrace the privatization of higher education, "including branch campuses run by overseas providers," in hopes that competition might spur domestic universities to improve. While partly successful in this endeavor, Monash University-Malaysia and RMIT in Vietnam raise difficult questions about the longer-term effects of FDI in higher-education services—from "the suitability of imported curricula and the readiness of foreign higher-education institutions to adapt knowledge to local conditions" to states' capacity to monitor branch-campus quality to foreign providers' commitment to equity and parity in wages and working conditions for staff in "home" and "foreign" campuses. Branch campuses, Welch finds, reveal both the advantages and the disadvantages of "globalization" in higher education.

In the next chapter, "Collegiality and Hierarchy: Coordinating Principles in Higher Education," professor Ivar Bleiklie of the University of Bergen elaborates on Mok's idea of internationalized "network governance" and uses this idea to illuminate key changes in the role that academics (both research and teaching faculty) play in university leadership. Tracing a shift from "collegial" to "hierarchical" structures of university administration since the 1970s (a gradual shift, he notes, that began much earlier), Bleiklie argues that, to understand the evolution of academic governance, "it does not suffice to look at how decision-making authority is distributed within academic institutions, but also how it is distributed across the institutional, national, and international arenas in which relevant decisions are made." Drawing historical comparisons between medieval, early modern, and modern universities, Bleiklie focuses on the final decades of the twentieth century, when the "massification" of higher education presented new concerns about efficiency and accountability to university managers at both the institutional and the system level. Top-down structures of institutional leadership replaced collegial structures worldwide. At the same time, however, new structures of interinstitutional (and often international) governance have given academics new levers of administrative power. Bleiklie identifies three such levers—editorial boards, peer-review panels, and funding councils—each of which has enabled academic elites to shape decisions that affect their work. Inasmuch as university funding increasingly hinges on institutional prestige, which, in turn, hinges on research publications vetted by international editorial boards and review panels, Bleiklie sees these interinstitutional structures as emerging forms of "network governance" that combine both collegial and hierarchical principles in university leadership for a "global" era. Bleiklie observes: "Although academic power has been weakened within individual universities, it is increasingly felt through decisions made by national and international peer-review mechanisms related to research funding, evaluation, and publication."

The next chapter takes a somewhat different view. In "The Twenty-First-Century University: Dilemmas of Leadership and Organizational Futures," Rosemary Deem, dean of history and social science at Royal Holloway in London, is less sanguine than Bleiklie about recent changes in university governance. In her contribution, professor Deem asks how shifting ideas about the purposes of universities have shaped "the practices, values,...and dilemmas of higher-education leaders and their senior teams." In an era of global competition, mass enrollments, quality audits, financial constraints, and entrepreneurial research, higher-education leaders have changed their views of the basic mission of the university. From the pursuit of world-class status to the commodification of knowledge, universities have come to serve commercial as much as social aims, private as much as public interests. Deem writes: "It is this tension—between a view of universities as an arm of economic policy and a notion that universities may serve wider social and cultural purposes—that lies at the heart of modern universities' struggle to decide what they are about, how they should be led, and how they should be organized." Drawing on data from three major studies of university leaders in the United Kingdom, Deem examines leaders' strategies for professional development (including their declining sense of institutional loyalty), their approach to personnel management (including their focus on hierarchical over collegial governance), and their core academic priorities (including their emphasis on research over teaching). She concludes that a growing—indeed global—pursuit of the "entrepreneurial university" may lead to a "retail model of the university in which neither teaching nor research is a vibrant or creative activity" and the production of knowledge serves narrowly instrumental rather than broader human needs. To avoid this fate, Deem offers a series of ideas to help university leaders envision more balanced "organizational futures."

The debate over the "purposes" of the university receives its deepest historical interrogation in the next chapter, "Medieval Universities and Aspirations to Universal Significance." Using the case of the medieval University of Paris, Ian Wei explores the ways in which thirteenth-century academics—particularly masters of arts and theology—imagined their roles as teachers and, ultimately, preachers of "universal" knowledge and truth. Scholarship, they believed, was intimately connected with the eternal salvation of souls, and the university's status as a privileged corporation rested on its contributions to this pastoral mission—a mission that extended beyond the university halls to encompass virtually all of western Europe. And yet, despite its "universal" project, the university as a community of scholars was never perfectly unified; rather, as Wei explains, it consisted of "communities within communities," its members separated by faculty affiliations (and hierarchies), regional loyalties (or nations), career ambitions (and social status), "college" associations, and ecclesiastical differences. Members of the university shared a common devotion to learning and spreading the sacred message of the church through preaching, but their identity as "scholars" was often divided—as their frequent disagreements (even brawls) indicated. Wei observes that "being a member of the university could mean very different things to different men, and the university environment was sometimes highly volatile." What is most remarkable to Wei, however, is the fact that, even with all these differences, the medieval academic community held together around a "set of values," a shared discourse, which, in times of crisis or conflict with external authorities, gave the university strength. Modern academics, he suggests, might have much to learn from their Parisian ancestors about effective negotiations with external stakeholders.

The debate over the purposes of the university continues in the sixth chapter, "The Changing Role of the Academic: Historical and Comparative Perspectives." Surveying the ways in which academics have balanced their responsibilities for teaching, research, and service over time, professor Xu Xiaozhou and Xue Shan of Zhejiang University note that "the external environment of the university has changed, and these changes have, in turn, affected the internal organization of academic life." Drawing comparative examples from medieval, early modern, and modern universities, Xu and Xue trace the emergence of an enduring compact between universities and society—an informal contract in which academics received both protection and prestige in exchange for their role in producing and transmitting knowledge. Granted autonomy and academic freedom, academics saw their role as cultivating talent and meeting public needs. Recently, however, as long-term public interests have given way to short-term private interests, the basic contract between universities and society has changed. Today, Xu and Xue argue, "external interest groups have essentially hired academics to do research by providing financial support." In this new context, academics pay less attention to teaching and devote themselves instead to profit-oriented research. The rise of "academic capitalism" has eroded academics' sense of loyalty to the university as a protected institution with a unique social purpose. The result has been a fundamental shift in the nature of the academic profession, a shift Xu and Xue view with grave concern. Without a certain degree of autonomy from external interests, they contend, academics' historic role as broad-minded scientific innovators—as well as their long-valued role as social commentators and critics—may be lost.

The volume's seventh chapter shifts the emphasis of the volume from faculty to students. In "Toward General Education in the Global University: The Chinese Model," professor Chen Hongjie, Shen Wenquin, and Cai Leiluo of Peking University chart the shift from general education to increasingly specialized education between the eighteenth and mid-twentieth centuries. This shift occurred not only in Western universities but also in Chinese institutions of higher education. Whereas, for centuries, Chinese scholars had stressed the Confucian classics, they came increasingly to pursue scientific and practical studies, particularly after China's military defeats in the Opium Wars. This emphasis on specialization culminated in the creation of Soviet-style research institutes in the 1950s and 1960s. Starting in the 1970s and 1980s, however, Chen, Shen, and Cai note a return to general education, particularly in elite universities. They attribute this renewed interest in general education to three factors: the need to serve more diverse students after the rise of "mass" higher education; the expansion of knowledge and the concomitant blurring of disciplinary boundaries; and the transfer of specialized learning to postgraduate, mainly doctoral, education. "In the postindustrial 'knowledge society' of the past few decades," they argue, "higher education has moved away from specialized education toward general education, especially at the undergraduate level in elite institutions." The primary models for general education were devised in prestigious American universities such as Harvard, Columbia, and the University of Chicago in the opening decades of the twentieth century and were revisited amid the so-called Culture Wars of the 1980s. Since then, the authors maintain, "Mainland China, Hong Kong, Japan, Hungary, Russia, Poland, South Korea, South Africa, and Sweden have all introduced general-education programs inspired by the American model." Describing several new programs in China, the authors foresee a "Chinese model" of general education arising to meet the country's rapidly expanding higher-education needs. Universities, they assert, "have no choice but to enable students to master various disciplines and develop transferable skills in order to equip themselves with a broader foundation of knowledge."

In the next chapter, professor Glen Jones and Bryan Gopaul of the University of Toronto continue the discussion of students' experiences by placing recent changes in Canadian doctoral training in historical context. In "Doctoral Education and the Global University: Student Mobility, Hierarchy, and Canadian Government Policy," Jones and Gopaul examine a series of policies that encouraged Canadian doctoral students to enroll in domestic universities. Tracing policies under both liberals and conservatives (Trudeau, Mulroney, Chretien, and Harper), they note: "Rather than supporting internationalization by funding Canadian students to learn about the world and attend 'global' universities," Canada's national graduate scholarship programs—guided by concerns about brain drain as well as efforts to meet growing instructional and research needs—sought to limit the mobility of Canada's "best and brightest." Insofar as most scholarship recipients enrolled in a handful of research universities, these aid programs fostered a process of institutional hierarchization, a trend amplified by competitive research-funding policies. Meanwhile, a growing emphasis on university-industry partnerships and commercializable knowledge led the graduates of Canada's most prestigious doctoral programs to pursue employment outside academia—and, in many cases, outside Canada. The result has not been optimal for Canada in the long run. Jones and Gopaul write: "just as on a national scale Canadian policies further advantaged universities in Toronto, Montreal, and Vancouver, so too on an international scale doctoral mobility concentrated in regions and careers that reinscribe historical inequalities and patterns of economic stratification." In a context of increasing national and international academic mobility, Canadian policies intended to strengthen doctoral education inadvertently reinforced inequality.

The final section of the volume examines the relationship between the university and external funding agencies. In the ninth chapter, "Can Modern Universities Learn from the Past? English Universities Working with Industry, 1870–1914," professor John Taylor of the University of Liverpool takes a closer historical look at an enduring phenomenon: university-industry partnerships. While many analysts characterize such partnerships as a recent innovation, Taylor reminds us that such relationships have been around for a very long time. Highlighting the role of business and industry in the development of Yorkshire College in Leeds, Owens College in Manchester, and Firth College in Sheffield, he shows how commercial interests (particularly in the chemical, textile, mining, and engineering industries) shaped everything from curriculum to community outreach to fundraising to governance to student-attendance patterns at these schools. While recognizing important differences between past and present university-industry partnerships, Taylor uses these historical examples to draw a series of lessons for U.K. universities today. Among these lessons, he stresses the "wide portfolio of courses" (both vocational and literary courses as well as "continuing professional development for academic staff") that appealed to a range of students, along with the close ties that bound universities and their communities. Even, perhaps especially, in today's global universities, Taylor argues, local ties need to be strengthened, not least because such ties may be the key to higher-education funding. He comments: "if links with business are to flourish, then local, regional, national, and international priorities need to be fused together." The great challenge, he observes, is to structure emerging university-industry partnerships in ways that draw on the lessons of the past.

The final chapter examines the debate over university funding and governance in comparative context. In "Universities and the Effects of External Funding: Sub-Saharan Africa and the Nordic Countries," professor Peter Maassen of the University of Oslo uses the extensive data collected by the Higher Education Research and Advocacy Network in Africa (HERANA) to compare the links between universities and economic development in six sub-Saharan African countries (Kenya, Tanzania, Ghana, Botswana, Uganda, and Mauritius) and four Nordic countries (Norway, Sweden, Finland, and Denmark). Looking at universities' external funding, the strength of their "academic core," and the dynamics of the social contract, or "pact," between universities and society, Maassen highlights a series of differences between African and Nordic universities that explain their divergent roles in economic development. For example, whereas Nordic universities enjoy a strong pact with their societies and thus stable government funding, universities in sub-Saharan Africa have a weak pact with their societies, unstable funding, and, therefore, a vulnerable academic core. In such circumstances, Maassen reveals, African universities must resort to other sources of funding, usually international donor agencies, even though university leaders have little power to influence the details of these funding relationships. While the lack of domestic resources compels African universities to seek external resources, donor funds typically support isolated, short-term projects and rarely strengthen the university's academic core. In the end, Maassen observes, a weak pact between university and society leads to funding that shortchanges the academic core and thus prevents universities from making long-term contributions to economic development.

Ironically, the forces affecting universities in sub-Saharan Africa—the search for external funds, the focus on short-term projects, the tenuous pact between the university and society—bear an eerie resemblance to forces now affecting universities in the United States, United Kingdom, and other countries that have adopted neoliberal reforms. More and more, a "global university" is one that prioritizes short-term over long-term interests and serves economic over humanistic ends. Rather than becoming more "universal" in a global era, many universities are becoming more narrow, perhaps (ironically) even more national, in the ways they are expected to secure the competitive advantage of the nation-state. The very structure of globalization has meant that universities are becoming, first and foremost, functional tools of industry and the state and, therefore, less autonomous in their approach to research and teaching. The result has been the steady commodification of knowledge. Both research and teaching have become tradable services, the value of which is determined by international markets. This volume does not celebrate the rise of the global university, nor does it offer any roadmaps or recipes for universities to become "global." Instead, it has a broader aim. It seeks to assess the state of the university in our time, taking stock of its core values (if it has any) and the extent to which its values might be changed—either subverted or subsumed—in favor of other values as history unfolds. While the contributors to this volume agree that universities are not, and should not be, merely businesses, they do not agree on alternatives, nor do they agree on any particular "model" of globalization in higher education. Rather, each author offers a unique vision of the global university, a vision informed by history in the belief that any possible future is necessarily embedded in the past.

PART I

Regionalism(s) and Global Higher-Education Reform

Global Aspirations and Strategizing for World-Class Status: New Modes of Higher-Education Governance and the Emergence of Regulatory Regionalism in East Asia

Ka Ho Mok

INTRODUCTION

Well aware of the growing importance of global university rankings, many governments in East Asia have introduced new strategies to enhance the global competitiveness of their universities. Determined to perform better in ranking exercises, leading universities have attempted to restructure their governance systems. One of the major trends of changing university governance is the emergence of regulatory regionalism, that is, new forms of regional governance that transcend the territorial spaces of nation states. As in Europe, university governance in Asia is now more international in scope; universities are increasingly subject to new external standards of measurement, even as their own internal governance procedures have become more managerial. This chapter examines policies and strategies employed by Mainland China, Taiwan, Hong Kong, South Korea, Singapore, and Malaysia to benchmark their universities with highly ranked (so-called world-class) universities. Specifically, this chapter reviews the strategies that selected Asian governments have adopted to make themselves into regional "hubs" of higher education, particularly the means they adopt to promote transnational higher-education governance.

GLOBAL UNIVERSITY RANKINGS

The popularity of global university rankings in recent years has undoubtedly contributed to universities' efforts to achieve or maintain "world-class" status. During the 1980s, university rankings tended to be domestically oriented and covered only universities in the countries that produced the rankings (e.g., the America's Best Colleges rankings in *US News & World Report*, published since 1983).[1] Since the year 2000, however, a variety of international university rankings have emerged. Among them, the Academic Ranking of World Universities (since 2003) and the World University Rankings (since 2004), managed by Shanghai Jiao Tong University and the *Times Higher Education Supplement*, respectively, have become particularly influential, so much so that the assessment indicators they apply have led to a new set of norms adopted by universities around the world as they endeavor to become world-class.

This obsession with global rankings may be a logical consequence of globalization and the worldwide massification of higher education. On the one hand, the dramatic advance of science and technology in a fiercely competitive knowledge economy has led to a rapid expansion of higher education in many developed countries. On the other hand, a dramatic increase in the number of higher-education institutions, coupled with a tendency toward privatization in the higher-education "market," has prompted concerns among the general public—both taxpayers and student-consumers—regarding the quality of these rapidly growing institutions. While recognizing the importance of expanding their higher-education systems, governments today seldom have sufficient financial resources to boost this sector single-handedly. A diversification of university funding sources has led to calls for more transparent quality indicators for the sake of fair competition. Today, higher-education consumers, following the logic of markets, hold university leaders accountable for quality, and university rankings are supposed to be a tool to compare and assess institutional performance.

But what does a higher spot on a global university ranking mean to students and faculty? What constitutes a world-class university, and what are its guiding values? These questions lie at the heart of this volume, and specifically at the heart of this chapter. We must ask these important questions as we engage in critical reflections upon the past, present, and future of universities and the growing prominence of "instrumentalist" approaches to transforming universities into world-class enterprises.

New Modes of Higher-Education Governance in East Asia

Recent changes taking place in the higher-education sector of various East Asian countries have clearly suggested a significant transformation in relation to university governance and regulatory regimes. To boost their universities' rankings, many Asian states have worked hard to benchmark their higher-education systems with international counterparts. Such moves are clearly indicated by the quest for world-class universities in Asia. Similarly, the rise of regionalization in Asian higher education can be understood as part of a broader strategy to assert both regional and (ultimately) global leadership. One of the major consequences of globalization seems to be the formation of regional collaborations to enable participating institutions to have a stronger regional voice in global policy dialogues (Robertson 2010). Many Asian universities have made efforts to form regional and international networks or alliances through research collaborations, joint academic programs, and academic exchanges. This chapter explores the causes and consequences of this new regionalism in higher-education governance in East Asia.

Public Universities and the State

Seeking Entrepreneurial Universities with a Strong State Presence

Even in the context of a push for more autonomous and entrepreneurial universities in East Asia, one cannot ignore the persistence of strong state intervention and regulation in Asian higher education. As they pursue world-class status for select universities, East Asian governments have aggressively sought to improve the efficiency of their higher-education systems. Within a very short time, they have adopted new strategies to respond to local, regional, and global challenges. First and foremost, they have adopted procompetition policies, which have imparted an ethos of "privateness" to East Asian higher-education systems. Private institutions have been allowed to prosper and have contributed much to the expansion of the East Asian higher-education sector since the 1990s. At the same time, public universities have undergone a similar process of incorporation (or corporatization) as East Asian states have made their public universities more autonomous (Mok 2009a). This is particularly the case in Malaysia and Singapore, where, since the late 1990s, all the region's prominent public universities have been incorporated as not-for-profit companies. The University of Malaya (UM), along with eight other Malaysian public universities, was reorganized in 1998, while the National University of Singapore (NUS) and Nanyang Technological University (NTU) were reorganized in 2005.[2] In theory, these public universities have become more self-governing and self-financing. They can now recruit and reward their staff with more flexibility so as to foster a vibrant entrepreneurial climate. They can also borrow money, engage in business ventures, and establish companies or consultancy firms.

Similarly, in Mainland China, Taiwan, Hong Kong, and South Korea, recent governance reforms have given more autonomy to university leaders and have reshaped internal administrative structures to give academics and university councils more decision-making power (Mok 2006). The transformation from state- and bureaucratic-dominated governance to a model that engages more academics has been particularly evident in Taiwan and Hong Kong (more than in Mainland China, where a party-government dual control system persists). For instance, the Taiwanese University Law has been frequently amended since 1993 to reinforce not only the autonomous power of universities but also various changes that permit a greater role for academic faculty in university governance.[3] In the case of Hong Kong, the establishment of a new public university (Hong Kong University of Science and Technology) in 1991 with a new model of governance catalyzed further changes in other universities. It should be noted, however, that greater autonomy in East Asian public universities has been accompanied by reduced state expenditures. Universities are now expected to raise funds through all sorts of channels, especially from nonstate sources (Mok 2009b).

Of course, the basic elements of these reforms are not exclusive to East Asia. In response to the challenges posed by globalization, most modern states around the world have sought to reinvent themselves by moving beyond the welfare state toward what some have called the competition state (Gill 1995; Moran 2002; Jordana and Levi-Faur 2005). Thus, attempts to privatize or corporatize the higher-education sector are part of a much broader regulatory shift. By deregulating certain sectors and enforcing competition in others, states have sought to become facilitators or even generators of markets. What appears to make the East Asian case different is the combination of deregulation (or decentralization) in market restructuring with—simultaneously—the persistence of a strong regulatory state. In contrast to Cerny's (1997) characterization of the competition state as basically a liberal state, Levi-Faur (1998) has pointed to a paradox wherein "the greater the commitment of the competition state to the promotion of competition, the deeper its regulation will be" (676). Thus, instead of a retreat of the state, actions taken by the competition state may in fact result in a reassertion of the role of the state (ibid.).

I would likewise argue that in order to promote essential national interests through the creation and enforcement of competition, rapidly developing states in East Asia have seized the opportunity of economic restructuring to transform themselves into either "market-facilitating states" or "market-accelerating states" by proactively regulating market institutions (Mok 2008b).[4] Unlike the regulatory framework in the United States, which evolved in the context of a liberal market economy, new regulatory frameworks in Asia have emerged from a combination of liberalizing markets and strong states. As Jayasuriya (2000) rightly points out, "this authoritarian liberalism presupposes the existence of a strong (or better described as politically illiberal) state with a capacity to regulate the economy" (329).

Governments in Mainland China, Taiwan, South Korea, Singapore, and Malaysia have played an active "market generator" role during the past two decades, not only in setting out strategic directions for economic development but also in orchestrating reforms in higher education to meet national goals. The proactive role of the state is evident, for example, in the cultivation of transnational (regional) higher-education partnerships. Singapore has been particularly effective and systematic in pursuing world-class status for its national universities and in promoting transnational higher-education partnerships as part of a grand strategy of nation-building. Singapore's hope is that significant state intervention and proactive guidance, implemented as indirectly as possible, will result in a well-managed regional hub of higher education (Lee and Gopinathan 2001, 2008; Tan 2006). Likewise, in the case of Mainland China, Taiwan, South Korea, and Malaysia, state-led measures have sought to boost the competitiveness of higher-education systems, although in some of these countries a lack of consistency in governance practices—owing to long traditions of highly centralized and state-dominated higher-education governance—has led to conflicting regulatory regimes characterized simultaneously by centralization and decentralization (Hawkins

2006; Mok 2003a, 2006; Kim 2006; Lee 2006a; Morshidi 2009). In Malaysia, for example, even after universities were made not-for-profit corporations, the establishment of the Ministry of Higher Education in 2004 clearly revealed the state's intention to retain its centralized control.[5] Similarly, in Mainland China, while the central government has devolved many of its administrative powers to local governments and university authorities since the 1980s, its strong intention to develop a few top-tier national universities into world-class institutions (through the big-budget 211 Project and 985 Project) has dominated the reform agenda of most of China's public universities (Min 2004; Mok 2005).[6]

The Hong Kong government, in contrast, has been committed to free-market principles and has acted more like a market facilitator. Nonetheless, it too has taken increasing steps to regulate the development of its higher-education sector. Since 2007, when its Task Force on Economic Challenges pinpointed "educational services" as one of the key industries for Hong Kong's future development, the Hong Kong government has played a more interventionist role. Besides its effort to construct a more inclusive Qualifications Framework, the Hong Kong government has become more aggressive in luring international students with talent and expertise (e.g., raising the current 10 percent threshold for international students) while at the same time relaxing immigration restrictions to facilitate students' stay in Hong Kong.[7] "Deep collaboration" among Hong Kong's public universities has fostered efficiencies in university governance, and the University Grants Committee (UGC)[8] has supported the notion of university mergers or other forms of basic restructuring to catapult Hong Kong's universities into a better position in global rankings (Lee 2005; Chan 2007).

Overall, these new forms of higher-education governance demonstrate that East Asia has not entirely given way to neoliberal globalization. A paradoxical model of "centralized decentralization" is evident in persistent state control over the details of entrance examinations and enrollment quotas, and in governments' role in setting tuition fees. While the intensity of state control over higher education has varied among East Asian countries (with Mainland China and Hong Kong at opposite ends of the spectrum), these states have gradually converged around a similar pattern of reform: rendering more autonomy and flexibility to public universities in order to promote their vitality, efficiency, and competitiveness while at the same time wielding regulatory power more aggressively to guide strategic developments. Thus, in terms of state regulation, the new East Asian model differs from the more liberal American model and resembles some European practices.

PRIVATE UNIVERSITIES AND THE STATE

The Undecided Role of Private Higher-Education Institutions

University reforms in East Asia have liberated the private sector, which has, in turn, contributed to the massification of domestic higher education and, in some cases, the growth of national economies. Since the 1990s, Singapore, Malaysia, Hong Kong, and to some extent the Chinese special economic zone of Shenzhen have all declared their intention to become regional hubs of higher education. Indeed, private universities have been promoted robustly in these territories, as have governance reforms undertaken in public institutions (Mok 2009b). When compared with American and European models, however, the growth of private universities in East Asia is still slow. Public institutions of higher education (e.g., national universities and research institutes) far outpace their private counterparts. Moreover, though fewer in number, public universities often garner more resources—on top of state funding—and thus tend to perform much better academically than private universities.

This is particularly the case for top public universities in East Asia, which aspire to practice the highly demanding Emerging Global Model (EGM) of the twenty-first-century research university.[9] EGM universities are characterized by an intensity of research that far exceeds past experience in East Asia. Mohrman, Ma, and Baker (2008) identify eight characteristics of EGM universities: research intensity, global mission, diversified funding, worldwide recruitment, increasing complexity, new roles for professors, new relationships with government and industry, and global collaboration with similar institutions. Most governments in East Asia have now realized that the quest for world-class universities is in fact a race among this subset of research institutions, and given their long traditions of state-dominated or even exclusively public higher-education systems (e.g., in Mainland China) it naturally follows that universities receiving aggressive promotion from the state are most often from the public sector. For instance, among the 12 universities included in the first phase of Taiwan's Development Plan for World Class Universities and Research Centers of Excellence (a two-phase program lasting from 2006 to 2015 with a total budget of NT$100 billion),[10] only two are private institutions.[11]

On the other hand, the South Korean higher-education system has a vibrant and long-established private sector, and several private universities have been chosen for public subsidies to strengthen South Korea's national research capacity. Of the seven universities supported by the two-phase Brain Korea 21 Project (see table 1.1),[12] which has a total budget of US$3.64 billion, only two are public institutions.[13]

Apart from universities, the privileged status of the public sector vis-à-vis the private sector in East Asian higher education is also evident in the persistence of a small group of specialized national (state-affiliated) research institutions, which are still influential.[14] The Academies of Sciences and Social Sciences in Mainland China, and the Academia Sinica and Industrial Technology Research Institute in Taiwan are excellent examples. Particularly in Mainland China, the heritage of China's Soviet-style command economy prior to the reforms of 1979 meant that research and teaching activities were separated, with national research institutes receiving a disproportionate share of national funding for research and development. While this dual system has undergone significant change since the 1980s, state-run research institutions continue to play a critical role in promoting national research capacity. This conspicuous domination and regulation by the state can also be found in Taiwan and, to some extent, in Singapore and Malaysia.[15] Thus, unlike the United States and Europe, where basic research is typically the province of research universities while applied research falls under the ambit of large and medium-sized private enterprises, China directs most of its research resources to public research institutes.

Table 1.1 The first and second phase of Brain Korea 21 Project, South Korea

	First phase	*Second phase*
Period	1999–2005	2006–2012
Budget	US$1.34 billion	US$2.3 billion
Participation	564 centers/teams and 89,366 students over the seven-year period	74 universities, 244 centers, 325 project teams, 20,000 graduate students per year
Support	$400 per month for masters, $600 for doctoral, $1,250 for postdoctoral researchers, $2,500 for contract professors	$500 per month for masters, $900 for doctoral, $2,000 for postdoctoral researchers, $2,500 for contract professors

Source: Korean Ministry of Education, Science, and Technology website: http://english.mest.go.kr/main.jsp?idx=0301020101&brd_no=52&cp=1&pageSize=10&srchSel=&srchVal=&brd_mainno=528&mode=v (Last accessed on December 15, 2005).

While the state remains a powerful player in East Asian higher education, the process of liberalization and privatization in the region during the past two decades has been impressive. As these states adjust their role from being the principal provider of higher education to being something more like a facilitator of higher-education development, private institutions have been encouraged to expand—particularly through various transnational arrangements. Since 1995, under the framework of General Agreement on Trade in Services (GATS), higher education has been regarded as a service to be liberalized and regulated by trade rules. In places like Singapore, Malaysia, and Hong Kong, which aspire to become regional hubs of higher education, collaborations with reputable Western institutions have become indispensable, given the region's pressing demand for higher education. Among these transnational higher-education arrangements—which include joint degree programs, twinning programs, and distance-learning programs—foreign academic institutions, especially from Australia, Britain, and the United States, have been allowed to set up local branch campuses (for more on this phenomenon, see the chapter by Anthony Welch in this volume). Private universities have played a key role in establishing transnational partnerships, and Singapore has been especially proactive in this regard.[16] Similarly, in cases like Malaysia, the more dynamic and creative private sector has become a balancing force that moderates state intervention in the pubic sector (Mok 2009b). Gradually, the marketization and commodification of private higher education have begun to affect the state's role.

ENGLISH-ORIENTED "INTERNATIONALIZATION" IN THE QUEST FOR WORLD-CLASS STATUS

Another new feature in East Asian higher-education governance—a feature often taken for granted—is the English-oriented "internationalization" of universities that have achieved, or are aspiring to, world-class status. Since all the East Asian cases selected here are not "native English-speaking societies" in the strictest sense[17] (if compared with their native English-speaking North American, British, and Australian counterparts), they are disadvantaged when it comes to the media of teaching, learning, research, and publication in an era of academic globalization. Mainland Chinese, Taiwanese, and South Korean research universities are particularly handicapped in their endeavor to achieve world-class status, since, unlike their counterparts in Hong Kong, Singapore, and Malaysia, they are unable to "benefit" from the linguistic legacy of British colonialism. These former British colonies, accidental beneficiaries in today's global language bias, have touted their "English milieux" as a selling point in their quest to become regional hubs of higher education.

Of course, language plays a significant role in assessment indicators used by global university rankings. For instance, to measure research outputs, the number of Science Citation Index (SCI) and Social Science Citation Index (SSCI) journal articles is an indicator used by almost all influential global rankings, including the two most prominent rankings managed by Shanghai Jiao Tong University and the *Times Higher Education Supplement*. Yet the SCI and SSCI journal databases—run by the American company Thomson Reuters—include mostly English-language journals, followed by those in other European languages, while journals in East Asian languages are almost completely excluded.[18] Moreover, the indicators used in the *Times'* assessment of internationalization are the proportion of an institution's faculty and students who come from other countries.[19] These metrics have put enormous pressure on East Asia's leading research universities to adjust their language policies to lure more foreign students and scholars. Typically, the process of internationalization involves a much stronger emphasis on English, or even a complete shift in an institution's teaching medium.

From 2005 to 2007, the Chinese University of Hong Kong had a heated debate regarding the adjustment of its bilingual language policy, with a result clearly in favor of English.[20] Likewise, a number of leading universities in Mainland China, Taiwan, and South Korea have shifted the teaching medium of certain courses, departments, or faculties from the national language to English. The PhD program at the Guanghua School of Management of Peking University, for example, is taught exclusively in English. In Malaysia, after two decades of struggle to consolidate the national language—Malay—the government in the 1990s reinstated English as the teaching medium for tertiary education. While similar reforms in language policy can also be found in European universities, particularly in those in Eastern Europe, this English-oriented process of internationalization has become pervasive among leading research universities in East Asia. It has been reinforced by the rapid development of transnational higher-education partnerships in the private sector (again predominantly in English).

Some may argue that, given the paradigmatic influence of the present Anglo-Saxon model—or more specifically the American model—of higher education, there is a danger of "recolonization" as East Asian societies pursue world-class universities. Having been strongly influenced by Anglo-Saxon standards of academic practice, East Asian universities may be engaged in a process of "policy copying" rather than "policy learning"—a process that may create a new "dependency culture" and reinforce an American-dominated "hegemony" (Mok 2007; Deem, Mok, and Lucas 2008). If so, the quest for world-class universities may prove counterproductive. Having said that, a closer scrutiny of the current reforms of higher education in East Asia may reveal further contrasts between East Asian models and prevailing American and European models, particularly in terms of university governance. The remainder of this chapter will focus on whether and how a new "regulatory regionalism" has evolved among major university systems in Asia.

THE EMERGENCE OF REGULATORY REGIONALISM

The recent transformation and restructuring of higher education in East Asia reflects a wider regional trend that began in the late 1980s to "reinvent the state" and improve the overall efficiency of the public sector (Mok 2006). Another important trend that began at the same time—a trend also evident in the accelerated integration of the European Union—is regulatory regionalism. While the contours of regulatory regionalism are slowly becoming visible in East Asian higher education, this trend is far less developed in East Asia than it has been in the higher-education sector of the European Union.

Regulatory Regionalism in the Making

Admittedly, the European higher-education sector has been dwarfed by its American counterpart since the end of World War II. The higher-education system in the United States is not only the most developed system in the world but also the most renowned for its diversity and flexibility in governance. This successful American model, particularly as it applies to research universities, has increasingly posed a challenge to relatively stagnant and conservative European institutions with their heritage of state control from the eighteenth and nineteenth centuries. Faced with global competition in the realm of higher education, the European Union has responded by attempting to synergize the competitive strengths of European universities through new forms of regulatory regionalism. The effort to improve the quality of European research universities can be found in the Lisbon Strategy initiated by the European Council in March 2000 (Deem, Mok, and Lucas 2008).[21] The Bologna Declaration[22] in 1999 and the subsequent Bologna Process[23] could be regarded as a second effort to regionalize university learning and teaching. Over the past decade, academic degree structures in EU universities have been harmonized to foster student mobility, facilitate credit transfers, and standardize quality assurance (Robertson 2008, 2009). Furthermore, the Bologna Declaration, with its goal of achieving a European Higher Education Area by 2010, has created a framework to promote EU universities within a global market, particularly in Asia. By 2009, membership of the European Higher Education Area included 46 countries with roughly 5,600 public and private institutions and more than 16 million students. Now that Russia and Southeastern Europe have joined the European Higher Education Area, the strategy of regulatory regionalism has the potential to extend far beyond the EU as a constitutional entity (Robertson 2009: 8).

To date, formal mechanisms to promote East Asian regional integration in higher education have not yet been developed; however, signs of regulatory coordination are evident in various regional organizations and in institutional interactions undertaken within a wider framework of ASEAN + 1 (the ten ASEAN countries plus China) or ASEAN + 3 (ASEAN plus China, Japan, and South Korea). For example, in 2007, China and the ASEAN countries signed an Agreement on Trade in Services under the ASEAN-China Free Trade Zone (ACFTA) arrangement, which was set to be realized in 2010. According to this agreement, education services will soon become a market item that can be "traded" transnationally within this zone. At the same time, NGOs such as the Association of Southeast Asian Institutions of Higher Learning (ASAIHL), a consortium of major public universities from various Southeast Asian countries, foster cooperation among member institutions, particularly through regional fellowships and academic exchange programs. A newer but even more relevant organization, the Association of East Asian Research Universities (AEARU) was founded in January 1996 as a forum for presidents of leading research universities in East Asia. Composed of 17 leading universities from Mainland China, Japan, Korea, Hong Kong, and Taiwan, AEARU carries out mutual exchanges among these institutions. AEARU has put an emphasis on the common academic and cultural backgrounds of its member universities, which form a union specifically for the Confucian Cultural Sphere.[24]

Compared with the nongovernmental ASAIHL and AEARU, the Southeast Asian Ministers of Education Organization (SEAMEO) has offered another framework of collaboration with semiofficial functions in the region. Given the fact that all its members, except the Timor-Leste, are also members of ASEAN, SEAMEO effectively acts as the educational wing of ASEAN. Among its 19 specialized centers, the Regional Center for Higher Education and Development (SEAMEO-RIHED) is particularly relevant in initiating reforms in higher-education governance. For instance, SEAMEO-RIHED has recently tried to establish an ASEAN Quality Assurance Network (AQAN) for the \ development of a common set of quality-assurance guidelines. After the first ASEAN Quality Assurance Roundtable Meeting in Kuala Lumpur in 2008,[25] the Kuala Lumpur Declaration recognized the crucial role of quality assurance in advancing the process of harmonization in regional higher education. Moreover, overseas study visits, regional workshops, and seminars regarding university governance or institutional restructuring have also been held by SEAMEO-RIHED over the past few years (SEAMEO-RIHED 2009).[26]

In a preliminary study titled *Harmonisation of Higher Education: Lessons Learned from the Bologna Process* (Supachai and Nopraenue 2008), SEAMEO-RIHED began to explore the creation of a common space of higher education in Southeast Asia. A further research project on that theme followed, and SEAMEO-RIHED subsequently initiated a conference series to raise "awareness" among key stakeholders about the process of higher-education harmonization in Southeast Asia (SEAMEO-RIHED 2009: 6). As the phrase "raising awareness" implies, even though deliberations about the construction of a broad higher-education framework within this region are underway, if compared with the EU's Bologna Process, concrete achievements remain to be seen in ASEAN.[27] Indeed, before 2007, most of the initiatives regarding higher education in ASEAN focused on creating a level playing field for its Indo-China members (Vietnam, Cambodia, Laos, and Myanmar) in terms of infrastructure and human resource development, rather than a systematic mechanism for policy harmonization across the region (IPPTN 2008: 1). Nonetheless, the broader principle of regional coordination lies behind all these efforts.

Close Interuniversity Collaborations and Regionalism in Formation

Major higher-education systems in East Asia have used the opportunity of globalization and the push for world-class university status to reach out to others in the region to strengthen the "Asian presence" in the global higher-education market. In the process, we have seen both competition and collaboration between different higher-education systems in Asia. For instance, Yonsei University in South Korea has set up an international college offering Korean studies in English to attract overseas students. Yonsei has also reached a regional collaboration with the Faculty of Social Sciences at the University of Hong Kong and Keio University in Japan to launch a three-campus program in Comparative Asian Studies. The program recruits students from all three partner institutions to enhance their learning experiences and overseas exposure (Faculty of Social Sciences, University of Hong Kong 2009). Similarly, a new regional research consortium on Asian Education and Development Studies in Asia has participants from all the major comparative education societies in Asia, including those in Mainland China, Hong Kong, Taiwan, Singapore, Japan, South Korea, Australia, and New Zealand (National Chung Cheng University 2009). This new regional research consortium has tried to provide a platform for scholars, academics, and practitioners who are interested in development studies and education in Asia to discuss issues related to development, policy, and governance. Most recently this consortium has launched a regional journal *Asian Education and Development Studies* to marry two fields of studies. The proposed journal will be published by an international publisher in 2012.

Meanwhile, more frequent collaborations and interactions among university systems have taken place between Mainland China, Hong Kong, and Taiwan, with more students and staff participating in academic exchanges and research collaborations. The author of this chapter is currently involved in setting up a new research consortium on comparative Greater China Studies, with positive responses from institutions based in Mainland China, Hong Kong, and Taiwan. A regional symposium on Rapid Social and Economic Change and Policy Response in Greater China was coorganized by the Center of Greater China Studies, the Hong Kong Institute of Education's College of Social Sciences, National Taiwan University, and the Institute for Social Policy and Social Security of Sun Yat-Sen University at the Hong Kong Institute of Education in December 2010. Participating institutions plan to strengthen their collaborations in promotion of Asian scholarship. During a recent visit to Taiwan, the author met the Dean of the College of Social Sciences of National Taiwan University to discuss further collaborations. One possible area for regional joint ventures is the creation of executive master's degree programs for civil servants from Mainland China, Taiwan, and Hong Kong. In view of the improved relationship between Mainland China and Taiwan, academic institutions consider Hong Kong an ideal place to facilitate academic exchange and professional training for students and civil servants from Taiwan and Mainland China. Hong Kong, recognized for its political neutrality, is well positioned to facilitate more regional collaborations for Greater China.

Perhaps the most dynamic aspect of regionalization in global higher education is the effort to create regional hubs of research excellence. Singapore, Malaysia, and Hong Kong are particularly keen to become regional hubs of research, making education services a pillar of economic development and state capacity-building (Mok 2009a). One key to the emergence of these regional hubs has been the aggressive cultivation of transnational higher-education links. Transnational higher-education arrangements are becoming increasingly popular as a way to diversify university systems not only in these places but also in developing economies like Mainland China, India, and the Southeast Asian countries. As Anthony Welch notes in his chapter in this volume, all these places have realized that the state alone does not have the capacity to meet pressing educational demands. East Asian societies have, therefore, allowed overseas academic institutions to mount off-shore programs to create additional education opportunities. Given the rapid expansion and improvement of higher education in East Asia, and in particular the growth and prosperity of the region's network of transnational higher-education arrangements, it is expected that the trend of regulatory regionalism will continue. Over time, China may become the center of this process owing to its remarkable size and its universities' aggressive strategies to achieve world-class status. Indeed, China has begun to use its higher-education sector as a means to exert its cultural "soft power" throughout the region.

Regional shifts are already apparent in various global university rankings. Taking the *Times'* World University Rankings for 2009 as an example, it appears that American supremacy is slipping, and efforts taken by certain East Asian governments have begun to pay dividends. While the United States still has the most institutions in the top-200 list (a total of 54), since 2008 it has lost five institutions from the top 100, and four have dropped out of the top 200 altogether. In the meantime, institutions from Japan, Hong Kong, South Korea, Taiwan, and Malaysia have all improved their rankings, as indicated in table 1.2 (Baty 2009).[28]

Similarly, it seems that the Bologna Process has successfully boosted the attractiveness of the Europe's higher-education market

Table 1.2 Number of institutions in the top-200 list of the *Times'* World University Rankings, 2008 and 2009 (selected cases)

Country / Territory	2008	2009	Difference
United States	58	54	−4
United Kingdom	29	29	0
Canada	12	11	−1
The Netherlands	11	11	0
Germany	11	10	−1
Australia	9	9	0
Japan	10	11	+1
China	6	6	0
Hong Kong	4	5	+1
South Korea	3	4	+1
Singapore	2	2	0
Taiwan	1	1	0
Malaysia	0	1	+1

Source: Adapted from data presented in the official website of *Times Higher Education*: http://www.timeshighereducation.co.uk/Rankings2009-Top200.html (Last accessed on December 18, 2005).

as a common area, particularly among Asian students. The number of Chinese students studying in France and Germany has increased by more than 500 percent (in each country) since early 2000; in comparison, the number of Chinese students in the United States grew by only 50 percent (Verbik and Lasanowski 2007, quoted in Robertson 2008). After examining the enrollment trends of international tertiary students in the top five destinations (the United States, United Kingdom, Germany, France, and Australia), a report issued by the Center for International Initiatives at the American Council on Education (ACE) warned in 2009[29] that competition from others had begun to erode the United States' position as the premier destination for international study. Moreover, this report highlighted the trend of regionalization in the mobility of international students, mentioning the increasing attractiveness of Singapore for Asian students and the United Arab Emirates and Qatar for students from the Middle East. Again, this tendency toward regionalization may spur further collaborations in higher-education governance and regulation in East Asia.

TENTATIVE CONCLUSIONS

New modes of regional higher-education governance are emerging in East Asia. During the past two decades, all the East Asian states discussed in this chapter have adjusted their approaches to higher-education governance, and while internal contexts differ from one case to the next, one common feature characterizes all these restructuring efforts: the persistence of effective state regulation in public institutions. Thus, despite efforts at incorporation and corporatization in university governance, the regulatory autonomy of most East Asian public (national) universities remains in doubt. At the same time, the private sector of higher education has grown dramatically since the 1990s, liberated and encouraged by East Asian states owing to various economic considerations and the need to expand the provision of higher education. Still, the private sector remains largely sidelined in the quest for world-class universities (with South Korea the only exception among the selected cases).

Going forward, government capacity to guide and dictate the developments of higher education in this region may still be the key. Governments have combined pro-world-class policies, including heavy investment from the state, a rapid process of internationalization (e.g., hiring faculty and luring students from overseas), and a strong emphasis on publishing in international—specifically English-language—journals. Yet, even as this quest for world-class universities has had benefits, it may also generate negative side-effects if pursued without proper local and regional contextualization. For instance, stressing the importance of publishing in English-language journals could divert research from issues more relevant to national development. Fostering the use of English may affect intellectual works in local languages and could also handicap nonnative-English-speaking students and scholars. In both the public and private sector, universities have pursued English-oriented internationalization. This trend is particularly evident among the most esteemed public institutions in the region. While the impact of this linguistic policy reform on higher-education governance remains to be evaluated, much debate has been aroused by the issue. Arguably, these shifts in regional higher-education policy have—in one way or another—contributed to the surge of East Asian institutions in global university rankings in the past few years.

A trend toward regulatory regionalism is clearly detectable in East Asia. Despite the fact that regionalization is still in an early phase in Asia, we should not underestimate the importance of the growing prominence of regional collaborations, which may well facilitate new governance models through "network governance." The increasing hybridization of organizations shaping global regionalization may render conventional governance models inappropriate, while new forms of governance may lead to the emergence of super- or mega-regional governance structures to manage the growing complexity of increasingly transnationalized education offerings (Ball 2009). A tangible effort to promote regional integration in higher education is now being attempted by ASEAN mainly through the semiofficial SEAMEO-RIHED. In the long run, however, China may take the lead and pursue further collaborations through a broader regional mechanism such as ASEAN + 3.

If an East Asian model of higher-education governance and regulatory regionalism emerges, could it eventually outpace other models? The American model is distinctive in the sense that it is not dominated by public institutions. In fact, most of its elite research universities are private. Some may argue (e.g., Ding 2004; Hou 2009) that the United States' diversity in higher-education governance and financing, combined with its milieu of academic freedom, has contributed to its supremacy and vigor. However, given that a world-class university must first be a *research* university, and that as Altbach (2007) points out, "almost all research universities outside the United States and Japan are public and state supported" (17), both the European and East Asian models may have good reason to maintain their public-dominated features, supplemented by a spirit of entrepreneurship and autonomy that mimics the private sector. Most leading universities in East Asia are learning from their American counterparts' emphasis on innovative research and their dynamic collaborations with industry. Yet a paradox persists. To promote competition, most East Asian states have resorted to *deeper* regulation (though less explicit than before), yet in the long run such regulation and state control may stifle the real spirit of competition. In the same way, private institutions of higher education have been encouraged as a way to activate the whole system, yet the private sector is largely sidelined in the pursuit of world-class universities. It is not easy—in theory or in practice—to strike a balance between neoliberal marketization and a strong regulatory state. The effectiveness of the East Asian model of higher-education governance, given its specific cultural and historical context, will likely remain open to debate.

Notes

This chapter is based upon a research project funded by the government of the Hong Kong Special Administrative Region. The author wants to thank the Research Grant Council for offering financial support to enable him to under the present report (HKIEd 7005-PPR-6). Thanks must be extended to Dr. OngKok Chung for offering research assistance on the present project.

1. Other prominent examples of national university rankings include those operated by the Maclean's (Canada), the *Times* (UK), the Center for Higher Education Development (Germany), and the Asahi Shimbum (Japan). However, these national rankings existed only from the 1990s onward after being inspired by the American model.

2. The third and also the newest public university in Singapore, Singapore Management University (SMU), was established in August 2000 in collaboration with the Wharton School of Business at the University of Pennsylvania. It in fact implied the first attempt of the Singapore government to adopt a more diversified governance and funding mechanism toward its public higher-education sector.

3. This University Law was thereafter amended in 2002, 2003, 2005, 2006, 2009. The 2005 amendment was particularly significant in the sense that a total of 42 articles were reviewed and revised.

4. A set of four possible regulatory regimes could be categorized from the perspectives of state regulation on the one hand and civil regulation on the other, as shown in table 1.3 (Mok 2008a: 153, developed and modified from Levi-Faur 1998):

Table 1.3 Civil and state regulation

	Civil regulation (strong/ organized)	Civil regulation (weak/ spontaneous)
State regulation (strong/centralized)	Authoritarian liberalism Market-accelerationist state	State socialism Interventionist state
State regulation (weak/decentralized)	Economic liberalism Market-facilitating state	Market socialism Market-coordinating state

5. For instance, although the Ministry of Higher Education in Malaysia has introduced the mechanism of search committees for the appointment of senior leaders of its public universities since 2005, the minister him/herself takes consideration of the committee's recommendations and makes the final decision. The fact that after more than a half century of nationhood, Malaysia has yet to see any non-Malay (roughly 45 percent of its population) appointed as vice-chancellor of any of its public universities shows that this is still a highly biased selection process based primarily on domestic ethnic-political considerations rather than meritocracy, and that the ministry still holds the final control. In fact, even the senior appointments of non-Malays as the deputy vice-chancellors are rare, and it was

only in 2007 that the ministry "decided" to create another position of deputy vice-chancellors to accommodate non-Malay candidates (Abdul Razak 2008: 14).

6. The 211 Project aimed to well-equip a total of 100 Chinese national universities for the twenty-first century, while the subsequent 985 Project intended to concentrate further the state's extra financial provision to a group of only around 40 top institutions that have the potential to achieve international reputations. Put simply, these projects were designed to pump enormous extra resources into China's best universities. For instance, in the first round of three-year grants under the 985 Project, Peking and Tsinghua Universities each received RMB1.8 billion (US$225 million), while Fudan, Zhejiang, and Nanjing Universities each received RMB1.2 billion (US$150 million) (Mohrman 2008: 35, 42).

7. The most recent effort is the Hong Kong PhD Fellowship Scheme, launched by the Research Grants Council (RGC) in 2009. This Fellowship will provide a monthly stipend of HK$20,000, as well as a conference and research-related travel allowance of HK$10,000 per year to qualified PhD students for a maximum period of three years. A total of 135 PhD Fellowships will be awarded for the 2010/2011 academic year.

8. UGC is the governmental organization responsible for shaping the direction of higher-education development in Hong Kong.

9. The Emerging Global Model (EGM) of the twenty-first-century research university is a new concept defined by the New Century Scholars group under a Fulbright program. For details, see (Mohrman, Ma, and Baker 2008).

10. The first target of this Taiwanese higher-education project is to cultivate at least one "world-class" university that could be included into the top-100 list in international league tables within 10 years; its second target is to develop at least 10 research centers of excellence in Asia within 5 years. Accordingly, the National Taiwan University (NTU) and National Cheng Kung University were selected by the Ministry of Education in 2005 as the only two promising universities capable of achieving the first target within 10 years. In fact, NTU has successfully scored 95th in the most recent 2009 World University Rankings (*Times Higher Education Supplement*) from the ranks of 102 in 2007 and 124 in 2008. For details of this project, see http://www.edu.tw/files/list/B0069/發展國際一流大學及頂尖研究中心計畫書(中文版).pdf.

11. In fact, one of the two private universities, Yuan Ze University, was excluded from the list two years after the implementation of the plan owing to an unsatisfactory assessment result.

12. The Brain Korea 21 Project stands for "Nurturing Highly Qualified Human Resources for the 21st Century Knowledge-Based Society." After its first-phase implementation (1999–2005), the South

Korean government claimed that BK21 had achieved: (1) an increasing number of SCI-level papers in science and technology: 3,765 (1998)→7,281 (2005); (2) the rise of SCI national ranking: 16th (1998)→12th (2005); (3) quality improvement as indicated by the average Impact Factor per article: 1.9 (1999)→2.43 (2005). http://english.mest.go.kr/main.jsp?idx=0301020101&brd_no=52&cp=1&pageSize=10&srchSel=&srchVal=&brd_mainno=528&mode=v (Accessed on December 15, 2005).

13. These two public institutions are Seoul National University and Korea Institute of Science and Technology; whereas the five private institutions are Pohang University of Science and Technology, Korea University, Yonsei University, Sungkyunkwan University, and Hanyang University. According to a statistics from the Ministry of Education & Human Resources Development, these top-seven research universities contributed 56 percent of the total number of SCI-level paper in 2001, a time when there were aggregately 192 four-year universities and colleges in Korea. http://unpan1.un.org/intradoc/groups/public/documents/APCITY/UNPAN015416.pdf (Accessed on December 15, 2009).

14. Again, the South Korean case is exceptional if compared with others. Since its economy is dominated by Chaebols (big enterprises) under the auspices of the state, these Chaebols, with abundant resources, usually set up their own in-house research units, and this could lower the necessity and importance of state-run research institutes.

15. For instance, in Singapore, A*STAR (Agency for Science, Technology & Research) is the leading government agency dedicated to fostering world-class scientific research and talent for the city-state. A*STAR actively nurtures public sector R&D in biomedical sciences and physical sciences & engineering through its 14 public research institutes and 7 consortia & centers located in Biopolis and Fusionopolis and their vicinity. Official website of A*STAR (Accessed on December 16, 2009): http://www.a-star.edu.sg/AboutASTAR/Overview/tabid/140/Default.aspx.

16. For instance, Singapore is today home to 16 leading foreign tertiary institutions and 44 pretertiary schools offering international curricula (official website of the Global Schoolhouse initiative: http://www.edb.gov.sg/edb/sg/en_uk/index/industry_sectors/education/global_schoolhouse.html). The prestigious INSEAD (Institut Européend' Administration des Affaires, established its Singapore branch campus in 2000), the University of Chicago Booth School of Business (2000), S. P. Jain Center of Management (2006), the New York University's Tisch School of the Arts (2007), Digi Pen Institute of Technology (2008) are among the list of these foreign tertiary institutions, ranging from business, management arts, media, and hospitality to information technology, biomedical sciences, and engineering.

17. Singaporean society may well be the closest to this title among these East Asian cases. However, though English has long been the first language to be taught in its education system and functions as the predominant official language (there are in fact four official languages in Singapore, namely English, Mandarin, Malay, and Tamil), according to a survey taken by the Ministry of Education since 1980, by the year of 2004, Mandarin was still the dominant home language for around half of the Chinese Singaporean Primary 1 students (http://www3.moe.edu.sg/press/2004/pr20040109.htm).

18. Before 2008, these two databases were run by Thomson Scientific, one of the five operating divisions of the Thomson Corporation. Thomson merged with Reuters to form Thomson Reuters in 2008.

19. There are four aspects of assessment in *The Times* annual rankings, namely, reputation (peer review 40 percent + recruiter review 10 percent), research (citations/faculty 20 percent), teaching (faculty/student 20 percent), and internationalization (international faculty 5 percent + international students 5 percent). It is, however, worth noting that *Times Higher Education* (previously the *Times Higher Education Supplement*) have signed an agreement with Thomson Reuters to provide all the data for its annual World University Rankings from 2010 onward and ended its relationship with the previous partner—QS. Accordingly, the company claims that it will develop a new methodology and will publish a revamped World University Rankings with separate rankings by subject areas starting in 2010. (http://www.timeshighereducation.co.uk/story.asp?sectioncode=26&storycode=408908&navcode=105)

20. For details of the university's current language policy after the debates, please refer to Report of the Committee on Bilingualism, the Chinese University of Hong Kong (July 16, 2007): http://www.cuhk.edu.hk/policy/english/bilingualism/downloads/cob-report-e.pdf

21. The Lisbon Strategy aims at making the EU the world's "most dynamic and competitive economy," and with respect to higher education, it has focused on the challenges of creating a knowledge economy and the necessity of innovation.

22. In 1999, the education ministers of 29 European countries and European university heads met to discuss the future development of European higher education, and subsequently issued the Bologna Declaration.

23. "Convinced that the establishment of the European area of higher education required constant support, supervision and adaptation to the continuously evolving needs" (Bologna Declaration 1999), the European education ministers decided to meet regularly to assess progress, thus transforming this commitment into an ongoing policy process.

24. AEARU's membership includes five top research universities from Mainland China (Peking, Tsinghua, Fudan, Nanjing, University of

Science & Technology of China); six from Japan (Tokyo, Kyoto, Osaka, Tohoku, Tsukuba, Tokyo Institute of Technology); three from South Korea (Seoul National University, Korea Advanced Institute of Science & Technology, Pohang University of Science & Technology); two from Taiwan (Taiwan, TsingHua); and one from Hong Kong (Hong Kong University of Science & Technology).

25. This roundtable meeting in 2008 was coorganized by SEAMEO-RIHED and the Malaysian Qualifications Agency (MQA). Since then, it has become an annual roundtable meeting with specific theme related to quality assurance of the region's higher education.

26. For instance, the Regional Seminar on University Governance in Southeast Asian Countries was held at Luang Prabang, Laos, on October 14, 2008 (SEAMEO-RIHED 2009).

27. For example, while academic mobility within the region has been improved and efforts have also been taken toward establishing a regional quality assurance system, there is by far no regional agreement on the comparability of degree programs.

28. Japan counts 11 institutions in the top 200, and its representatives in the top 100 rose in number from 4 to 6. As regards Hong Kong, despite having only a total of 8 public tertiary institutions, it has 5 institutions in the top 200, up from 4 in 2008. And most remarkably, its tally includes 3 in the top 50. South Korea has 4 universities in the top 200, up from 3 in 2008. Malaysia returned to the top 200 with its Universiti Malaya entering at 180th place (Baty 2009). Taiwan eventually secured a place in the top 100 (National Taiwan University, 95), yet it is also the only score for Taiwan in the top 200. As for the Mainland China, there remain two institutions in the top 100 and a total of 6 in the top 200. Singapore has also continued to secure 2 institutions in the top 100.

29. http://www.acenet.edu/Content/NavigationMenu/Programs Services/cii/pubs/ace/SizingUptheCompetition_September09.pdf

BIBLIOGRAPHY

Abdul Razak Ahmad. 2008. "The University's Governance in Malaysia: Re-examining the Role of the State," paper presented at the symposium on *Positioning University in the Globalized World: Changing Governance and Coping Strategies in Asia*, the University of Hong Kong, Hong Kong, December 10–11.

Altbach, Philip G. 2003. "The Costs and Benefits of World Class Universities," *International Higher Education* 33: 5–8.

Altbach, Philip and Daniel C. Levy (eds.). 2005. *Private Higher Education: A Global Revolution*. Rotterdam: Sense.

Altbach, Philip G. and Jorge Balán (eds.). 2007. *World Class Worldwide: Transforming Research Universities in Asia and Latin America*. Baltimore: Johns Hopkins University Press.

Ball, Stephen. 2009. "Global Education, Heterarchies and Hybrid Organizations," paper presented at the 2009 Asian-Pacific Forum on Sociology of Education: Social Change and Education Reform, May 6–8, National University of Tainan.

Baty, Phil. 2009. "Rankings 09: Asia Advances," *Times Higher Education,* October 8. http://www.timeshighereducation.co.uk/story.asp?storycode =408560

Bologna Declaration. 1999. *The European Higher Education Area.* Joint Declaration of the European Ministers of Education Convened in Bologna, June 19.

Cerny, Philip G. 1997. "Paradoxes of the Competition State: The Dynamics of Political Globalization," *Government and Opposition* 32(2): 251–274.

Chan, David K. K. 2007. "Global Agenda, Local Responses: Changing Education Governance in Hong Kong's Higher Education," *Globalisation, Societies and Education* 5(1): 109–124.

Chan, David K. K. and William Lo. 2008. "University Restructuring in East Asia: Trends, Challenges and Prospects," *Policy Futures in Education* 6(5): 641–652.

Chan, David K. K. and Pak Tee Ng. 2008. "Developing Transnational Higher Education: Comparing the Approaches of Hong Kong and Singapore," *International Journal of Educational Reform* 17(3): 291–307.

Chou, P. 2006. "Taiwan's Higher Education at the Crossroad: Implications for China," paper presented at the International Forum on Education (IFE) Senior Seminar EWC, Hawaii, United States.

Deem, Rosemary, Ka Ho Mok, and Lisa Lucas. 2008. "Transforming Higher Education in Whose Image? Exploring the Concept of the 'World-Class' University in Europe and Asia," *Higher Education Policy* 21(1): 83–97.

Ding Xueliang (丁學良). 2004. 什麼是世界一流大學? *(On University Reform and Development).* 北京: 北京大學出版社. Beijing: Peking University Press.

Faculty of Social Sciences, the University of Hong Kong. 2009. "3 Campus Programme in Comparative Asian Studies," website of Faculty of Social Sciences, HKU, www.hku.hk/socsc.

Federkeil, Gero. 2008. "Ranking Higher Education Institutions: A European Perspective," *Evaluation in Higher Education* 2(1): 35–52.

Fong, Pang Eng and Linda Lim. 2003. "Evolving Great Universities in Small and Developing Countries," *International Higher Education* 33: 9–10.

Gill, S. 1995. "Globalization, Market Civilization and Disciplinary Neoliberalism," *Millennium* 24(3): 399–423.

Hanson, E. Mark. 2006. "Strategies of Educational Decentralization: Key Questions and Core Issues," in Christopher Bjork (ed.), *Educational Decentralization: Asian Experiences and Conceptual Contributions,* pp. 9–25. Dordrecht: Springer.

Hawkins, John N. 2006. "Walking on Three Legs: Centralization, Decentralization, and Recentralization in Chinese Education," in

Christopher Bjork (ed.), *Educational Decentralization: Asian Experiences and Conceptual Contributions*, pp. 27–41. Dordrecht: Springer.

Hou, Yung-Chi (侯永琪). 2009.〈二十一世紀美國研究型大學的研究競爭力——由高等教育分類與排名分析〉"Research Performance of American Research Universities in the 21st Century in Classification and Ranking," *Journal of Higher Education* 4(1): 1–38.

Huang, Mu-Hsuan (黃慕萱). 2008.〈華人四地大學研究競爭力分析〉"Research Competitiveness of Universities in Taiwan, China, Hong Kong, and Singapore," *Evaluation in Higher Education* 2(1): 77–105.

IPPTN (Institut Penyelidikan Pendidikan Tinggi Negara). 2008. "Harmonisation of Higher Education (Part 2): Initiatives and the Future for Southeast Asia," *IPPTN Updates on Global Higher Education*, no. 39, September 15. Penang, Malaysia: IPPTN, Universiti Sains Malaysia.

Jayasuriya, K. 2000. "Authoritarian Liberalism, Governance and the Emergence of the Regulatory State in Post-Crisis East Asia," in R. Robinson, M. Beeson, K. Jayasuriya, and H. R. Kim (eds.), *Politics and Markets in the Wake of theAsian Crisis*, pp. 315–330. London: Routledge.

———. 2008. "Regionalizing the State: Political Topography of Regulatory Regionalism," *Contemporary Politics* 14(1): 21–35.

Jordana, J. and Levi-Faur, D. 2005. "Preface: The Making of a New Regulatory Order," *Annals of the American Academy of Political and Social Science* 598(1): 1–6.

Kaneko, M. 2004. "Japanese Higher Education: Contemporary Reform and the Influence of Tradition," in P. G. Altbach and T. Umakosji (eds.), *Asian Universities: Historical Perspectives and Contemporary Challenges*, pp. 115–143. Baltimore: Johns Hopkins University Press.

Kim, Ee-gyeong. 2006. "Educational Decentralization in Korea: Major Issues and Controversies," in Christopher Bjork (ed.), *Educational Decentralization: Asian Experiences and Conceptual Contributions*, pp. 115–128. Dordrecht: Springer.

Knight, J. 2006a. *Higher Education Crossing Borders: A Guide to the Implications of the General Agreement on Trade in Services (GATS) for Cross-Border Education*. Paris: United Nations Educational, Scientific and Cultural Organization & Commonwealth of Learning.

———. 2006b. "The Role of Crossborder Education in the Debate of Education as a Public Good and Private Commodity," paper presented at the International Forum on Education (IFE) Senior Seminar EWC, Hawaii, United States.

Lee, Michael H. H. 2005. "Major Issues of University Education Policy in Hong Kong," *Asia Pacific Education Review* 6(2): 103–112.

Lee, Michael H. H. and Saravanan Gopinathan. 2001. "Centralized Decentralization of Higher Education in Singapore," *Education and Society* 19(3): 79–96.

———. 2008. "University Restructuring in Singapore: Amazing or a Maze?," *Policy Futures in Education* 6(5): 569–588.

Lee, Molly N. N. 1999. "Corporatization, Privatization, and Internationalization of Higher Education in Malaysia," in P. G. Altbach (ed.), *Private Prometheus: Private Higher Education and Development in the 21st Century.* New York: Greenwood Press.

———. 2004. *Restructuring Higher Education in Malaysia.* Penang, Malaysia: School of Educational Studies, Universiti Sains Malaysia.

———. 2006a. "Centralized Decentralization in Malaysian Education," in Christopher Bjork (ed.), *Educational Decentralization: Asian Experiences and Conceptual Contributions*, pp. 149-158. Dordrecht: Springer.

———. 2006b. "Public vs. Private Higher Education: Tensions or Partnerships? A Southeast Asian Perspective," paper presented at the International Forum on Education (IFE) Senior Seminar EWC, Hawaii, United States.

Lee, Molly N. N. and Stephen Healy. 2006. "Higher Education in South-East Asia: An Overview," in UNESCO (ed.), *Higher Education in South-East Asia*, pp. 1–12. Bangkok: UNESCO Asia & Pacific Regional Bureau for Education.

Levi-Faur, David. 1998. "The Competition State as a Neo-mercantilist State: Understanding the Restructuring of National and Global Telecommunications," *Journal of Socio-Economics* 27(6): 655–686.

Liu, Nian Cai and Ying Cheng. 2005. "The Academic Ranking of World Universities," *Higher Education in Europe* 2 (30): 127–136.

Lo, Y. W. and F. Y. Weng. 2005. "Taiwan's Responses to Globalization: Decentralization and Internationalization of Higher Education," in K. H. Mok and R. James (eds.), *Globalization and Higher Education in East Asia*, pp. 137–156. Singapore: Marshall Cavendish Academic.

Min, W. F. 2004. "Chinese Higher Education: The Legacy of the Past and the Context of the Future," in P. G. Altbach and T. Umakosji (eds.), *Asian Universities: Historical Perspectives and Contemporary Challenges*, pp. 53–83. Baltimore: Johns Hopkins University Press.

Mohrman, Kathryn. 2008. "The Emerging Global Model with Chinese Characteristics," *Higher Education Policy* 21(1): 29–48.

Mohrman, Kathryn, Wanhua Ma, and David Baker. 2008. "The Research University in Transition: The Emerging Global Model," *Higher Education Policy* 21(1): 5–27.

Mok, Ka Ho. 2000. "Marketizing Higher Education in Post-Mao China," *International Journal of Educational Development* 20(2): 109–126.

———. 2003a. "Beyond Decentralization: Changing Roles of the State in Education," in Ka Ho Mok (ed.), *Centralization and Decentralization: Educational Reforms and Changing Governance in Chinese Societies*, pp. 203–217. Hong Kong: Comparative Education Research Center, University of Hong Kong.

———. 2003b. "Education," in I. Holliday and P. Wilding (eds.), *Welfare Capitalism in East Asia: Social policy in the Tiger Economies*, pp. 37–69. Basingstoke: Palgrave Macmillan.

———. 2003c. "Similar Trends, Diverse Agendas: Higher Education Reforms in East Asia," *Globalization, Societies & Education* 1(2): 201–221.

———. 2005. "Globalization and Educational Restructuring: University Merging and Changing Governance in China," *Higher Education* 50(1): 57–88.

———. 2006. *Education Reform and Education Policy in East Asia.* London: Routledge.

———. 2007. "Questing for Internationalization of Universities in Asia: Critical Reflections," *Journal of Studies in International Education* 11(3–4): 433–454.

———. 2008a. "Positioning as Regional Hub of Higher Education: Changing Governance and Regulatory Reforms in Singapore and Malaysia," *International Journal of Educational Reform* 17(3): 230–250.

———. 2008b. "Varieties of Regulatory Regimes in Asia: The Liberalization of the Higher Education Market and Changing Governance in Hong Kong, Singapore and Malaysia," *Pacific Review* 21(2): 147–170.

———. 2008c. "When Domestic Forces Meet the Global Trends: The Liberalization of the Privateness in East Asian Higher Education," *Evaluation in Higher Education* 2(1): 53–76.

———. 2009a. "The Quest for Regional Hub of Education: Growing Heterarchies, Organizational Hybridization and New Governance in Singapore and Malaysia," *Journal of Education Policy* 26(1): 61–81.

———. 2009b. "When State Centralism Meets Neo-Liberalism: Managing University Governance Change in Singapore and Malaysia," paper accepted for publication by *Higher Education.*

Mok, Ka Ho and A. Welch (eds.) 2003. *Globalization and Educational Restructuring in the Asia Pacific Region.* Basingstoke: Palgrave Macmillan.

Mok, Ka Ho and H. H. Lee. 2000. "Globalization or Re-colonization: Higher Education Reforms in Hong Kong," *Higher Education Policy* 13(4): 361–377.

Mok, Ka Ho and Richard James (eds.) 2005. *Globalization and Higher Education in East Asia.* Singapore: Marshall Cavendish Academic.

Mok, Ka Ho and Ying Chan. 2008. "International Benchmarking with the Best Universities: Policy and Practice in Mainland China and Taiwan," *Higher Education Policy* 21(4): 469–486.

Moon, Mugyeong and Ki-Seok Kim. 2001. "A Case of Korean Higher Education Reform: The Brain Korea 21 Project," *Asia Pacific Education Review* 2(2): 96–105.

Moran, M. 2002. "Review Article: Understanding the Regulatory State," *British Journal of Political Science* 32: 391–413.

Morshidi Sirat. 2008. "Incorporation of State-Controlled Universities in Malaysia, 1996–2008: Flirting with the Market," *Global Higher Education*, June 8, 1–5.

————. 2009. "Strategic Planning Directions of Malaysia's Higher Education: University Autonomy in the Midst of Political Uncertainties," *Higher Education*, DOI 10.1007/s10734-009-9259-0.

National Chung Cheng University, Graduate Institute of Education. 2009. Comparative Education and Development Studies Research Consortium. Paper presented at the Comparative Education and Development Regional Symposium, September 2009, National Chung Cheng University, Chaiyi, Taiwan.

Robertson, Susan L. 2008. " 'Europe/Asia' Regionalism, Higher Education and the Production of World Order," *Policy Futures in Education* 6(6): 718–729.

————. 2009. "The EU, 'Regulatory State Regionalism' and New Modes of Higher-Education Governance," paper presented to the panel on *Constituting the Knowledge Economy: Governing the New Regional Spaces of Higher Education*, International Studies Association Conference, New York.

————. 2010. "Global Regionalism and Higher Education: Reimagining Policies, Projects and Politics," paper presented to the CIES Annual Conference on *Reimagining Education*, March 1–5, Chicago, United States.

Rozman, G. 1992. "The Confucian Faces of Capitalism," in M. Borthwick (ed.), *Pacific Century: The Emergence of Modern Pacific Asia*, pp. 308–316. Boulder, CO: Westview Press.

Salmi, Jamil and Roberta Malee Bassett. 2009. "Rankings 09: Measures Matter," *Times Higher Education*, October 8. http://www.timeshigher education.co.uk/story.asp?storycode=408566

Scott, C. 2004. "Regulation in the Age of Governance: The Rise of the Post-Regulatory State," in J. Jordana and D. Levi-Faur (eds.), *The Politics of Regulation: Institutions and Regulatory Reforms for the Age of Governance*, pp. 145–177. Cheltenham: Edward Elgar.

SEAMEO-RIHED. 2009. *Annual Report*. Bangkok: Regional Center for Higher Education and Development, Southeast Asian Ministers of Education Organization (SEAMEO-RIHED).http://www.seameo.org /images/stories/SEAMEO_General/About_SEAMEO /SEAMEO%20Units/Centers_Annual_Rpt/RIHED_Executive _Summary_2008_2009.pdf

Shin, Jung Cheol. 2009. "Building World-Class Research University: The Brain Korea 21 Project," *Higher Education* 58(5): 669–688.

Song, Mei-Mei and Hsiou-Hsia Tai. 2007. "Taiwan's Responses to Globalization: Internationalization and Questing for World Glass Universities," *Asia Pacific Journal of Education* 27(3): 323–340.

Supachai, Y. and S. D. Nopraenue. 2008. *Harmonisation of Higher Education: Lessons Learned from the Bologna Process*. Bangkok: SEAMEO-RIHED.

Tan, Charlene and Pak Tee Ng. 2007. "Dynamics of Change: Decentralised Centralism of Education in Singapore," *Journal of Educational Change* 8(2): 155–168.

Tan, Jason. 2006. "Limited Decentralization in the Singapore Education System," in Christopher Bjork (ed.), *Educational Decentralization: Asian Experiences and Conceptual Contributions*, pp. 59–70. Dordrecht: Springer.

Tien, F. 2006. "Incorporation of National University in Taiwan: Challenges for the Government and the Academics," paper presented at the International Workshop on University Restructuring in Asia, Hiroshima, Japan.

World Bank. 2007. *Malaysia and the Knowledge Economy: Building a World-Class Higher Education System (Report No. 40397-MY)*. New York: Human Development Sector, East Asia and Pacific Region, the World Bank.

CHAPTER 2

Contributing to the Southeast Asian Knowledge Economy? Australian Offshore Campuses in Malaysia and Vietnam

Anthony R. Welch

INTRODUCTION

This chapter reviews the recent rise in foreign direct investment (FDI) in offshore campuses of Australian universities, in Malaysia and Vietnam, in the context of a rise in global trade in services, including educational services. The first section traces the rise of service-sector trade, especially in higher education, and assesses its significance in the context of a so-called knowledge economy with marked differences between the global "North" and "South." The next section charts the rise of FDI related to higher education, revealing a similar dominance by wealthier nations. The chapter examines the changing patterns of investment for Vietnam and Malaysia as each government has allowed greater privatization in its higher-education sector. This shifting context—driven in part by responses to globalization and structural adjustment measures since the 1980s—has encouraged Australian universities to invest in branch campuses in both Vietnam and Malaysia. Exploring the different pattern of growth of each branch campus and its business model, the chapter concludes with an assessment of the potential benefits of FDI in branch campuses for developing countries, and the very real problems these campuses can bring, or aggravate.

For decades, the model for international education was a mix of aid to developing countries (as with the Colombo Plan or other such scholarship schemes), the promotion of cultural exchanges, the draw of national prestige, and/or the expression of international goodwill. In the new millennium, characterized by ubiquitous rhetoric about the "knowledge economy," education is increasingly treated as an engine of economic growth and international competitiveness. This framework very much includes international education, or as it is now coming to be termed, transnational trade in education services. Current estimates put this trade, largely in the higher-education sector, at more than US$50 billion annually worldwide, a figure that has attracted increasing interest among economists from organizations such as the World Trade Organization, the World Bank, the Asian Development Bank, and the Organization for Economic Cooperation and Development (OECD 2002, 2004a, 2004b; WTO 2001, 2002; APEC 2001).

The trend toward the commercialization of transnational education was accelerated in 1995 by the passage of the Global Agreement on Trade in Services (GATS), to which more than 140 nations are now signatories. The four modes by which trade in education services occurs can be summarized as shown in table 2.1. As indicated in table 2.1, Mode 2, or students studying in another country, has been the dominant form of transnational education thus far, but the other modes are growing fast. FDI in transnational higher education— including the establishment of foreign branch campuses—falls under Mode 3 (Commercial Presence).

The trend to view international higher education as a form of trade rather than aid raises a number of questions. First, trade is rarely conducted on the much-touted level-playing field; rather, there are almost always winners and losers. Analysis of trade in education services shows that winners fall into two categories: (1) providers from richer countries; and (2) providers from English-speaking countries (OECD 2004; Welch 2011c). Mode 2 exchanges in education provide confirmation of the unequal flow of resources from poorer to richer countries. It has been estimated that OECD nations host 85 percent of all international enrollments in higher education worldwide (OECD 2002: 95), with six countries—the United States, United Kingdom, France, Germany, Australia, and Japan—accounting for 75 percent of all international students. Similarly, the dominance of Mode 2 trade in higher-education services by English-speaking nations is clear, with the four main English-speaking countries (the United States, United Kingdom, Australia, and Canada) accounting for 54 percent

Table 2.1   Modes of provision of cross-border education services under GATS

Mode	Explanation	Examples	Size and potential
1. Cross-border supply	The service, not the person, crosses the border	- Distance Education - Education Software - Virtual Education (including Corporate Training)	Small so far, but growing rapidly, with great growth potential, especially via Information and Communications Technology (ICT)
2. Consumption abroad	The consumer moves to the country of the supplier	- Students who study overseas	Still the largest share of transnational education
3. Commercial presence	Provider uses or establishes facilities in a second country	- Local university or satellite campus - Private providers (often business, IT, and languages)	Growing phenomenon, with strong likelihood of further growth
4. Presence of natural persons	Persons traveling to a second country to provide a service	- Professors, teachers, consultants	Given greater mobility among professionals, likely to grow strongly

Source: Adapted from OECD 2002.

of all international enrollments (94) and some 70 percent of students from Asia/Oceania. Table 2.2 shows how Mode 2 trade in higher-education services has grown among three major English-language providers over the past three decades. Even this table, however, underestimates the dominance of the English language in trade in education services, as an increasing number of non-English-speaking countries, including several within the Asia-Pacific region, are now offering programs in English.

This dominance of English also includes programs at branch campuses. For example, table 2.2 does not reveal the disproportionate growth in Australian "offshore" enrollments, that is, students who remain in their home country but are officially enrolled in an Australian university. Offshore enrollments can take two forms: (1) distance-education programs (Mode 1 in the GATS table above); or (2) enrollment at a branch campus of an overseas university (Mode 3). A dramatic rise in offshore enrollments has been a key feature of international student enrollments within the Australian

Table 2.2 International student enrollment growth, Australia, the United Kingdom, and the United States, 1980–2002

Year	Australia	Growth	United States	Growth	United Kingdom	Growth	Japan	Growth	Germany	Growth
1980	8,777	–	311,822	–	56,003	–	–	–	–	–
1985	13,047	8.6	342,113	.7	53,694	4.3	–	–		
1990	47,065	60.7	386,851	3.1	77,800	4.8				
1994	69,819	8.3	449,749	6.2	97,188	53.4				
1999	84,304	0.7	490,933	.2	213,000	.0	56,552		187,195	
2006	166,954	8.0	572,509	6.6	300,056	0.9	117,903	08.5	260,314	39.1

Source: Data compiled from *Overseas Student Statistics* (1994; 1999; 2003) Canberra: Australian Education International [AEI]; *Open Doors* (1993–1994; 1998–1999; 2004). Washington: Institute for International Education; *UNESCO Statistical Yearbook* (1998; 1983; 1993; 1989; [1989–1998 = Paris, UNESCO); *Global Education Digest* (/2006) Montreal: UNESCO Institute for Statistics; Department of Education and Science (1991) *Statistical Bulletin*. London: Department of Education and Science; HESA (2000; 2004) *Higher Education Statistics*. London: Higher Education Statistics Agency.

Note:

1. For consistency, UNESCO statistics used for the UK, but compared with DES sources.
2. Large rises in Australia 1985–1990 and the United Kingdom 1990–1994 partly result from changed institutional arrangements within each higher-education system, notably mergers.

system in recent years. More students from the Asia-Pacific region are seeking qualifications from Australian universities while at the same time avoiding the high costs (and perhaps the interruption to career and family life) associated with living in Australia. Many offshore students are enrolled in Australian branch campuses.

The increase in offshore enrollments was initially fueled by the effects of the regional economic crisis that hit Southeast Asia in the 1990s, and by significant shifts in the value of the Australian dollar. The more recent global financial crisis of 2008–2009 has produced similar effects (*Star Online* 2009). Figures show that, until the mid-1990s, demand for offshore programs was modest; since then, growth has been rapid. Whereas in 1996 some 21 percent of Australian universities' international enrollments fell into this category, by 1999 this figure had risen to 33 percent (IDP 2002). In 2002 it was 35 percent, with 28 percent, or some 45,000 students, at offshore campuses and the other 7 percent enrolled via distance-learning technology. By 2004, offshore enrollments totaled some 73,000 students, 70 percent of whom were in Southeast Asia and China (AVCC 2003). In recent years, offshore enrollments have grown at a significantly faster rate than onshore international enrollments, and the number of offshore programs has proliferated. In 1997, there were 341 offshore programs (AVCC 1998); by 2003, this number had risen to 1,569 (NTEU 2004). For onshore/offshore enrollments at selected universities in the year 2000, see table 2.3.

Notwithstanding this dramatic rise of international trade in higher-education services, countervailing forces are at work. Higher-education systems are both important repositories of national cultures and treasured national status symbols. For these reasons, reform is often resisted, particularly reform that originates externally. It is notable, for example, that very few of the signatories to GATS listed their higher-education sector as open to competition. In practice, then, the focus of this study—transnational higher education under Mode 3—involves a delicate mix of competition, cultural sensibilities,

Table 2.3 International students in selected Victorian universities by onshore/offshore status, 2000

University	Onshore	Offshore	Total
Monash	5,648	3,204	8,852
RMIT	4,912	4,123	9,035
Melbourne	4,902	–	4,902

Source: Compiled from Victorian Auditor General 2002.

and (as Ka Ho Mok notes in his chapter in this volume) both national and regional regulatory regimes.

Higher Education and the Knowledge Economy

The rise in cross-border trade in education services in Australia and Southeast Asia is part of two wider trends. The first is the admittedly uneven rise of regional economies and the increasing economic integration of Australasia with ASEAN. The signing of an ASEAN trade agreement at the Vientiane Summit in 2004 aimed to *double* two-way trade and investment between the ASEAN group and Australasia—then valued at A$50 billion annually—over the next decade (Australian 2004a). If achieved, this aim will certainly enhance regional service-sector trade, including trade in education. The second trend affecting cross-border trade in education services is a shift in Southeast Asian regional economies from agriculture and manufacturing to service-based growth, underlined in the title to the 2004 World Investment Report of the UN Conference on Trade and Development (UNCTAD): *The Shift towards Services.*

This shift toward services places great emphasis on investments in human capital. In the so-called post-Fordist economy, productivity and efficiency are in large measure viewed as outcomes of workers' skill levels and their capacity to work both individually and in teams to anticipate and solve production problems. In most OECD countries, knowledge-based industries (including education) account for an increasing share of national employment as well as the value added to the business sector. Knowledge-based industries now account for more than 50 percent of total GDP in OECD countries, a proportion that continues to grow (OECD 2000).

Steep growth in higher-education enrollments is evident in the Asia-Pacific region (albeit differentially in Australia and ASEAN) and is related to an increasing demand for more highly educated and highly skilled workers (OECD 2001). This upskilling and the increasing demand for competencies that are themselves knowledge-based (e.g., the capacity to communicate effectively with people from other cultures) are now often claimed to be constitutive of the new millennium's globalized knowledge economy. Reich (1991) estimated that "symbolic analysts" (generally agreed to refer not merely to science and technology specialists but also to highly skilled white-collar workers who are involved in some aspect of knowledge creation, management, or coordination) account for about 20 percent of the US workforce. While some workers continue to gain required competencies via nonformal means, most recruitment within OECD countries still strongly emphasizes higher levels of formal education.

Although the paradigm for knowledge-based economies is that of OECD member states, the benefits of knowledge-based economies are by no means limited to such countries. Ministries of Trade, of Education, of Science and Technology, of Finance, and of Human Resource Development in countries across the Asia-Pacific region extol the virtues of knowledge-based economies for advancing national development. International organizations are not shy about proclaiming the capacity of knowledge institutions to promote growth in developing countries. As one UNCTAD report put it,

> Knowledge-based economies are an effective response to the challenges currently faced by developing countries, especially those whose savings rates and direct investment are not sufficient to stimulate sustainable economic development from capital accumulation alone. (UNCTAD 2004a)

This emphasis on knowledge-based economies to make up for low domestic savings and investment rates describes the situation in both Vietnam and Malaysia. Both have liberalized their regulatory regimes to allow for the establishment of more private higher-education institutions, including branch campuses run by overseas providers.

NORTH-SOUTH DIFFERENCES IN THE KNOWLEDGE ECONOMY

As many observers have noted, the knowledge economy has taken hold in greater density among developed economies than in developing economies, and the process of globalization is in some respects widening this gap. A World Bank study in 2000 noted that the global North had roughly ten times more research and development personnel (scientists and technicians) per capita than the South (3.8 percent compared to 0.4 percent) and spent about four times more of its GDP on research and development (2.0 percent compared to 0.5 percent). In addition, the North was responsible for some 97 percent of all patents registered in the United States and Europe and, together with the newly industrializing countries of East Asia, accounted for 84 percent of all scientific articles published (World Bank 2000: 69). While it must be admitted that indices such as the Science Citation Index (SCI), Social Science Citation Index (SSCI), and Engineering Index (EI) are biased in favor of English-language journals (thus adding linguistic disadvantage to existing disparities of wealth), the North-South gap in academic output and impact is illustrative (table 2.4).

Comparative figures put these data into perspective: Australian publications for 1995 totaled 18,088, and Japanese publications totaled 58,910. Citation counts for each country in the period from 1993 to 1997 were 301,320 and 930,981, respectively. Later data indicate real growth in innovation measures in Southeast Asia but still a significant gap between Southeast Asia and the developed world. (Similar disparities arise in the case of patents; see table 2.5.) While Welch (2010c, 2010d, 2011a, 2011c) has shown that both Vietnam and Malaysia made giant strides with regard to such research indicators in the past 20 years or so—as have East Asian countries such as China, Korea, and Taiwan (Yang and Welch 2010)—a huge gap remains between ASEAN states and developed economies with comparatively advanced infrastructure and longstanding higher education and research systems. The global knowledge economy is no level-playing field.

Table 2.4 Papers and citations, by country, 1980s and 1990s

Country	Number of papers 1981	Number of papers 1995	Number of citations 1981–1985	Number of citations 1993–1997
Malaysia	229	587	1,332	3,450
Vietnam	49	192	203	1,657

Source: Compiled from *Higher Education in Developing Countries*, 125–127.

Table 2.5 US patents granted, by region, country, and level of development

	Number of patents			Patents per 100,000 people		
	1990–1994	2000–2004	% Change	1990–1994	2000–2004	% Change
Southeast Asia	31	140	450	0.01	0.04	15.3
Indonesia	6	15	250	0.00	0.01	8.8
Malaysia	13	64	492	0.07	0.28	15.3
Philippines	6	18	300	0.01	0.02	10.4
Thailand	6	43	717	0.01	0.07	20.9
Developed (Average)	104,170	168,017	61	12.88	19.58	4.3

Source: Compiled from World Bank 2006.

The Rise of Service-Sector Foreign Direct Investment

How have countries like Vietnam and Malaysia used foreign direct investment in higher education to position themselves in a rapidly—if still unevenly—changing global knowledge economy? The answer to this question reveals similarities and differences between the two countries. In the late 1990s, Vietnam established a Foreign Investment Bureau in its Ministry of Planning and Investment to supervise and coordinate foreign investment in its main service-sector industries: call centers, data processing, and consulting and information services. Vietnam also revised its Law on Corporate Income Tax in 2003 to end discriminatory policies for foreign enterprises (UNCTAD 2004b: 53). In the wake of these reforms, Vietnam has seen a swift rise in FDI from the Vietnamese diaspora (known as *Viet Khieu* and numbering 2.7 million worldwide), many of whom are now visiting or returning to and establishing businesses in Vietnam. FDI inflow from *Viet Khieu* doubled in four years, rising to US$6 billion in 2006. This inflow "now outstrips the amount Vietnam receives in either foreign aid or international investment" (SCMP 2005a). Malaysia has followed a similar path, encouraging FDI into call centers and software development within its Multimedia Super Corridor. Capital inflows for both Vietnam and Malaysia for the period from 1970 to 2003 are shown in table 2.6, with comparative data for China and East Asia overall.

One of the most visible trends in this table is the rise of China as a magnet for FDI. Whereas in 1970 China did not register on this scale at all, it now attracts almost half of all FDI in Asia (49.9 percent). Notwithstanding some growth in trade in (educational) services

Table 2.6 FDI inflows to Malaysia and Vietnam, China and Asia, 1970–2003 (US$ billion)

Year	Asia	China	Malaysia	Vietnam
1970	811	0	94	0
1980	407	57	934	0
1990	24,310	3,487	2,611	180
1995	79,589	37,521	5,815	1,780
2000	146,067	40,715	3,788	1,289
2001	111,854	46,878	554	1,300
2002	94,383	52,743	3,203	1,200
2003	107,120	53,505	2,474	1,450

Source: Compiled from UNCTAD 2004: 368–370.

between China and ASEAN (Welch 2011b, 2011c), this growth has come at the expense of parts of Southeast Asia, as the data for Malaysia show. Whereas in 1970 Malayasia attracted 11.6 percent of total Asian FDI, by 2003 it attracted only 2.3 percent. Certainly, the Asian currency crisis had a dramatic impact, with FDI into Malaysia falling precipitously between 1995 and 2001. It fell again between 2002 and 2003, despite a 27 percent rise in FDI into Southeast Asia (UNCTAD 2004b: 50). The picture for Vietnam is broadly similar, though the numbers are smaller and the trend more positive. In 1980 (barely a year after the country finally became free of war), Vietnam did not register any significant FDI, and even as late as 1990, Vietnam attracted a mere 0.74 percent of the total for Asia. The picture changed, however, during the 1990s, reaching a peak in 1995 (as with Malaysia). Once again, the regional currency crisis brought a slump in FDI in Vietnam, although the figures show that Vietnam recovered more ground proportionally than Malaysia, attracting some 1.4 percent of total Asian FDI in 2003. Overall, FDI has risen dramatically over the past two decades in both countries, in Malaysia from US$5.2 billion in 1980 to US$59 billion in 2003, and in Vietnam from US$9 million to US$18.6 billion over the same period (UNCTAD 2004b: 379). China, by comparison, attracted $72 billion in FDI in 2006, and US$101 billion in 2010, as compared with US$7 billion for Malaysia and an estimated US$9–10 billion for Vietnam (UNCTAD 2011; FDI Vietnam [n.d.]).

What is not revealed in these tables is the changing balance of FDI, especially the trend toward the service sector. From 1990 to 2002, the proportion of total FDI in the service sector rose in developed economies from 49 percent to 62 percent, and the same trend was evident in developing countries, where FDI in the service sector rose from 47 percent to 55 percent (UNCTAD 2004b: 30). The proportion of FDI occupied by the service sector grew from 58 percent to 73 percent in developed countries and from 35 percent to 50 percent in developing countries (263). This increase was mirrored in ASEAN, where the service-sector share of FDI rose from 30 percent in 1992 to 48 percent in 2003 (52). This growth has probably been, at least in part, an effect of the *ASEAN Framework Agreement on Services* (1995)—which prioritized four service-sector industries: air travel, tourism, health, and e-ASEAN—and the China ASEAN Free Trade Agreement (CAFTA), initiated in January 2010 (although most liberalization has thus far been restricted to goods rather than services). While this list excluded educational services (54), education

Table 2.7 Estimated world inward FDI, average annual flows, education (US$ million)

1989–1991			2001–2002			
Developed countries	Developing countries	World	Developed countries	Developing countries	Central and Eastern Europe	World
8	5	12	–8	31	6	29

Source: Compiled from UNCTAD 2004: 318.

has become one of the fastest-growing sectors with respect to FDI in developing countries (see table 2.7).

Attitudes toward FDI in education services have begun to change for various reasons. First, host countries have recognized that, where state capacity is limited, FDI can help to bridge the gap between educational supply and demand. In some places, this greater openness to FDI is related to the strictures of structural adjustment, which significantly eroded funding available to public-sector services, including education (Welch and Mok 2003). Second, the traditional view that only manufacturing could promote technology transfer is changing, as states realize that wider forms of skills transfer, including information processing, management, and organization, are also transferable (always allowing, of course, for differences of culture and tradition). Moreover, FDI can help to spur local industries. UNCTAD (2004b) notes: "FDI can add to the availability of competitive services, and therefore help domestic firms become internationally competitive in an increasingly globalised and knowledge-based world economy" (124).

Even as FDI in education services grows, concerns persist. For example, a common concern in many developing countries is that foreign providers of higher education may come to dominate the local scene in a sector that has considerable cultural significance, acting as both a repository of cultural traditions and a locus of cultural development. Hence there is often a concern that "Some services are...susceptible to exploitation of power by [foreign providers]...unless the government can set up and manage a complex regulatory system" (UNCTAD 2004b: 124). Yet, the capacity of the state to regulate foreign providers cannot always be taken for granted, at least not in Southeast Asia (see, for example, Welch 2010b, 2010d, 2011c, 2011d). Moreover, the question of the suitability of imported curricula and the readiness of foreign higher-education institutions to adapt knowledge to local conditions and priorities has arisen in various countries. Finally, there is a concern that FDI in educational services may result in a net loss of foreign exchange earnings via repatriated profits.

While governments see the injection of new ideas and knowledge via FDI in higher education as a means to internationalize their domestic university systems and perhaps raise the quality of local higher-education institutions, these concerns cannot be ignored. Improving local higher-education institutions can make local economies more attractive to knowledge- and skill-intensive industries from abroad and perhaps stimulate demand, competitiveness, and quality in associated local industries (indeed, increases in FDI in the services sector can boost local training and education, for example, via collaboration with local universities, and research and development projects in local science parks where these exist). But there is nothing necessary about this virtuous cycle, especially given the dominance of FDI flows by wealthy nations. Nor is there anything necessary about wealthy nations offshoring higher education into poorer nations. On the contrary, UNCTAD notes that "So far, most offshoring has taken place *among* developing countries, which underscores that it is not primarily a North-South issue" (UNCTAD 2004b: 147, emphasis added).

THE RATIONALE FOR FDI IN HIGHER EDUCATION AND THE ROLE OF OFFSHORE CAMPUSES

Both Malaysia and Vietnam have long been net importers of education services, although the former's 60,000 international enrollments in its higher-education system has substantially tipped the balance over recent years (Welch 2011d). In both countries, the investment regime has been liberalized in recent years and policies have been introduced to allow more foreign providers into the higher-education sector. Moreover, both Malaysia and Vietnam have relatively strong economic growth rates. Malaysia's GDP rate per capita signifies its status as a middle income, albeit still developing, country, and in Vietnam, especially in the more prosperous and entrepreneurial south, disposable income levels are rising and interest in education is keen. The traditional importance attached to learning within Southeast Asia is driving FDI in higher education in both countries. Table 2.8 gives relevant economic indicators for Malaysia and Vietnam, with comparative data for China and Australia.

Table 2.8 Comparative economic indicators, Malaysia and Vietnam

	Average GDP growth 1992–2002 (%)	GDP per capita
Malaysia	5.3	4,022
Vietnam	6.7	417
Australia	3.9	19,923
China	9.0	902

Source: Compiled from UNCTAD 2004: 286–288.

Table 2.9 Private higher-education institutions in Malaysia, May 2001

Institution Type	Number of institutions		Number of students		Number of academics	
	Total	Kuala Lumpur	Total	Kuala Lumpur	Total	Kuala Lumpur
College Status	652	158	209,589	48,512	8455	1808
University Status	10	2	20,839	933	855	45
University Branch Campus	4	2	1,641	110	95	11
Total	666	162	232,069	49,555	9395	1864

Source: Compiled from Sohail and Saeed 2003: 175.

FDI and Branch Campuses in Malaysia

Traditionally, enrollment in Malaysian universities has been limited, both in the public system (from which Chinese Malays, approximately one quarter of the population, were largely excluded by ethnic quotas) and in the private system, which is substantially funded by local investment. Notwithstanding substantial public investment, ever-rising demand has tested state capacity. A shortage of university places in the public sector has led to increasing privatization, underpinned by new legislation passed in the mid-1990s. The extent of change is indicated by the fact that, until the passage of the Private Higher Education Act (1996), the National Council on Higher Education Institutions Act (1996), the Universities and University Colleges (Amendment) Act (1996), the National Accreditation Board

Act (1997), and the National Higher Education Fund Board Act (1997), there were no private universities in Malaysia. By 2010, there were 20 private universities and some 650 private colleges, as well as 4 branch campuses of overseas universities (see table 2.9).

Current policy has moved from a heavy dependence on the state toward a "Malaysia Inc." approach, which embraces both domestic private-sector higher-education institutions and foreign higher-education institutions. As the ministry's website indicates,

> To take full advantage of the opportunities offered by an increasingly borderless world, foreign universities are being encouraged to set up offshore branches in Malaysia, but only the best will receive approval. At the same time, corporations have been given the mandate to establish private universities. This dynamic relationship between government, the private sector, and strategic foreign academic partners will no doubt help us realise our goals. (Study Malaysia 2003)

In keeping with this message, the Malaysian Association of Private Colleges and Universities (MAPCU) advertises its interest in promoting Malaysian education abroad, including via international partnerships and the establishment of foreign branch campuses in Malaysia, and Malaysian Ministers regularly promote the country's higher-education system abroad (Welch 2011d).

Monash University-Malaysia

This new environment has proved congenial to overseas providers, who have in recent years sought to establish branch campuses with Malaysian partners. The earliest example was the Australian institution Monash University-Malaysia, formed in early 1998 in partnership with the Sunway Group Malaysia (Banks and McBurnie 1999). An incorporated company called Monash University Sunway Campus Malaysia SdnBhd (MUSCM) was established to operate the institution, with Monash University and Sunway as shareholders. The issued capital of MUSCM consisted of 5 million ordinary shares, divided between Sunway, which has a majority 76 percent interest (3.8 million shares), and Monash University, which holds the remaining 24 percent (1.2 million shares). Monash University paid a total of A$503,000 for its shares in MUSCM. While the balance of power on the Board of Directors is with Sunway, academic matters fall entirely under the authority of Monash University and its relevant faculty boards, academic board, and university council. Under the operating agreement,

Sunway provides infrastructure facilities under a lease arrangement while Monash University provides the university's teaching staff (it should be noted that local academic-staff pay and working conditions differ significantly from those of Monash's Australian staff, who may teach in Malaysia from time to time). The Monash University-Malaysia campus offers undergraduate programs in engineering, arts and science, information technology, nursing, and business (though comparatively few students are enrolled in arts subjects). All students taking courses at Monash University-Malaysia are enrolled as Monash students and are awarded a Monash degree or diploma.

The website of Monash University-Malaysia claims that students may save around 40 percent in tuition and associated costs as compared with studying at Monash's campus in Australia. Any costs that Sunway incurs for providing and maintaining facilities are recovered via management fees and rental charges. Any costs that Monash incurs for providing education services and materials are recovered via royalties from the Monash Sunway Operating Company. A study to determine the costs of the Monash University-Malaysia campus concluded that annual support costs for the university were around A$832,000 for the 2000 financial year, offset by A$1.4 million in royalties and administration charges. While revenue targets were not met between 1998 and 2001, expenditures were lower than expected owing to decreased academic costs (a result of lower-than-expected student enrollments) and royalties paid by the operating company. Hence, the campus exceeded its budgeted profit expectations in the initial years.

Since it opened, Monash University-Malaysia has continued to expand its programs. In 2005, 50 students enrolled in medicine at MUSCM, taking the first two years of their medical education at Monash in Melbourne and their subsequent training in Malaysia. The medical course at Monash University-Malaysia has the same structure as the course in Australia, with the same admission requirements and the same assessment content and standards. Students who complete the course receive the same international degree as graduates from Monash University-Australia. The medical program plans to make resources available for medical research that is relevant to Malaysia. Indeed, the university has been able to leverage its presence to attract research investment by local firms. For example, National Instruments-ASEAN joined Monash University-Malaysia to create a pilot remote-access electrical engineering laboratory that enables students to conduct experiments over the Internet. The opportunity for Monash students at one campus to take a semester or more at the university's other campus is seen as an additional advantage, while the prospects of studying in another language (Behasa Melayu) may also prove attractive to some.

Monash University-Malaysia has been a success, but such a positive outcome cannot be taken for granted. A very different outcome befell a joint-venture campus in Malaysia between the Royal Melbourne Institute of Technology (RMIT) and Adorna Institute of Technology (AIT), Penang, which opened in 1996 but failed three years later. Attracting only about 300 students, issues such as a poor choice of site (50 km from the closest city), poor building standards, poor prospects for private education, lack of experience in education on the part of the Malaysian partner, difficulties in attracting appropriate local staff, overcapitalization, and the impact of the Asian currency crisis on the value of the local partner's property portfolio led to failure. Ultimately, A\$2.3 million was written off by RMIT (though it subsequently claimed that many Malaysian students transferred to RMIT's Melbourne campus to finish their studies, thereby allowing the institution to recoup its investment). The different experiences of Monash and RMIT in Malaysia show that success is not guaranteed in the establishment of foreign branch campuses. As it happened, RMIT enjoyed considerably more success in Vietnam.

RMIT Vietnam

While Vietnam has a long history of higher education, poverty and a century of war against colonialism and foreign incursions limited both the quantity and the quality of higher-education opportunities in that country (Tipton, Jarvis, and Welch 2003; Welch 2010a). Moreover, Vietnam's specialist research institutions—largely a legacy of Russian influence—were ill-adapted to the needs of a modernizing economy. Only in the 1980s did the situation begin to change. The year 1988 saw the establishment of the first People's University, a virtual copy of the Chinese Minban, or private university (as in China, the term *private university* was eschewed in favor of People's University). Four years later, the state formally loosened its grip over higher education, and within a decade, enrollment patterns showed a steady growth of private universities in Vietnam.

Private-sector higher education doubled its share of enrollments in Vietnam during the three years from 1996 to 1999, and current government plans are to raise the private share of total enrollments to 30 percent by 2010 and 40 percent by 2020 (Welch 2010a). It was in this context that the establishment of private branch campuses began (see table 2.10).

Table 2.10 Enrollments, public, semipublic, and private higher-education institutions, 1996–1997 and 2006–2007

Type of HEI	Number 1996–1997	% 1996–1997	Number 1997–1998	% 1997–1998	Number 1998–1999	% 1998–1999	Number 2006–2007	% 2006–2007
Public	525,596	88.50	631,994	88.35	696,375	87.17	1,346,529	87.40
Semipublic	42,448	7.15	37,518	5.25	33,254	4.16	—	—
People's	25,840	4.35	45,719	6.39	69,288	8.67	193,471	12.60
Total	593,884	100.00	715,321	100.00	798,817	100.00	1,540,000	100.00

Source: Compiled from Information Section MOET 2002; Welch 2010a.

Note: The semipublic category was formally abandoned in 2005.

The case of RMIT's branch campus in Vietnam reveals a complex mix of entrepreneurialism, strong bilateral relations between the two countries, support from local firms, philanthropic support, an established in-country presence of many years, and government commitment to open the country to service-sector trade and FDI in higher education. In this case, the foreign branch campus was associated with RMIT (then also engaged in what became its failed venture in Malaysia). For the Vietnamese government, a key factor shaping the branch campus was the state's insistence on full foreign ownership and independent international curricula so that a new university, with a technical and vocational emphasis, might quickly come into being as a model and training ground to assist the development of capacity across the education, training, and research sectors (Wilmoth 2004: 4).

RMIT promised to fulfill all these conditions in its Vietnam branch campus. The origins of RMIT's branch campus in Ho Chi Minh City predate its formal opening. As early as August 1994, RMIT had established links with Vietnam National University in Hanoi. In 1995, the two universities founded a joint Center for Systems Development (Nguyen 2000). Through the Center for Systems Development, nearly 50 students obtained their master's degrees in Systems Engineering, conferred by RMIT. Besides this program, RMIT forged links with other institutions to train executive staff for such corporations as Ford Vietnam, Telstra, Petro Vietnam, Vietnam Post and Telecommunications, the Bank of Investment and Development of Vietnam. Based on these and other projects, RMIT was invited in May 1996 to consider establishing an RMIT International University in Vietnam. In January 1998, RMIT received in-principle approval for this venture and, with this endorsement, spent A$2.8 million to locate a suitable site, conduct feasibility studies, pursue market research, draft a business plan, and prepare a formal application for an investment license. In April 2000, after more than two years of preparation, RMIT received its license, which allowed the RMIT International University to operate for a 50-year term under the Law on Foreign Investment in Vietnam.

RMIT Vietnam commenced operations in Ho Chi Minh City in January 2001, with Michael Mann (former Australian ambassador to Vietnam) as CEO. The choice of Ho Chi Minh City proved to be a good one. A city of some 7 million inhabitants, Ho Chi Minh City now accounts for 18.4 percent of national GDP. Foreign investment in Ho Chi Minh City increased by some 40 percent in 2004, and Ho Chi Minh leaders have made the development of the service sector an economic priority (SCMP 2005c). The creation of RMIT Vietnam fit this service-sector emphasis. Programs include university-preparation programs; intensive English classes; undergraduate programs in information technology and commerce; master's degree programs in systems engineering, education, architecture, and information technology; and postgraduate degrees in various fields of scientific and technological research. RMIT's cross-sectoral profile, in which it offers both traditional higher-education programs and vocational courses, meant that the Ho Chi Minh campus was well-placed to offer both industry training and short courses as well as higher-education programs. Courses at RMIT Vietnam are generally the same as those at RMIT's campus in Melbourne, but delivery structures differ, requiring extensive use of distance-learning technology. The medium of study in all cases is English.

As with Monash University-Malaysia but more explicitly in the case of Vietnam, the intention of RMIT Vietnam is to use the branch campus to promote local university reform. RMIT Vietnam has led other universities in Vietnam to compete with its standards, even as RMIT itself expands into new areas. A new 60-hectare site in South Saigon has been located within a designated development zone and plans to have 10,000 students by 2012. Industry links were a key component of the planning for this new site. The new campus includes research institutes in fields such as environmental studies, information technology, urban planning and infrastructure, business management and finance, biotechnology and food, and product innovation and manufacturing design. Along with industry links, a core element of the plan for the new campus was the idea that "each area would work with and attract funds from corporate, government, non-governmental, and philanthropic sponsors" (Willmoth 2002).

RMIT Vietnam differs from Monash University-Malaysia in several ways, including its financial planning and structures, which were underpinned by key loans from the Asian Development Bank (ADB) and the International Finance Corporation (IFC), each of which provided A$13.5 million. In addition, a key gift of US$18.9 million was received from the US philanthropic foundation, Atlantic Philanthropies (at the time, this gift was valued at A$27.6 million). This gift helped to finance start-up debt and equity injections estimated at A$30.4 million. This financial arrangement was unique. First, RMIT entered into a Debt Service Reserve Account Agreement together with the Commonwealth Bank, the ADB, and the IFC. Under this agreement, RMIT could be required to deposit up to A$12.9 million in a Debt Service Reserve Account (the amount deposited was to be reduced by any amount contributed under the terms of the Financial Support Agreement). Other agreements then limited RMIT's liability to $12.9 million in the event of project failure (Auditor General 2002). This agreement sustained the venture in its early years, since RMIT Vietnam was not expected to be profitable before 2007, nor was it expected that any dividends would be paid to RMIT before 2011.

The experiences of Monash University-Malaysia and RMIT Vietnam reveal both similarities and differences. Both cases are part of a wider strategy of internationalization within Australian universities, and both seek to extend training opportunities not merely to local students in each setting but also to students from across the region. They also seek to use their branch campuses to extend international opportunities to students at their Australian campuses. At the same time, Monash University-Malaysia and RMIT Vietnam have key differences. First, the RMIT Vietnam case illustrates that an early in-country presence was significant in laying the groundwork for a later branch campus. Second, it reveals that philanthropy and external support via scholarships and infrastructure support were key factors in the university's growth and development. Third, while FDI was crucial in the establishment of each university, the business structure of each investment was different. RMIT Vietnam was supported by key loans from international agencies and a major gift. At this point, RMIT Vietnam remains the only fully owned offshore campus of an Australian university and possibly the only fully foreign-owned university in Asia. RMIT Vietnam also offers a wider educational profile than Monash University-Malaysia (an understandable difference given that RMIT Melbourne began life more than a century ago as a working men's college and remains a cross-sectoral institution with substantial involvement in both vocational training and conventional higher education). Thus while Monash University has been able to leverage its presence in Malaysia to secure support from Malaysia-based industry, RMIT Vietnam has established a larger footprint among local firms.

CONCLUSION

In the context of what UNCTAD (2004b) rightly characterizes as a "shift toward services" in global trade, trade in *education* services forms a key component. The much-touted knowledge economy of the twenty-first century depends on a new generation of knowledge workers. While governments everywhere extol the virtues of this new economy to lift growth rates and enhance global economic competitiveness, few if any can sustain the costs entailed in supporting the increasing demand for higher education. This tension between ever-increasing demand and limited state capacity poses a particular challenge for developing countries, which, while keen to deploy higher education in the service of national development, face major financial and infrastructural constraints (Johnstone 2009; Welch 2010a, 2011c). A demographic profile characterized by a high proportion of young people, growing aspirations for higher education, and limited state finances has led many Southeast Asian governments to turn to privatization—including investments from foreign providers—as a means of extending opportunities in higher education without extending state liabilities (Welch 2010a, 2011c).

In this context, FDI in higher education has been a significant means to increase higher-education opportunities and promote higher quality and greater competitiveness among domestic higher-education institutions. This chapter's account of the rationale for and development of Australian branch campuses in Vietnam and Malaysia reveals that FDI has played a critical role in each case. While Vietnam will remain a net importer of education services for the foreseeable future, Malaysia has moved vigorously to export its education services, most notably to China and Muslim countries (Welch 2011c). And yet, the potential benefits of branch campuses and their associated FDI need to be weighed against the genuine problems that such ventures present. Questions of equity and parity, for example, obtain for both students and staff. The Australian Universities Quality Agency (AUQA), a national agency charged with quality assessment of universities has highlighted problems of parity in relation to branch campuses. The lower pay and employment conditions of academic staff appointed under local conditions and the lower level of student facilities and experience have been cited as problems in studies of overseas branch campuses (indeed, these problems have led one recent study to describe the branch-campus approach in terms of a "core" and "periphery" model (Coleman 2001). Steps to enhance branch-campus conditions have now been taken by more than one Australian university in light of critical reviews by AUQA.

A second key issue also relates to quality assurance. Several of the ASEAN states have difficulty regulating the quality of their domestic higher-education institutions, especially in an era of accelerating privatization (Tipton, Jarvis, and Welch 2003; 2010a). The demands of ensuring the quality of hundreds of higher-education institutions with only a small national agency often taxes state capacity, quite apart from issues of corruption and cronyism that obtain in some states and limit capacity to control quality (Welch 2007a and 2007b). If the ability to oversee domestic institutions is already beyond the reach of several Southeast Asian states, how much more might this be the case when offshore campuses are added to the mix? While a "well-designed regulatory regime, aimed at ensuring the quality, scope, and availability of a given service, contributes to improvements expected from FDI, just as it contributes to improvements under local (public or private) owners" (UNCTAD 2004b: 191), such a regime cannot be taken for granted in several Southeast Asian states.

This lack of regulatory capacity may limit the potential benefits of foreign branch campuses. According to UNCTAD (2004b),

> A weak regulatory framework in some developing countries may be a factor limiting the extent to which certain services are offshored from Europe or North America.... Various observers suggest that stricter regulations in some developing countries (notably India) may be necessary to avoid a backlash. (207)

While branch campuses can spur quality improvements and competitiveness among domestic institutions, the absence of a solid regulatory regime may encourage the proliferation of spurious or poor-quality branch campuses, with potential losses accruing to both students and investors.

Who, then, are the winners and losers regarding FDI in branch campuses? Certainly, FDI in branch campuses can be a means to increase access to higher education beyond the small percentage in developing countries who have traditionally been able to gain scholarships to study abroad, or pay the substantial fees and living expenses that studying abroad entails (Wilmoth 2004: 3). If it is true that enrolling in a branch campus can save as much as 40 percent of the total costs of a university degree, this may explain some of its growing appeal. At the same time, given the climate of increasing privatization in global higher education, it is crucial that the needs of the poor, rural dwellers, women, and other marginal groups are not overlooked in the rush to promote higher-education development. Scholarships are one means to make opportunities more widely available for students who are unable to afford the high fees that private universities command, but scholarships are few while able students are many. It is, therefore, necessary to maintain a well-financed, widely available public higher-education system that serves the many who are unable to afford other options. FDI by wealthy countries in branch campuses in poor countries can assist in development and equalizing opportunity or it can deepen divisions between the haves and the have-nots, both within and between nations. The two cases analyzed above look more promising than most, but each must be evaluated in terms of practical outcomes over time.

BIBLIOGRAPHY

Altbach, P. and T. Umakoshi (Eds.) (2004) *Asian Universities. Historical Perspectives and Contemporary Challenges.* Baltimore: Johns Hopkins University Press.

APEC (2001) *Measures Affecting Trade and Investment in Education Services in the Asia-Pacific Region.* Singapore: APEC Secretariat.

Auditor General Victoria (June 2002) "Case Studies of Selected Associated Entities and Joint Ventures of Victorian Universities," http://www.audit.vic.gov.au/reports_mp_psa/psa0202.html#P1355_42164 (Accessed December 23, 2004).

Australian Broadcasting Commission (ABC) "Australia to Sign Southeast Asian Non-Agression Pact," http://www.abc.net.au/am/content/2005/s1528168.htm (Accessed June 10, 2010)

Australian Vice Chancellors' Committee (1998) *Australian Universities Offshore Programs.* Canberra: AVCC
——— (2003) *Offshore Programs of Australian Universities.* Canberra: AVCC.

Australian, The (2004a) "ASEAN Deal to Double Trade with the Region," September 27.
———(2004b) "Joining the ASEAN Club," September 27.
———(2004c) "PM's Parting Shot at WTO," September 27.

Banks, M. and G. McBurnie (1999) "Embarking on an Educational Journey—The Establishment of the First Foreign Full University Campus in Malaysia under the 1996 Education Acts: A Malaysian-Australian Case Study," *Higher Education in Europe*, 24 (2): 265–272.

Coleman David (2001) *The Core and the Periphery: Organizational, Educational and Transformative Trends in the Internationalization of Higher Education.* Unpublished PhD, University of New South Wales.

Davis, D., A. Olsen, and A. A. Bohm (Eds.) (2000) *Transnational Education Providers, Partners and Policy: Challenges for Australian Institutions Offshore.* Canberra: IDP

FDI Vietnam (2011) Official Statistics and News, http://www.fdivietnam.com/tag/fdi-vietnam-2010 (Accessed January 20, 2011)

IDP (2002) *International Students Enrolled in Australian Universities 1994–2002.* Canberra: IDP.

Johnstone, B. (2009) "Worldwide Trends in Financing Higher Education," J. Knight (Ed.) *A Conceptual Framework: Financing Higher Education, Access and Equity.* Rotterdam: Sense.

Lee, M. (2004) Malaysian Universities. Towards Equality, Accessibility and Quality. P. Altbach and T. Umakoshi (Eds.) *Asian Universities. Historical Perspectives and Contemporary Challenges.* Baltimore: Johns Hopkins University Press, pp. 221–238.

National Tertiary Education Union (2004) *Excess Baggage: Australian Staff Involvement in the Delivery of Offshore Courses.* NTEU Research Report, Melbourne.

Nguyen, X. (2000) *RMIT International University Vietnam: An Innovative Vision for Developing Vietnamese Studies.* Unpublished Paper, University of California,

Organization for Economic Cooperation and Development [OECD] (2000) *Science, Technology and Industry Outlook.* Paris: OECD.

―――― (2001) *Education Policy Analysis 2001.* Paris: OECD.

―――― (2002) *Education Policy Analysis 2002.* Paris: OECD.

―――― (2003) *Education at a Glance 2003.* Paris: OECD.

―――― (2004a) "Cross Border Education. An Overview," *Internationalization and Trade in Higher Education. Opportunities and Challenges.* Paris: OECD, pp. 17–38.

―――― (2004b) "Cross Border Post Secondary Education in the Asia-Pacific Region," *Internationalization and Trade in Higher Education. Opportunities and Challenges.* Paris: OECD, pp. 137–204.

―――― (2004c) *Innovations in the Knowledge Economy.* Paris: OECD.

Pham, Luan huong and G. Fry (2004) "Universities in Vietnam. Legacies, Challenges and Prospects," P. Altbach and T. Umakoshi (Eds.) *Asian Universities. Historical Perspectives and Contemporary Challenges.* Baltimore: Johns Hopkins University Press.

Pritchard, W. (2005) "Trends and Contexts for Foreign Direct Investment in Southeast Asia" In B. Pritchard et al. (Eds.) *Regulating Foreign Direct Investment: Southeast Asia at the Crossroads.* Sydney: Research Institute for Asia and the Pacific (RIAP), pp. 1–29.

Pyvis, D. and A. Chapman (2004) "Student Experiences of Offshore Higher Education: Issues for Quality," Australian Universities Quality Agency (AUQA) Occasional Publications Number 3.

Reich, R. (1991) *The Work of Nations.* New York: Simon and Schuster.

Senate Employment, Workplace Relations, Small Business and Education References Committee (2001) *Universities in Crisis.* Canberra: Parliament of Australia.

Shinn, Chris, A. Welch, and N. Bagnall (1999) "Culture of Competition. International Student Policies in the United States and Australia," *Journal of Further and Higher Education,* 23, 1: 81–100.

Sohail, M. Sadiq and M. Saeed (2003) "Private Higher Education in Malaysia. Students' Satisfaction, Levels, and Strategic Implications," *Journal of Higher Education Policy and Management,* 25, 2: 173–181.

South China Morning Post (2005a) "Foreign Direct Investment Reaches a Record US$60b," January 15.

———— (2005b) "Ho Chi Minh City Goes Furthest and Fastest in Market Makeover," January 12.

———— (2005c) "Rich Returning Boatpeople Give Buoyancy to Growth," January 14.

Star Online (2009) "Education Industry Expected to Remain Positive This Year," http://biz.thestar.com.my/news/story.asp?file=/2009/1/12/business/2933045&sec=business

Tipton, Ben, D. Jarvis, and A. Welch (2003) "Vietnam," *Re-Defining the Borders between Public and Private in Southeast Asia.* Tokyo: Ministry of Finance/RIAP, University of Sydney, pp. 212– 254.

United Nations Conference on Trade and Development (UNCTAD) (2004a) New Partnership for the Mediterranean Region. UNCTAD and the Institut de la Méditerranée sign agreement. Press Release December 17.

———— (2004b) *World Investment Report 2004. The Shift towards Services.* UN, New York and Geneva.

———— (2011) *Global Investment Trends Monitor. Global and Regional FDI Trends in 2010,* www.unctad.org/en/docs//webdiaeia2011_en.pdf

Welch, A. (2002) "Going Global. Internationalising Australian Universities in a Time of Global Crisis," *Comparative Education Review,* 46, 4 (November 2002): 433–471.

———— (2004) "Internationalising Australian Universities. Two Case Studies," B-S. Rhee (Ed.) *Internationalization of Higher Education.* Seoul, Korean Educational Development Institute/Ministry of Education and Human Resource Development. (In Korean).

———— (2005b) "New Millennium, New Milieu," A. Welch (Ed.) *The Professoriate. Profile of a Profession.* Amsterdam: Springer.

———— (2007a) "Blurred Vision? Public and Private Higher Education in Indonesia," *Higher Education,* 54, 5: 665–687.

———— (2007b) "Ho Chi Minh Meets the Market. Public and Private Higher Education in Vietnam," *International Education Journal,* 8, 3: 35–56.

———— (2010a) *Financing Higher Education for Inclusive Growth in Asia.* Manila: Asian Development Bank.

———— (2010b) "Internationalization of Vietnamese Higher Education: Retrospect and Prospect." G. Harman, M. Hayden, and N. Pham (Eds.) *Reforming Vietnamese Higher Education. Challenges and Priorities.* Dordrecht: Springer, pp. 197–214.

———— (2010c) "Measuring Up? The Competitive Position of South East Asian Higher Education," M. Sirat, S. Kaur, and W. Tierney (Eds.) *Critical Issues in Quality Assurance and University Rankings in Higher Education in the Asia-Pacific.* Penang: University Sains Malaysia Press.

———— (2010d) "Vietnam, Malaysia, and the Global Knowledge System," L. Portnoy, V. Rust, and V. Bagley (Eds.) *Higher Education, Policy and the Global Competition Phenomenon.* London: Palgrave Macmillan.

——— (2011a) "Changing Balance, Blurring Borders: South East Asian Higher Education in the Global Era," *Higher Education in Southeast Asia. Blurring Borders, Changing Balance.* London: Routledge.

——— (2011b) "The Dragon the the Tiger Cubs. China-ASEAN Relations in Higher Education," D. Jarvis and A. Welch (Eds.) *ASEAN Industries and the Challenge from China.* London: Palgrave Macmillan.

——— (2011c) *Malaysia, Higher Education in Southeast Asia. Blurring Borders, Changing Balance.* London: Routledge.

——— (2011d) *Vietnam, Higher Education in Southeast Asia. Blurring Borders, Changing Balance.* London: Routledge.

Welch, A. and B. Denman (1997) "The Internationalization of Higher Education: Retrospect and Prospect," *Forum of Education,* 51, 1: 30–52.

Welch, A. and Ka Ho Mok (Eds.) (2003) "Conclusion. Deep Development or Deep Division?" *Globalization and Educational Re-structuring in Asia and the Pacific.* London: Palgrave Macmillan.

Wilmoth, D. (2002) "Planning a New University in Vietnam: Innovation in Urban Development," *Eastern Regional Organization for Planning and Housing, 18th World Congress,* Kuala Lumpur, October (unpublished paper).

——— (2004) "RMIT Vietnam and Vietnam's Development: Risk and Responsibility," *Journal of Studies in International Education,* 7, 10: 1–20.

World Bank (2000) (Task Force on Higher Education and Society) *Higher Education in Developing Countries.* Washington: World Bank

——— (2006) *An East Asian Renaissance. Ideas for Economic Growth.* Washington, DC: World Bank.

World Trade Organization (WTO) (2001) *Annual Report 2001.* Geneva: WTO.

——— (2002) *Services Negotiations Offer Real Opportunities for All WTO Members and More for Developing Countries.* (Press Release, June 28), Geneva: WTO.

Yang, R. and A. Welch (2010) "Does China Have a World Class University? The Case of Tsinghua," *AC21* Conference, Zhejiang University, Hangzhou, China, October.

RELATED WEBSITES

ASEAN, www.aseansec.org
ASEAN member economies basic indicators, http://www.aseansec.org/macroeconomic/aq_sel1.htm
APEC, www.apecsec.org.sg
ASEAN Statistics Unit, *Statistical Yearbook,* www.aseansec/org/macroeconomic/aq
Ministry of Education, Malaysia, http://keduak.moe.gov.my/english

Monash Malaysia, www.monash.edu.my/
Related ESCAP data is available at http://www.unescap.org
Related OECD data is available at www.oecd/org/edu/eag2003
Related UNCTAD data is available at UNCTADwww.unctad.org
RMIT Vietnam, http://www.rmit.edu.vn/public/asp/home.asp
Victorian Auditor General's Report, http://www.audit.vic.gov.au/reports
_mp_psa/psa0202.html
WTO/GATS http://www.wto.org/english/tratop_e/serv_e/gatsqa_e.htm

PART II

The Changing Dimensions of University Governance

CHAPTER 3

Collegiality and Hierarchy: Coordinating Principles in Higher Education

Ivar Bleiklie

INTRODUCTION

Since their origin in medieval Europe, university power arrangements have been shaped by a tension between two principles of coordination: collegiality and hierarchy. The collegial principle holds that academics as a group of peers make decisions on behalf of the institution. Institutional leaders are elected by and among members of the academic community and negotiate on behalf of the academic peer group with funders and stakeholders to secure the flow of resources to the institution while preserving its autonomy. Collegiality has traditionally been supported by academics who strive to control the working conditions of the institutions in which they work. The hierarchical principle, on the other hand, holds that institutional leaders (rectors, vice-chancellors, presidents) make decisions on behalf of the institution with a view to the interests of major funders and other stakeholders and apply the means necessary to see their decisions implemented by subordinate faculty and department levels. They may be appointed by or otherwise depend upon other actors than their academic peers, be it the government, board of trustees, or private donors. They are, therefore, inclined to try to control the institutions and the academics within them from above. The hierarchical principle has traditionally been promoted by actors (e.g., public or religious authorities, business interests) who wish to use academics and their knowledge in pursuit of their own ends.

The balance between the principles of collegial and hierarchical coordination has shifted throughout history and varies from country to country. The major research question asked in this chapter is how this tension is developing today. The chapter gives a short historical account of how this tension has played out under different conditions in different historical periods, distinguishing the medieval university, the university of the Enlightenment, and the modern research university. It then discusses the main topic: how the tension between collegial and hierarchical coordination has played out in recent years through the rise of mass higher education, the "knowledge society," and current higher-education reforms. To what extent do current developments move universities toward more hierarchical forms of coordination, and to what extent are collegial forms of coordination sustained or promoted? The main thrust of the argument is that, to understand the changing nature of academic autonomy, it does not suffice to look merely at how decision-making authority is distributed within academic institutions, but also how it is distributed across institutional, national, and international arenas in which relevant decisions are made.

COORDINATING UNIVERSITY AFFAIRS: THE HISTORICAL LEGACY

In his chapter on the history of the universities in the *International Handbook of Higher Education* (Forest and Altbach 2007), Harold Perkin points out that, although institutions for elite training already had emerged in many parts of the world, only in Europe, from the twelfth century onward, "did an autonomous, permanent, corporate institution of higher learning emerge and survive, in varying forms, down to the present day" (Perkin 2007). Medieval European society was "fractured and divided on every dimension: between church and state, and within them between multiple layers of authority from emperor and pope through baron and bishop." These competing powers—church and state—"demanded the allegiance of society and imposed two systems of law, canon and civil, with equal jurisdiction over the faithful. In the mutually destructive strife between empire and papacy, power was 'up for grabs' and fractionated out in a hierarchy of competing authorities: king and archbishop, duke and abbot, free county and free city, manorial lord and parish priest. In the interstices of power, the university could find a modestly secure niche, and play off one authority against another" (159). Another factor that protected universities against unwanted outside interference was the fact that universities were the alma mater of bishops, judges, and high officials in civil and ecclesiastical administration. Under these conditions, Perkin's argument goes, the university evolved into an immensely flexible corporate institution capable of adapting to almost any kind of social and political environment. During the gradual transformation of the medieval university into the modern research university from around 1500 to the end of the nineteenth century, universities remained autonomous in important respects. Although the state won its power struggle with the papacy, Europe was divided between rival dynastic states competing among other things to attract academics and was, therefore, sufficiently pluralistic for universities to retain their ability to keep rival authorities at a certain distance.

The German research university is usually considered the most influential university model in the nineteenth and early twentieth centuries. It came with an innovation, the specialized single-subject professor, as opposed to the master professor who might teach the whole syllabus during a career. Moreover, the German research university emphasized, at least rhetorically, a need for academic freedom and institutional autonomy. The German model thus represented the clearest example of a professorial university wherein the combination of institutional autonomy and individual academic freedom meant that the collegial principle was a predominant form of coordination, securing for German professors independence as well as domination over the university. The model of the German research university was copied across Northern Europe, the United States, Russia, and Japan, and as it was transported across the world it underwent significant changes. In terms of coordinating principles the exported version often came without the degree of independence and control over university affairs that was found in Germany (Perkin 2007). Nevertheless, the research university as it developed from the nineteenth century until the 1960s featured collegiality as a basic coordinating principle, crucial both to the autonomy of the university and to the academic freedom that was considered necessary to secure the economic and cultural progress of advanced, democratic societies.

Since the great post–World War II expansion of higher education, university reformers have sought to increase the capacity of higher-education institutions to deal effectively and efficiently with growing and increasingly diversified tasks. While reform efforts have been directed in part toward the expansion and development of higher-education systems, increasing efforts have been directed toward the improvement of organizational capacity, efficiency, and quality. In many cases, this pursuit of organizational efficiency has meant that university leaders have sought to strengthen the hierarchical principle at the systems level as well as the institutional level. Since the 1960s, politicians and administrators have tended to base their reform attempts on the assumption that universities are poorly managed. Universities have thus been regarded as insufficiently developed organizations, lacking structures and leadership that permit them to operate as goal-oriented and efficient strategic actors (Keller 1983). As in other types of organizations, the reformers' aim is to introduce better steering mechanisms to make independent subunits and individuals contribute to the goals of the organization in a more disciplined way. Universities, therefore, need to strengthen their formal hierarchies by strengthening leadership, developing a common set of goals and management structures capable of implementing them (or what Rosemary Deem in this volume calls the "line management" of universities) (Brunsson and Sahlin-Andersson 2000; Whitley 2008).

In contrast to this hierarchical view, some continue to maintain that universities should be organized in collegial ways that permit them to fulfill their specific mission (Ben-David and Zloczower 1991; Musselin 2007; Olsen 2007; Pelikan 1992; Weick 1976). According to this view, be it based on a functional necessity or a normative value, universities must have the autonomy and provide the academic freedom to allow independent, high-quality scholarly research. Given the inclination of university reformers to opt for greater efficiency and stronger leadership, their critics often accuse them of undermining faculty autonomy and academic freedom. In recent decades, these two views have been pitted against one another in debates over university reform (Bleiklie 1998; Bleiklie and Kogan 2007).

THE RESEARCH QUESTION

This chapter begins with the following assumption: until the 1970s European universities were characterized by relatively strong collegial coordination and weak hierarchical coordination, at least in comparison with other kinds of organizations such as public bureaucracies or business enterprises. After decades of higher-education expansion and university reform, however, the coordination of (and within) universities has changed. To what extent has hierarchy been strengthened and collegiality weakened by these reforms? From a European perspective this question entails two related problems. The first concerns stability and change: to what extent do new higher-education policies have an effect? The second concerns national peculiarities and global modernizing processes: to what extent do national higher-education policies effectively converge around a common pattern based on internationally shared goals and standards? If higher-education policies are in fact changing from more collegial to more hierarchical models of coordination, to what extent do national peculiarities likely shape these changes—perhaps despite shared goals for and ideologies about higher education at a general (or international) level? To shed light on these questions I will first outline three broad transformation processes that have characterized the development of higher education as a "field of social action" (Bleiklie and Kogan 2006). I will then discuss the implications of these processes for coordination within the sector, particularly with a view to the development of academic "autonomy" as a dynamic phenomenon (1) within universities; (2) within national systems of higher education; and (3) in relation to international higher-education policy shifts. After addressing these general questions about change and continuity, I will look briefly into the questions of cross-national convergence or sustained diversity.

THREE PROCESSES OF INSTITUTIONAL TRANSFORMATION

Although I am specifically focusing on change processes over the past 30 years or so, this should not prevent us from looking at longer historical trajectories. I start, then, with the long-term process of *rationalization* in university governance. Anyone familiar with the writings of Max Weber (1978) is likely to know that he regarded the process of rationalization—the introduction of formal procedures and the progressive formalization of social relationships—as an essential characteristic of the modernization of the Western world. Weber's focus was on the transition from a feudal to a modern society as it emerged during the latter half of the second millennium CE, a transition brilliantly analyzed by Clark (2006) in his consideration of fundamental changes within European universities. The literature on the development of higher education demonstrates that processes of rationalization still loom large. Thus rationalization—in the sense of an increasing formalization of social relations and procedures covering a steadily wider number of areas of academic life—is an essential element in the processes of change that have characterized European higher education in recent decades. It is evident in the introduction and proliferation of quality-assurance protocols, performance evaluations, accountability procedures, and incentive systems. The bodies involved in these activities increasingly base their decisions on formal criteria and the collection of standardized data in order to measure the efficiency and quality of academic work. Rationalization is often justified in the name of improved democratic control and increased transparency, both of which are supposed to ensure more efficient use of (public) funds. Public-sector movements such as New Public Management and the ensuing transformation of the general discourse on public-sector reform—and, more specifically, higher-education governance—represent this trend (Magalhães and Amaral 2009). Although rationalization in earlier periods differed from current processes in terms of motivation, manifestations, and consequences, it turned, then as now, on the formalization of social relationships.

STRENGTHENING GOVERNMENT STEERING AND THE MANAGERIAL CAPACITY OF UNIVERSITIES

Since the managerial revolution of the 1970s, intrainstitutional hierarchization has occupied a central position on public university reform agendas. Universities have, partly at the initiative of ministries and partly at their own initiative, started to formulate goals, develop strategies, and strengthen leadership while reducing rank-and-file academic influence. Two issues in this tug-of-war for power are easily identified. One turns on academic representation on decision-making bodies. The other turns on the authority of elected bodies. The tendencies of the past 30 years are twofold. First, during the 1970s, universities saw an extension of the privileges of representation to include not only full professors but all members of the university community (Clark 1987). Second, since the 1980s, universities have seen a tendency to reduce the size of elected bodies, and more recently (since the 1990s) to turn these bodies, excepting institutional boards, into advisory rather than decision-making bodies (Paradeise, Reale, Bleiklie, and Ferlie 2009). The latter process of hierarchization is represented by the abolition of "shared" leadership structures, replacing elected academic leaders with appointed ones and redefining elected bodies from decision making to advisory functions.

EMERGING ARENAS OF COLLEGIAL INFLUENCE

The increasing hierarchization of university governance—particularly at the level of intrainstitutional organization—is not, however, the whole story. The growing influence of *inter*institutional arenas means that power is spread beyond the borders of individual institutions, residing in relations across organizations through formal and informal networks. The idea of "network governance" (also addressed by Ka Ho Mok in this volume) is associated with the development of new forms of governance since the 1980s, conceptualized as an alternative to traditional bureaucratic top-down steering. There are many reasons to consider decision-making power based in horizontal networks as an alternative form of—or a possible challenge to— top-down bureaucratic power (Byrkjeflot and Guldbrandsøy 2009; Theisens and Enders 2007). For example, interinstitutional networks may displace decision-making authority from leaders within single institutions to leaders across several institutions. At the same time, network influence may emerge from needs that are felt and expressed by traditional hierarchic power holders. Some of those needs may be better understood in the context of rationalization and the long-term movement from the typical orientation of traditional groups toward a modern orientation that has been in the making for a long time (some would say, since the sixteenth century). In the field of university governance, this movement has involved a slow shift in decision-making ideals based on local, intramural, familial, personal, and short-range considerations toward decision-making ideals based on cosmopolitan, extramural, occupational, impersonal, and long-range considerations (Clark 2006: 294f.).

Two important manifestations of this trend in recent decades are, first, that bodies involved in national evaluation and quality assurance boards, research funding councils, and publishing bodies operate at the supranational level, and second, that decisions made by these supranational bodies are often based on academic peer-review panels. Although academic power has been weakened *within* individual universities, it is increasingly felt through decisions made by national and international peer-review mechanisms related to research funding, evaluation, and publication. A further manifestation of stronger network influence in higher-education governance is increasing external representation on university boards. Also, we have witnessed in recent decades a tremendous growth, differentiation, and formal integration of higher-education systems, including a differentiation of government agencies involved in higher-education governance. Increasing network governance is thus a phenomenon caused by several developments: the growth and differentiation of the higher-education system itself; the differentiation of public bodies involved in higher-education governance; the involvement of a broader range of stakeholders in higher education; and the increasing number of extrauniversity bodies related to evaluation, funding, publishing, and so on. Taken together, these trends have implications for core elements of higher education such as academic autonomy, the leadership of academic institutions, and the steering of national higher-education systems.

THE ACADEMIC POWER BASE: FROM INSTITUTIONS TO INTERNATIONAL NETWORKS?

In a somewhat romantic rendition, historians of the modern university tell a tale in which, once upon a time (or at least since the early nineteenth century), universities and their professors found themselves in a world characterized by institutional and individual autonomy and academic freedom (in fact the two—institutional autonomy and academic freedom—were scarcely differentiated since the university was perceived as a collegium of professors, and the university was an expression of their collective will). The German model (a.k.a. the Humboldtian University) came to be perceived as the most prominent embodiment or symbol of the modern research university. In recent decades (since the 1980s), however, historians have suggested that this autonomy was gradually undermined by policymakers, administrators, and external stakeholders as academics lost their influence over and freedom within their institutions. Thus, we are told, a schism and a contradiction developed in which *institutional* autonomy and *individual* autonomy became pitted against one another. In this account, academic power is presented as a phenomenon first located in—and then removed from—professorial privilege and academic control over decision-making bodies within universities. The salient change concerns the extent to which academics first gained and then lost power in these arenas.

In contrast to this romantic (and reductive) history, the argument put forward in this chapter is that the history of a gradual loss of professorial power is merely part of a much bigger picture. No doubt, with what we called the intrainstitutional hierarchization process, academics as a group nowadays often have to share power with other actors, such as external stakeholders and nonacademic colleagues on institutional boards. Nevertheless, one might also argue that academic power has shifted from elected bodies to leadership positions. The new leaders are appointed, not elected, but they are still academics. The new leaders obviously operate within a more hierarchical system in which decision premises are formulated by institutional leaders and boards before being implemented in a top-down process.

Subordinate leaders at all levels have their authority delegated to them from above. This stands, formally at least, in clear contrast to the previous system of elected leaders who at every level had their authority delegated from the body of peers who elected them. Thus the transition from elected to appointed leaders may be seen as a transition from a system designed to express the collective will of academics from the bottom-up to a system designed to implement the will of the leadership from the top-down.

The tightening of hierarchical control over decisions made within institutions has been paralleled by an increasing institutional dependence upon and penetration by decisions made by actors from external arenas. These external actors, in turn, often make decisions that are strongly influenced by academics. Consider research funding. As many chapters in this volume note, research universities are increasingly dependent on external funding. Their access to research funds depends partly on the activity of individual researchers within institutions and partly on decisions made by (usually academic) review panels associated with national and international funding agencies. Furthermore, these agencies often demand matching funds from receiving institutions. The relationships between universities and funders have a networked character: they depend first on the behavior of individual academics and the research networks they belong to. They also depend on peer-review panels that tend to be products of established collegial relationships. Review panels as collegial bodies are thus making decisions that affect university funding decisions, sometimes in a binding way. Thus, depending on the success of individual researchers and the conditions imposed by the funding agencies, substantial parts of university budgets may effectively be decided by internal and external academic actors.

Funding is but one example of academic power in the context of network governance. Evaluation panels that assess institutional or disciplinary performance work in a similar way. They may make recommendations that are less immediately binding than funding decisions, but in the long run they represent important ways of communicating performance criteria that are difficult for an academic institution to ignore. Similarly, the publication process hinges on academic decision makers. Since the publication of articles in academic journals or books by academic publishers is the most important criterion for hiring and promotion in universities, publishing decisions made by editorial reviewers have an important effect on university personnel decisions. Through their participation in funding agencies, evaluation panels, and editorial boards, academics exert a degree of (indirect) power over higher-education systems at both the interinstitutional and the intrainstitutional levels. Taken together, these network-based collegial decision-making arenas penetrate and limit in various ways the power of university leaders.

Academic power is a dynamic phenomenon, and research on higher-education governance should not be confined to gauging how much power academics enjoy within universities. Since academic power is exercised in different and changing decision arenas, research should focus not only on how but also on *where* academic power is exercised. In addition to intramural collegial bodies it is exercised by extramural, often international, academic bodies, based on networks through which the members of these bodies are selected. As for *how* academic power is exercised, the traditional conception is that it is mainly exercised by traditional groups with jurisdictional monopolies over certain decisions. Increasingly, though, while it cohabitates with the influence of other intramural groups (students, administrators, and external stakeholders), academic power also penetrates academic institutions from the outside (Byrkjeflot and Guldbrandsøy 2009).

THE TRANSFORMATION OF ACADEMIC INSTITUTIONS

Academic institutions have changed. According to traditional historical accounts, the European research university has been an institution typically located within public administrative settings, its operating conditions determined by a legal framework within a public administrative order. Within this context, state intervention was limited and circumscribed in important ways, leaving decisions on the content of teaching and research largely to academics (Bleiklie 1998). The dominant account of recent change holds that universities are in the process of becoming more hierarchically integrated and tightly managed and that the position of academics is similar to that of any employee group in a business enterprise (again, see Rosemary Deem's chapter in this volume). Yet, empirical studies have provided ample evidence that this stylized picture misses the actual variation one finds across institutions and national systems, and it certainly misses the many practices that unfold behind the veil of academic rhetoric (Hood et al. 2004; Kehm and Lanzendorf 2006; Lepori et al. 2007a, 2007b; Paradeise, Reale, Bleiklie, and Ferlie 2009). The research question, therefore, turns on the extent to which universities have changed from bureaucratically regulated, decentralized institutions, collegially managed by academics, as depicted by idealized accounts

(Pelikan 1992), to autonomous, hierarchically managed institutions run by nonacademic administrators (Brunsson and Sahlin-Andersson 2000; Musselin 2007).

The problem with the picture above is not only that it plays down a great deal of cross-institutional and cross-national variation but also that it takes the trend of hierarchization for granted and questions only its strength and uniformity. The position taken here is different. The argument here is that the penetration of universities by external networks is likely to generate new sources of academic power that *sustain* decentralization and *undermine* hierarchic control. If university governance arrangements traditionally have been perceived as some sort of compromise between (1) academic collegial power and administrative power internally and (2) institutional autonomy and government steering externally, emerging forms of network governance have complicated the picture in two ways. First, universities are increasingly integrated in horizontal as well as hierarchical governance patterns, and second, the division between academic collegial jurisdictions and administrative external oversight are becoming blurred (Bleiklie 2007; Enders and Fulton 2002; Huisman 2009; Teichler 2007). When analyzing academic institutions we thus need to look at them from more than a top-down perspective. A network approach will reveal little if we look at university governance only from such a perspective, because we are likely to focus exclusively on the active decisions of institutional leaders and government actors. In this case we would end up with a decent representation of processes of rationalization and intrainstitutional hierarchization, but we would miss the horizontal dimensions of interinstitutional decision-arena formation and their implications for power relationships within intrainstitutional decision arenas.

The research question, therefore, turns on how and to what extent universities have been affected by the three processes of rationalization, intrainstitutional hierarchization, and interinstitutional networking. One such effect may have deep implications for the position of academics in universities. If we look at the "academic profession" and how it has developed in Europe, the 1970s and 1980s witnessed a profound change (with some notable exceptions) from a situation in which only fulltime professors enjoyed the broad privileges of academic freedom, autonomy, and control over internal decision-making bodies, to a situation in which all or nearly all academic personnel came to enjoy such privileges and influence. Recent decades, in turn, may represent a new transition—a transition from a situation in which nearly all academic personnel enjoyed a role in intrainstitutional governance to a situation in which a new academic elite emerges to reinforce the vertical dimension within the academic collegium. In this new era, elite academic influence is based not just on full professorship but on network position gained through participation on national and international peer-review panels of all sorts: research funding panels, evaluation bodies, hiring committees, editorial boards, and so on. While such an elite may enjoy high aggregate influence, its members operate in highly decentralized ways. They are organized in a relatively loose set of networks around a series of decision arenas internally divided by disciplinary and functional lines. These networks of decision makers are blurred at the edges and involve considerable mobility among participants. Although many of the decision arenas in question consist of academic review panels, others, such as research funding bodies, often draw their members from a wider set of backgrounds, including politicians, civil servants, business representatives, and so forth. In such cases their modi operandi are based on criteria that represent compromises between more diverse sets of considerations and decision premises than purely academic ones. Individual members usually acquire their positions on these decision-making panels based on research reputation. Within individual universities such elites may be highly influential, even as rank-and-file academics find themselves in a gradually weaker position. In addition to the hierarchization represented by tighter management of universities, we may thus see a new emerging hierarchy among academics, based on research reputation transformed into network positions (or vice versa).

Let us now return to the initial question: to what extent has hierarchy been strengthened and collegiality weakened in the modern university? In this chapter it is argued that, rather than answering "little" or "much," we need to develop a third set of options. Alongside the introduction of hierarchical features of more tightly managed, vertically integrated universities, we also see the proliferation of collegial decision making within increasingly influential network structures. The sources of collegial power that limit the power of institutional leaders have moved from a decentralized structure of independent collegial groups and strong bottom-up processes to the external network penetration of institutions. Universities still seem to be decentralized in ways that limit the effect of strengthened top-down leadership structures. Accordingly, the most important source of decentralization that has emerged as part of the process of change is interinstitutional network structures often dominated by academics. We might, therefore, ask four questions: First, to what extent have universities become more tightly managed and integrated than before? Second, to what extent has a new academic elite emerged, once again strengthening the vertical dimension of the academic collegium? Third, to what extent has academic power reasserted itself through the many decision-making arenas affecting institutional policies? Fourth, to what extent do actors within universities perceive the division between academic and administrative power to be important?

HIGHER-EDUCATION SYSTEMS: FROM INSTITUTIONAL AGGREGATES TO STANDARDIZED ORDERS

In the 1970s, the higher-education sector in Europe was constituted by aggregates of institutions that allegedly showed little interest in coordinating their activities or cooperating to achieve national priorities. In recent years, however, we have seen much stronger integration, both nationally and internationally, as well as emerging institutional hierarchies with formally common standards intended to make cooperation, coordination, mobility, and flexibility possible (in this volume, Ka Ho Mok as well as Glen Jones and Bryan Gopaul observe similar changes in East Asian and Canadian universities). While we know much about academic behavior *within* academic institutions, we know relatively little about academic behavior *between* institutions. It is assumed that governance and steering as well as the competitive strategies of individual institutions have an effect on the shape and content of national higher-education systems (Bleiklie 2007; Huisman, Meek, and Wood 2007; Meek, Goedegebuure, and Huisman 2000; Meek, Goedegebuure, Kivinen, and Rinne 1996), but we do not have solid—let alone comparative—evidence as to how exactly government policies and market strategies affect the hierarchical (vertical) and functional (horizontal) *diversity* of higher-education systems (Teichler, 2007). Furthermore, few, if any, researchers have analyzed the reciprocal effects between national higher-education systems and their broader environments—including how policymakers and markets respond to various higher-education system characteristics and developments.

What we know is that both national and international higher-education systems have been formally redefined during the past decades, and that governments have tried to establish various formal orders, such as hierarchical, competitive systems, or binary systems in which some institutions have been assigned status equivalent to research universities while others have been given a status equivalent to teaching- and vocationally oriented colleges (Teichler 2007). Moreover, there is a supranational dimension to the issue: whereas diversity used to be a national concern, the current interweaving of European and national higher-education policies—for example, through the Bologna and Lisbon processes—brings the issue of diversity to a European level (Huisman 2009; Witte, 2006; Witte, Van der Wende, and Huisman 2008). The suggestion here is that, to understand higher-education system development, we should look not only at governance and market forces at the national level but also at the increasingly international processes of rationalization that flow from common legislation, degree systems, evaluation criteria, and so on. Do academic institutions act differently when they perceive themselves as part of a supranational system? What have been the reciprocal effects of governance, market forces, and emerging higher-education systems at the national as well as supranational levels? To what extent are institutional strategies responses to universities' formal or perceived positions within supranational systems? How are perceptions and practices of academic autonomy and academic freedom shaped when they are integrated in increasingly rationalized national and supranational spaces?

One observation shared by students of university policy is that politicians tend to give higher education much more attention now than they did a couple of decades ago. Resorting to a stylized argument again, a standard description would note that, whereas policies in the 1970s were the product of the actions of individual institutions, in the 2000s they came to be formulated by national governments in a much more integrated process for the entire sector. Furthermore, whereas national policies previously were concerned with legal regulation and the overall size of the system, they are now much more directly targeted at teaching and research activities. In this sense, national governments have apparently become much more forceful in their capacity and willingness to formulate policies for the sector from the top-down. At the same time, several trends seem to move decisions *away* from national political authorities. In many cases, national university policies have granted a higher degree of formal autonomy to institutions, expecting that they then will act strategically based on their own long-term aims (see both Ka Ho Mok and Anthony Welch—as compared with the African perspective of Peter Maassen—in this volume). Furthermore, national political authorities are looking to supranational bodies like the EU and the OECD for guidance and inspiration in order to promote "excellence," a "European dimension," and the international standing of their institutions (Corbett 2005; Olsen 2007). Central government apparatuses have at the same time become more diversified, with intermediate bureaucracies charged with teaching, research funding, evaluation, and innovation often operating in semiautonomous ways (Verhoest et al. 2010).

TOWARDS A COMMON MODEL, OR CONTINUED DIVERSITY?

Although supranational reform trends have received much attention in the literature on higher education in recent decades, an important strand of literature has focused on national reforms, and during the past ten years several comparative studies of national reforms have emerged (de Boer, Enders, and Schimank 2007; Hood et al. 2004; Kehm and Lanzendorf 2006; Kogan et al. 2006; Paradeise, Reale, Bleiklie, and Ferlie 2009). A recent comparison of higher-education governance reforms in seven European countries (Paradeise, Reale, Goastellec, and Bleiklie 2009) found support for Pierson's (2000) claim that reform attempts tend to face "path dependency," that is, forceful established norms and practices tend to absorb change efforts and limit their effects. The study demonstrated that national reform processes, often justified in similar terms, have varied considerably across countries with regard to pace, rate, emphasis, and implementation. Geographically one may distinguish national reform processes along an East-West dimension (e.g., distinguishing the United Kingdom from continental Europe) and a North-South dimension (e.g., distinguishing Northern British and "Humboldtian" Germanic countries from Southern "Napoleonic" ones). The United Kingdom and to some extent the Netherlands stand out as early and comparatively radical reformers while continental European countries have lagged behind as slower and more consensus-oriented reformers.

However, the resilience of established local arrangements are not just demonstrated by national peculiarities in terms of the pace, rate, emphasis, and implementation of reforms. There were strong "path dependent" forces in action that helped both to slow down and absorb reforms by adapting them to established institutional patterns in each country (Paradeise, Reale, Goastellec, and Bleiklie 2009). This latter point may be illustrated by the observation that reform emphases have tended to vary from country to country. For example, in terms of the choice of national steering instruments, it is fair to say that, whereas French reforms have had a strong focus on contracts between institutions and government (Musselin and Paradeise 2009), German reforms have focused on competition between institutions (Schimank and Lange 2009), UK reforms have focused on quality assessment through national ranking exercises of research and teaching performance (Ferlie and Andresani 2009), and Norwegian reforms have focused on leadership restructuring (Bleiklie 2009; Bleiklie and Lange 2010). In short, national peculiarities can—and usually do— shape more general international reform trends.

CONCLUSION

Let me conclude by adding one final comment underlying the arguments set forth in the previous pages. Much of the research on higher-education governance and steering operates with a tacit assumption that major actor groups like academics and administrators have stable interests and values. Policy change based on new value paradigms or perceived needs is, therefore, cast in terms of external shocks or influences brought about by policymakers or other external stakeholders. The argument pursued here points out that perceptions and definitions of core values and needs in academic institutions are not static but dynamic (see also the chapter by Xu Xiaozhou and Xue Shan in this volume). Given the dynamism of academic values, institutions respond in different ways to broader changes. One overarching process that may be seen as a common denominator for the growing and increasingly diverse higher-education systems in Europe is the steady process of standardization that aims to create transparency, flexibility, and mobility within academic systems. To what extent these processes represent a fundamental change is open to question, but they do seem to represent a change in some of the fundamental operating conditions for actors within higher education, including their values and perceived interests. As both national and supranational standardization policies unfold, institutions respond—and, increasingly, they respond through the involvement of new governance networks. Network structures are changing patterns of interaction among major actor groups in ways that may make it more difficult to distinguish clearly among these groups. Although change followed from attempts at transforming universities into more tightly managed organizations, these changes were also part of more comprehensive transformation processes that entailed emerging network structures, which, in turn, have generated new sources of academic power and arenas for collegial decision making. Universities are still decentralized, but because their recently strengthened hierarchic structures are penetrated by networks, they are now decentralized for different reasons than were universities in the 1970s.

National university policies and reform processes have become more ambitious and forceful during the past decades, and they are characterized by similar goals and justifications. This convergence of goals may tempt observers to assume that national higher-education reforms are pushing university systems toward one common form. Yet, national reforms still face important policy traditions and preferences at the level of national politics as well as the level of university institutions. At the national level the rate, pace, emphasis, and implementation of higher education reforms vary according to national traditions that affect the interpretation of relevant reform measures and adapt reforms to fit the preferences and values of major stakeholders. This variation indicates that the forces sustaining national and institutional particularities are strong and that in spite of sometimes fundamental transformations, universities are not necessarily converging toward one common model.

BIBLIOGRAPHY

Ben-David, J. and A. Zloczower (1991) "Universities and Academic Systems in Modern Societies," in J. Ben-David (ed.) *Scientific Growth. Essays on the Social Organization and Ethos of Science.* Berkeley, LA, London: University of California Press.

Bleiklie, I. (1998) "Justifying the Evaluative State. New Public Management Ideals in Higher Education." *European Journal of Education*, 33 (3): 299–316.

———(2007). "Systemic Integration and Macro Steering." *Higher Education Policy*, 20 (4): 391–412.

——— (2009) "Norway: From Tortoise to Eager Beaver?" in C. Paradeise, E. Reale, I. Bleiklie, and E. Ferlie (eds.) *University Governance: Western European Comparative Perspectives.* Dordrecht: Springer.

Bleiklie, I. and H. Kogan (2006) "Comparison and Theories," in M. Kogan, M. Bauer, I. Bleiklie, and M. Henkel (eds.) *Transforming Higher Education. A Comparative Study* (2nd edition). Dordrecht: Springer.

——— (2007) "Organisation and Governance of Universities." *Higher Education Policy*, 20: 477–493.

Bleiklie, I. and S. Lange (2010) "Competition and Leadership as Drivers in German and Norwegian University Reforms." *Higher Education Policy*, 23 (2): 173–193.

Brunsson, N. and K. Sahlin-Andersson (2000) "Constructing Organisations: The Example of Public Sector Reform." *Organisation Studies*, 4: 721–746.

Byrkjeflot, H. and K. Guldbrandsøy (2009) "From Governance to Government in the Norwegan Hospital Sector." Draft. Bergen: Rokkan Center.

Clark, B. R (ed.) (1987) *The Academic Profession. National, Disciplinary and Institutional Settings.* Berkley, LA, London: University of California Press.

Clark, W. (2006) *Academic Charisma and the Origins of the Research University.* Chicago and London: University of Chicago Press.

Corbett, A. (2005) *Universities and the Europe of Knowledge: Ideas, Institutions and Policy Entrepreneurship in European Community Higher Education Policy, 1955–2005.* Palgrave: Macmillan.

de Boer, H., J. Enders, and U. Schimank (2007) "On the Way towards New Public Management? The Governance of University Systems in England, the Netherlands, Austria and Germany," in D. Jansen (ed.) *New Forms of Governance in Research Organizations—Disciplinary Approaches, Interfaces and Integration.* Dordrecht: Springer.

Enders, J. and O. Fulton (2002) "Blurring Boundaries and Blistering Institutions: An Introduction," in J. Enders and O. Fulton (eds.) *Higher Education in a Globalising World. International Trends and Mutual Observations.* Dordrecht, Boston, London: Kluwer Academic, pp. 1–16.

Ferlie, E. and G. Andresani (2009) "United Kingdom from Bureau Professionalism to New Public Management?" in C. Paradeise, E. Reale, I. Bleiklie, and E. Ferlie (eds.) *University Governance: Western European Comparative Perspectives.* Dordrecht: Springer.

Forest, J. J. F. and P. G. Altbach (eds.) (2007) *International Handbook of Higher Education.* Dordrecht: Springer.

Hood, C., O. James. B. G. Peters, and C. Scott (eds.) (2004) *Controlling Modern Government.* London: Edward Elgar.

Huisman, J. (2009). "Institutional Diversification or Convergence?" in B. Kehm, J. Huisman, and B. Stensaker (eds.) *The European Higher Education Area: Perspectives on a Moving Target.* Rotterdam: Sense, p. 21.

Huisman, J., V. L. Meek, and F. Q. Wood (2007). "Institutional Diversity in Higher Education: A Cross-national and Longitudinal Analysis." *Higher Education Quarterly*, 61 (4): 563–577.

Kehm, B. M. and U. Lanzendorf (eds.) (2006) "Reforming University Governance. Changing Models and Patterns of Higher Education Funding: Some Empirical Evidence," in A. Bonaccorsi and C. Daraio (eds.) *Universities and Strategic Knowledge Creation.* London: Edward Elgar, pp. 85–111.

Keller, G. (1983). *Academic Strategy. The Management Revolution in American Higher Education.* Baltimore: Johns Hopkins University Press.

Kogan, M., M. Bauer, I. Bleiklie, and M. Henkel (eds.) (2006) *Transforming Higher Education. A Comparative Study* (2nd edition). Dordrecht: Springer.

Lepori B., M. Benninghoff, B. Jongbloed, C. Salerno, and S. Slipersaeter (2007a) *Changing Conditions for Research in Four European Countries.* Bonn: Lemmens.

Lepori B., P. van den Besselaar, M. Dinges, B. van der Meulen, B. Potì, E. Reale, S. Slipersaeter, and J. Theves (2007b) "Comparing the Evolution of National Research Policies: What Pattern of Change?" *Science and Public Policy,* 34 (6) (July): 372–388.

Magalhães, A. and A. Amaral (2009) "Mapping Out Discourses on Higher Education Governance," in Jeroen Huisman (ed.) *Governance in Higher Education Systems.* London: Routledge, Taylor & Francis.

Meek, V. L., L. Goedegebuure, and J. Huisman (2000) "Editorial: Diversity, Differentiation and the Market." *Higher Education Policy,* 13 (4): 1–6.

Meek, V. L., L. C. J. Goedegebuure, O. Kivinen, and R. Rinne (eds.) (1996). *The Mockers and Mocked: Comparative Perspectives on Differentiation, Convergence and Diversity in Higher Education.* Oxford: Pergamon.

Musselin C. (2007) "Are Universities Specific Organizations?" in G. Krücken, A. Kosmützky, and M. Torka (eds.) *Towards a Multiversity? Universities between Global Trends and National Traditions.* Bielefeld: Transcript Verlag.

Musselin, C. and C. Paradeise (2009) "France: From Incremental Transitions to Institutional Change," in C. Paradeise, E. Reale, I. Bleiklie, and E. Ferlie (eds.) *University Governance: Western European Comparative Perspectives.* Dordrecht: Springer.

Olsen, J. P. (2007) "The Institutional Dynamics of the European University," in J. P. Olsen and P. Maassen (eds.) *University Dynamics and European Integration.* Dordrecht: Springer.

Paradeise, C., E. Reale, I. Bleiklie, and E. Ferlie (eds.) (2009) *University Governance: Western European Comparative Perspectives.* Dordrecht: Springer.

Paradeise, C., E. Reale, G. Goastellec, and I. Bleiklie (2009) "Universities Steering between Stories and History," in C. Paradeise, E. Reale, I. Bleiklie, and E. Ferlie et al. (eds.) *University Governance:* Western European

Pelikan, J. (1992) *The Idea of a University. A Re-examination.* Cambridge, MA: Harvard University Press.

Perkin, H. (2007) "History of Universities," in J. J. F. Forest and P. G. Altbach (eds.) *International Handbook of Higher Education.* Dordrecht: Springer, pp. 159–205.

Pierson, P. (2000) "Increasing Returns, Path Dependence, and the Study of Politics." *American Political Science Review,* 94 (2): 251–267.

Ridder-Symoens, Hilde de (ed.) (1992) *A History of the University in Europe. Universities in the Comparative Perspectives.* Dordrecht: Springer.

Schimank, U. and S. Lange (2009) "Germany: A Latecomer to New Public Management," in C. Paradeise, E. Reale, I. Bleiklie, and E. Ferlie (eds.) *University Governance: Western European Comparative Perspectives.* Dordrecht: Springer.

Teichler, U. (2007) "The Changing Patterns of the Higher Education Systems in Europe and the Future Task of Higher Education Research," in *European Science Foundation (ESF) Higher Education Looking Forward: Relations between Higher Education and Society.* Strasbourg: ESF, pp. 79–103.

Theisens, H. C. and J. Enders (2007) "State Models, Policy Networks, and Higher Education Policy," in G. Krücken, A. Kosmützky, and M.Torka (eds.) *Towards a Multiversity? Universities between Global Trends and National Traditions.* Bielefeld: Transcript Verlag.

Verhoest, K., P. Roness, B. Vershuere, K. Rubecksen, and M. MacCarthaigh (2010) *Autonomy and Control of State Agencies. Comparing States and Agencies.* Houndmills, Basingstoke: Palgrave Macmillan.

Weber, M. (1978) *Economy and Society. An Outline of Interpretive Sociology,* vol. 1 and 2. Berkeley, LA, London: University of California Press.

Weick, C. E. (1976) "Educational Organizations as Loosely Coupled Systems." *Administrative Science Quarterly,* 21 (1): 1–19.

Whitley, R. (2008) "The Changing Nature of Universities as Strategic Actors: From Hollow Organisations to Project-Based Firms?" Chapter Presented to a Workshop on Science and Society Relationships in the Age of Globalization Organised by the Research Council of Norway in Oslo on May 8, 2008.

Witte, J. (2006) *Change of Degrees and Degrees of Change. Comparing Adaptations of European Higher Education Systems in the Context of the Bologna Process.* Enschede: CHEPS.

Witte, J., M. Van der Wende, and J. Huisman (2008) "Blurring Boundaries: How the Bologna Process Changes the Relationship between University and Non-university Higher Education in Germany, the Netherlands, and France." *Studies in Higher Education,* 33 (3): 217–231.

CHAPTER 4

The Twenty-First-Century University: Dilemmas of Leadership and Organizational Futures

Rosemary Deem

INTRODUCTION

Conceptions of the purposes of universities have been a source of debate for many centuries, but in the twenty-first century, the worldwide expansion of higher-education systems, the pressures of globalization, the growing competition to attract overseas students, the rise of international rankings and league tables, and pressures on both public and private funding of universities have led to fresh questioning about what purposes universities should serve—and how universities should be funded. Questions about whether universities should be part of the public or the private sector have also fed into this debate, as higher-education institutions have increasingly been permeated by markets (markets for students, for scholars, and for knowledge). Meanwhile, universities' traditional missions of teaching and research have been joined by new requirements for entrepreneurial and public-engagement activities. This chapter explores the ways in which current debates about the purposes of universities have informed the practices, values, development, and dilemmas of higher-education leaders and their senior teams. It will also consider the ways in which new conceptions of the purposes of universities could lead to reshaping the future organizational structures and cultures of higher-education institutions. In so doing, the chapter will draw on recent research about leadership in public-service organizations and the management of universities. In particular, it will draw on three projects: (1) "New Managerialism and the Management of UK Universities," funded (1998–2000) by the Economic and Social Research Council (ESRC); (2) "Negotiating Equity in Higher Education Institutions: A Case-Study Analysis of Policies and Staff Experiences," funded (2004) by the Higher Education Funding Council for England; and (3) "Developing Organization Leaders as Change Agents in the Public Services," funded (2006–2009) by the ESRC.

Debates about the Purposes of Universities

Questions about the purposes of universities are longstanding and predate even the well-known nineteenth-century views of Cardinal John Henry Newman (1852) in Britain and Ireland and Wilhelm von Humboldt (1970) in Germany, as Wei's (2007) work on the medieval university of Paris demonstrates. Questions have focused mainly on the nature of teaching and research, the creation and transmission of knowledge, and the respective roles of professors and students. More recently, the scope of debates about university purposes has shifted. First, the move from elite to mass systems of higher education in most Western societies has exerted financial and other pressures on systems that are largely publicly funded. Massification, in turn, has led to significant concerns about institutional missions and structural differentiation within higher-education systems (Palfreyman and Tapper 2009). As higher education becomes more commonplace (in many societies), questions arise that take very different forms than they do in the context of elite higher education. Such questions range from where universities fit in the hierarchy of priorities for public funding (Kwiek 2003, 2005, 2007) to the extent to which higher education is a public or private good (Nyborg 2003; Marginson 2007). Further enquiries encompass the extent to which higher education exhibits good governance or "value for money" (Shattock 2006; Kehm and Lanzendorf 2006) and concerns about the maintenance and improvement of quality in teaching and research as part of stakeholder and public accountability processes. The latter have brought into play various systems of quality audit (Shah and Brennan 2000; Strathern 2000; von Tunzelmann and Mbula 2003; Lucas 2006; Cheng 2009), which are now found all over the world but had their origins in the United Kingdom, in what Leisyte and colleagues refer to as the prototype of the "evaluative state" (Leisyte et al. 2006).

Second, the traditional focus on research and teaching in most universities has been challenged not only by the expansion of higher education but also by the need for each institution to search for fresh sources of funding. This search had led to what some call "academic capitalism" (Slaughter and Leslie 1997, 2001). Increasingly, funding flows to applied rather than basic research, and support comes from other entrepreneurial activities such as technology transfer, knowledge exchange to nonacademic users, and the exploitation of intellectual property rights or spin-off companies. Universities are driven to pursue these sources of funding not only because they need more resources but also because the very pursuit conforms to wider visions about the commodification of higher education (Bok 2004), thereby making academic entrepreneurialism a key factor in governments' economic strategy. Such ventures clearly lead to the generation of additional funds, but there are many pitfalls in these so-called third-mission undertakings. They have the potential to alter the value basis of those who work and study in universities (Marginson and Considine 2000).

Third, as Ivar Bleiklie notes in this volume, a growing emphasis on leadership and management, particularly the movement toward corporate management and new managerialism (Deem et al. 2007) as a means of supervising formerly more collegially based institutions, has caused much more attention to be paid to the ways in which academic institutions are governed. This in turn has led to the use of new control technologies such as performance management for both academic units and individual academics and an emphasis on audit and self-governmentality. Control technologies have enabled closer surveillance of what academics do and have raised questions about academic freedom (Keenoy and Reed 2008).

Fourth, the significant expansion and use of new technologies in higher education, from the Internet to mobile smartphones, has made possible the sharing of learning activities between students and academics who are in different locations and time zones in ways that would not have been possible even two decades ago (Garrison et al. 2003; Conole and Oliver 2007). In helping to create what Castells (1997) refers to as the network society, the Internet has also placed vast amounts of information in the public domain and has encouraged people to think of information as rapidly and easily available; this, among other developments, has reduced the extent to which universities have a monopoly over certain kinds of knowledge and information (Lyotard 1984) and has made students want instant responses to queries. In addition, the use of networked technologies in universities has raised questions about the need for higher education to be in a particular place or physical space and—as Glen Jones and Bryan Gopaul observe in this volume—has made possible greater mobility for both students and faculty (Savin-Baden 2008). New technologies have overturned some of the traditional hierarchies between learners and teachers, which in itself has produced fresh questioning about what higher education can and should offer.

Finally, an emphasis on the role of universities in engaging with a wider public than their own students and alumni (Laing 2009), though not new in itself, has drawn fresh attention to universities' purpose. Laing argues that public concerns with knowledge in all its forms—its "development and discovery, its preservation and conservation, its transmission and application"—place the university at the heart of life in society, but "public engagement" is not welcomed by everyone in the university, perhaps because such engagement itself can seem like a form of instrumentalism imposed by government. There is a suspicion that any knowledge not immediately relevant to public interests will be seen as less valuable. Such scepticism is not surprising, because governments' enthusiasm for public engagement usually sits alongside an enthusiasm for paying less for higher education while expecting those who work in universities to dance to the government tune.

Contemporary debates over the purposes of universities typically fall into three categories: (1) debates that focus on what defines "world-class," global, and elite universities; (2) debates that deal with "entrepreneurial" universities; and (3) debates that ask what universities have become (and de facto what they should or should not become). The first of these categories—the debate over what defines a world-class university—has produced a burgeoning literature on the effects of globalization and international rankings on higher-education institutions (King 2009; Salmi 2009; Stensaker and Kehm 2009; Hazelkorn 2010). This debate itself is mainly about research outputs, how academic research is managed, and the recruitment of international students and staff to conduct advanced research. Some of the work in this area is critical—for example, King's work on how globalization is affecting governance in universities—but most of this literature concerns how university leaders can achieve world-class status in elite institutions (Salmi 2009). The negative implications of the quest for world-class status, even for those institutions that are successful in developing a truly international reputation (Deem et al. 2008, 2009), are less often considered than recipes for achieving "global" prestige (however elusive this ideal remains). Often omitted in the debate about world-class universities is what happens to the focus and purposes of all those institutions that are *not* part of the world-class-status quest and thereby risk losing resources, students, and staff to those that are.

The second strand of the debate over the purposes of universities—the strand dealing with entrepreneurialism—reflects a 1990s preoccupation with the ways in which universities shifted from traditional academic concerns toward the pursuit of additional funding through applied research and various commercialized activities (Slaughter and Leslie 1997, 2001; Clark 1998; Marginson and Considine 2000). Slaughter and Leslie (1997) documented the evolution of this new entrepreneurialism in various ways. They drew on quantitative data about the funding of US universities and qualitative interview data from academics to develop what they called a theory of "resource dependency." Marginson and Considine (2000) subsequently undertook similar research in Australia to underpin Slaughter and Leslie's claims. Clark (1998), meanwhile, compiled case studies of a small number of institutions that used central steering mechanisms to create entrepreneurial universities; he thus created a recipe that proved irresistible to many university leaders (Deem 2008), despite the fact that his case studies were based on "heroic narratives" rather than empirical analysis (Deem 2001). Sporn (1999) focused on how university structures in Europe and the United States adapted to funding changes. These analyses were written when public university funding, in the West at least, was still relatively generous; one might ask what scope is left in the realm of "entrepreneurialism" to deal with the effects of the 2008–2009 world financial crisis on higher-education institutions.

The third strand of the purposes-of-universities debate—the strand that asks what universities should or should not be—is the most enduring. Unlike the other two strands, this strand is more open-ended and imaginative in its conceptions (Readings 1996; Barnett 1999; Delanty 2001; Kwiek 2006; Peters 2007). Often focused on teaching and research as core activities in the academy, some of the contributions to this strand of the debate are pure future-gazing (Fuller 2007), others comment on present trends that seem to be establishing themselves (Boulton and Lucas 2008), and still others take a more historical perspective (Delanty 2001; Peters 2007). A few concern themselves with what they see as the demise of the "traditional" university and its disciplines (Readings 1996). What this strand generally overlooks, however, is the fact that the range of desirable purposes of universities is expanding well beyond teaching and research as conventionally conceived. Similarly, the notion that publicly funded universities have some kind of public-service function is rapidly receding (Deem 2007b). As the longer-term implications of the latest financial crisis become clear, some governments have broached the possibility of withdrawing public money from higher education on the grounds that it is now an entirely private service for which potential clients and students must pay. Of course, private higher education is already a burgeoning sector in many countries, but to make *all* higher education private, which now seems to be happening in the United Kingdom, is quite a different thing.

There is thus a strong tension between the notion that higher education is essentially an arm of industry and commerce and the notion that higher education is a social and developmental activity. As Patricia Gumport (2000) has noted, writing about the curriculum in American universities, "[T]he dominant legitimating idea of public higher education has been moving away from the idea of higher education as a social institution, and moving toward the idea of higher education as an industry... to produce and sell goods and services, train some of the workforce, advance economic development, and perform research.... In contrast, from the perspective of higher education as a social institution, public colleges and universities by definition must preserve a broader range of social functions that include such essential educational legacies as the cultivation of citizenship, the preservation of cultural heritage(s), and the formation of individual character and habits of mind. The tension between the two legitimating ideas is profound" (pp. 70–71). It is this tension that lies at the heart of modern universities' struggle to decide what they are about, how they should be organized, and how they should be led.

LEADERSHIP DILEMMAS

In this section I want to explore some of the dilemmas that leaders of twenty-first-century universities face as they seek to decide what universities are for. Since an entire chapter could be written on this topic, selections must be made. I have chosen to present the dilemmas that arose in some of the research I have done over the past 12 years, but these dilemmas also lie, I think, at the very heart of the leadership of the twenty-first-century university. These dilemmas are framed around the following three binaries: (1) leadership development: doing the day job or planning for a career?; (2) administrative strategies: line management or collegiality?; and (3) organizational priorities: research or teaching? It was suggested above that the most difficult tension for contemporary universities qua universities is the tension between the conception of a university as an arm of economic policy judged on the basis of its contribution to wealth, industry, and commerce, and the conception of a university as an organization with broader social purposes. It is still not clear how university leaders will deal with this fundamental contradiction between economic and social/cultural purposes, but the following discussion may provide some hints. Of course, as Ivar Bleiklie and various others in this volume note, in an increasingly international higher-education policy environment, there are likely to be different views in different countries as both national and supranational actors consider higher-education strategies. Despite this variety, however, the three dilemmas of leadership identified here seem to apply, in diverse ways, across national contexts.

Leadership Development: Doing the Day Job or Planning for a Career?

Whether considered in a national or an international context, the leadership of universities is undergoing significant change. No longer is it sufficient for a university rector, vice-chancellor, or president to be a leading academic in his or her institution; such leaders must also be fundraisers, networkers, and bearers of their institution's national and international profile. As Breakwell and Tytherleigh (2008) found when they interviewed university leaders in their study of UK vice-chancellors, what is needed now is very different from the needs of the past:

> Several [respondents] alluded to the fact that "a successful VC also couldn't afford to be a worrier"; a VC who was "would be dead quite quickly."...Another commented: "The 'fast moving situations' of today's universities also required a leader 'capable of dealing with, not just complexity, but things which shift from one thing to another very quickly."...Having "sheer physical stamina" was also emphasised by another VC... "a very stamina sapping job," not "a job for an elderly retired sort of civil servant like the VCs used to be in the fifties." (32)

Similarly, in the ESRC "New Managerialism" study (1998–2000), we noted three different paths that individuals took into higher-education leadership: the "career track" (which at that time was really possible only in the former polytechnics since most manager-academic posts in pre-1992 universities were fixed-term and not externally advertised);

the "good citizen route" (taking on a role because colleagues had asked one to do so or because one felt a sense of institutional obligation); and the "reluctant manager route" (in which people took on managerial roles, often with grave misgivings, because they were told they had to do so or because it was "their turn") (Scase and Goffee 1989; Deem et al. 2001). Though a more recent UK study noted that these three routes were still in evidence (Bolden et al. 2008), the "good citizen" and "reluctant manager" routes were fast disappearing in favor of the "career track" route. A vice-chancellor about to retire, whom we interviewed as part of the ESRC "New Managerialism" project, noted that his successor would play a very different role than he had played:

> I believe that I only have certain sorts of abilities and they're not particularly to be a front person. That is not where I would say I was at my best. I am probably much better at the internal management and the academic leadership. And I assumed that that's likely true for most people, because I think those three roles require very different characteristics in a person....therefore I sold the notion to senate and eventually to council, that of these four people [3 PVCs and a VC], one should be the real deputy and should be essentially the provost, in the American model, running the internal institution, being the chief executive, and that the other, the vice-chancellor would then still be the academic leader...and also be the outside face. So...now we've started recruiting for my successor. (Vice-chancellor, Furzedown)

The old idea of a vice-chancellor as an end-of-career role had its limitations, but at least those who saw their positions this way expressed a sense of abiding institutional loyalty. The career patterns that have developed in the twenty-first-century universities are very different. Today, there is a sense in which leaders' ambitions and career trajectories exist independently of the particular organizations in which they work (Martin and Wajcman 2004). This idea is very much in keeping with the "networked" academic elite that Ivar Bleiklie describes in his chapter in this volume. As one associate dean explained of his participation in a leadership-development course,

> I'm looking to the future, to be honest with you. I've chosen to go on the course which is aimed at, well, it's sort of aimed at associate deans, and newly appointed deans, and it's preparing for senior strategic leadership, with a view to being able...to be in a position to apply for a dean's post. (Male associate dean, Little Oaks)

A pro-vice-chancellor expressed a similar rationale for her decision to enroll in a leadership-development course:

> The most recent thing is that I've been accepted on to the Top Management programme...I had to have the support of my vice-chancellor, and the financial support, because it's jolly expensive, I mean it's about, I think, about £14,000...that is both to support me in my current role, but I've also got a very strong eye on its use in terms of my further career paths...I was interviewed for a vice-chancellor position recently, and the first question that I was asked was why I hadn't been on the TMP. (Female pro-vice-chancellor, Longley, post-1992)

Because being a manager-academic and leader is now much more of a career choice on both sides of the Atlantic (arguably it always was in North America), this does produce a new dilemma for those in leadership positions. There is a delicate balance to be struck between actually doing the day job and thinking about how to position that day-to-day activity so that it bolsters a case for the next move up the ladder. Going on a training course (especially an expensive one) helps in the current job and proves to be an advantage while looking for a new job.

In the twenty-first-century university, leaders often find themselves choosing between showing loyalty to their institutions and moving aggressively up the career ladder. Like the academics they supervise, they adopt the perspective of employees in a broader higher-education system—a system, either national or supranational, that runs like a business and is constantly on the lookout for top talent. In ways that Ivar Bleiklie makes clear in his contribution to this volume (which Xiaozhou Xu and Xue Shan also examine with considerable concern), the hierarchization of modern universities profoundly shapes the professional strategies of all who inhabit them—academics and administrators alike. Increasingly, university managers seem to value their own careers more than the institutions they serve (or, rather, lead).

Administrative Strategies: Line Management or Collegiality?

In recent decades, a shift in fashions in how to run public-service organizations in the United Kingdom has moved to place even more emphasis on leadership than new managerialists did in the 1980s and 1990s (Clarke and Newman 1997; Exworthy and

Halford 1999; Deem and Brehony 2005). The "Developing Organization Leaders as Change Agents in the Public Services" study (RES-000-23-1136-A), led by Mark Wallace, John Morris, and Mike Reed of Cardiff Business School, and myself, from 2006 to 2009 and known as the CAP project, explored how the second term of Tony Blair's New Labour government focused on "transformational leadership" as a way to achieve reform in the public sector. The project noted that mid-level "leaderism," or "a novel synthesis of efficient managerial coordination and effective expert accountability within new forms of organizational governance...promoted via the reprofessionalisation...of senior service organization staff as leaders" (Wallace et al. 2009), had to some extent replaced top-level management as the critical axis around which public-service organizations revolved. Inasmuch as UK manager-academics have a long-established preference for "leadership" rather than "management" (Middlehurst 1993; Deem et al. 2001), the move to leaderism was seen as relatively unproblematic in most UK universities. Certainly this was the view of most of those we interviewed in the CAP study. As one vice- chancellor observed,

> Having an organization where either things trickle up from the bottom or trickle down from the top...may have served the university well when it was devised in the 1950s...[but] it doesn't serve us well [now]...you need a sort of quick turnaround and you need an agreement among those who head up organizational units, whatever those units might be, in order to implement the policy, the agreed policy very quickly, and I think that's why, to me, a [new organizational] model is most appropriate. (Male VC, Hopton)

The growing focus on mid-level leaderism rather than top-level management has led, as this interviewee noted, to an emphasis on streamlined decision making, or what Burton Clark termed acentral steering core (Clark 1998)—a crucial feature of what Bleiklie calls the hierarchization of institutional decision making. This emphasis on leaderism has also drawn more attention to the use of line management as a way to execute decisions.

At the same time, the move to leaderism also has its dilemmas, notably in the conflict between line management and collegiality, which in turn impinges on issues of trust within institutions. The issue of trust came up repeatedly in the ESRC New Managerialism project, especially in focus groups with the members of learned societies. Academics with whom we spoke felt they were not trusted at all by senior managers. Two respondents put it thus:

> [First participant]: Well, I think they don't trust us, even Heads of Department, they don't trust us completely with money...I'm talking about elementary decisions...
> [Second participant]: I was looking at the managerial part and I feel that they don't *really* trust even up to the Head of Department, they don't *really* trust you (science learned society).

Trust and collegiality are key values that make shared decision making possible. As a New Managerialism focus group noted:

> If by collegiality you mean shared vision and values, that's one thing...which we all strive enormously hard to try to maintain. If you mean by collegiality the sorts of...democratic processes, I mean I think this is historically but I mean, I mean it was largely an illusion in many universities anyway....I think the tension is between how you try to maintain and move along with largely disparate and dispersed communities with a shared vision and values and wrestle with the problem of how you actually enable people both to make some influence and genuinely listen to what they have to say and to make decisions (Focus group, Generic academic body)

Thus, collegiality may have its challenges, but line management may have even more. Although in theory academics can be told what and how to teach, line management does not make them teach well, nor does it fit the culture of academic research, which rarely leads to straightforward or predictable results (Deem 2010). Some university leaders admit that hierarchical line management does not work when you are herding academic cats. According to one research dean,

> You can't drive academics and tell them what to do....I mean they run around all over the place, don't they? And the more you try pushing them in one direction, the more obstinate they become....I don't think even the vice-chancellor could persuade them, with professors, to do things that they don't want to do. (Research dean, pre-1992 university)

Despite the challenges with line management in universities, some leaders still try it, even if, as a consequence, the cats disappear in several directions and fail to return home. To use another metaphor, the implications for the university of making people do things and constantly checking that they have done so is akin to planting seedlings in a garden and digging them up each week to see if they are growing. It is not a good idea.

The New Managerialism study clearly showed that, within universities, hierarchical line management erodes collegiality as well as trust, turns people who should be colleagues against one another, and assumes that both research and teaching are mechanical tasks that can be done as and when instructed. That way lies the retail model of a university in which neither teaching nor research is a vibrant or a creative activity. Yet, as funding constraints and audit demands tighten their grip on publicly supported higher education, it is likely that line management—or its cozier-sounding cousin, "performance management"—will become more common, thereby moving us closer to a conception of universities as industries and further away from a conception of universities as institutions with broader social purposes.

Organizational Priorities: Research or Teaching?

Choosing whether to emphasize research or teaching may not sound like a leadership dilemma, since most universities encompass both activities. The real dilemma concerns which of these activities takes priority in terms of resources, strategic direction, effort, and status. When we begin to examine the relative status of research and teaching, it is evident that research is far more easily measured and quantified than teaching (hence all those international league tables based on citations and publications) and that, since the early nineteenth century, institutions focusing on research have had more status than those based on teaching. Furthermore, the career rewards and promotions prospects of research are often much greater than those available to academics who excel in teaching. Though some have argued that research and teaching have no real connections and are not positively correlated (Hattie and Marsh 1996), others have shown that research and teaching have many synergies (Jenkins 1998; Deem and Lucas 2006; Jenkins et al. 2007). Given the opportunity, many academics will discuss at length how their teaching and research flow into one another and are mutually reinforcing. There are clear positive benefits for students who are given access to research skills and problem-based learning, even at the undergraduate level and certainly for all postgraduates (Robertson and Bond 2005; Brew 2006; Deem and Lucas 2006; Lucas and Turner 2007).

Some university leaders actually place teaching ahead of research in their lists of institutional priorities. Consider the words of this respondent from the ESRC New Managerialism project:

> Very first thing I ever said...first speech...what I said was "students come first."...I would say 80 percent of the organization breathed a sigh of relief...well I believe in that, but I also believe it's right for this organization at this time in its history. (Female vice-chancellor, post-1992 university)

Of course, such a view would not go down well in research-oriented universities. Nevertheless, in talking with university leaders and their senior teams, two policy levers were regarded as having the greatest effect on the management of publicly funded English universities: (1) the Research Assessment Exercise (RAE) and (2) the National Student Survey. The focus on the RAE was not unexpected, inasmuch as this audit of academic outputs and research infrastructure has been in place since 1986 and has led to significant funding for research-oriented institutions. The National Student Survey, on the other hand, was more surprising. It surveys final-year undergraduates in UK universities about their degree experiences. Individual institutions have long had at their disposal much more sophisticated, locally tailored information about how students respond to their teaching and assessment. Nonetheless, it seems to many that research-oriented universities pay attention to teaching only when they are subject to some form of national scrutiny. In England this started to happen in the mid-1990s with the creation of the Funding Council and Quality Assurance Agency (QAA) (though far more attention was paid to paper audit trails than to actual teaching). Since the early 2000s, the QAA has retreated from close investigations of subject departments in favor of a meso-level analysis of how academic standards are guaranteed and how universities comply with codes of institutional practice. Starting in 2005, the well-funded Higher Education Funding Council for England Centers for Excellence in Teaching and Learning (CETLs) focused on teaching, learning, and assessment and were seen as a way to invest in teaching at a level comparable to UK investment in research (Gosling and Hannan 2007). However, as the CETL funding drew to a close in 2010, it was not at all clear that the impact of the CETLs had been significant outside the institutions in which the centers were located. Moreover, at least one university cut some of its CETL staff who had won the funding in the first place.

Former Harvard president Derek Bok observed that, in the United States, academics pay far less attention to new discoveries about teaching than they do to new discoveries in research, and they are less inclined to investigate their teaching when it fails to achieve expected results (Bok 2004). Similarly, in the United Kingdom, teaching innovation rarely brings rewards to those who pursue it (Hannan and Silver 2000). Though the situation with regard to teaching has become somewhat better in the United Kingdom since the late 1990s (new higher-education teachers now receive some training), it is often the case that nonteaching-intensive universities pay far less attention to teaching than they do to research—even though teaching often brings in more revenue than research. It is not surprising, then, that many pre-1992 universities have struggled to offer promotion to full professorships to those who excel in teaching rather than research. This dilemma can be resolved only by paying attention to both research *and* teaching.

ORGANIZATIONAL FUTURES

Ivar Bleiklie's chapter in this volume notwithstanding, there is surprisingly little written on the internal organizational structures of universities. Classic studies of US universities in the 1970s and 1980s pointed out the extent to which universities' loosely coupled and anarchic structures—rather than being chaotic and inefficient—actually worked very well (Meyer and Rowan 1977; Cohen et al. 1988; March and Olsen 1989, 1989). Other single-case studies of individual institutions documented patterns of organization that worked in particular places, but more general—let alone comparative—theories of university organization are rare. Some studies consider how to position institutions for entrepreneurial change (Clark 1998) or reflect on changes already made to existing institutions (Sporn 1996, 1999; Taylor 2006), but these studies often imply that only a limited number of (sometimes contradictory) changes can be made in universities, such as (1) increased centralization (Clark's central steering core); (2) decentralization and devolution of power and resources to basic academic units; (3) a move to interdisciplinary units designed to pursue entrepreneurial activity (Marginson and Considine 2000); or (4) a combination of new supersized academic units (such as superfaculties or colleges), which have devolved powers but also report to a central core (Taylor 2006). Some universities veer between different organizational structures, from departments to faculties to schools and back again, and in the United Kingdom, colleges (which are really just faculties by another name) have recently become quite fashionable (Taylor 2006). Given this rather limited range of organizational options, many changes in academic institutions may be no more than the equivalent of moving the deck chairs on the Titanic.

Some writers question the extent to which publicly funded universities, as compared with mainstream private-sector institutions, are even capable of undergoing major change and hence also contend that the impact of leaders on higher-educational organizations may be quite limited. Burgoyne et al. (2009) suggested that

> For U.K. universities, and particularly the ancients…they are led as much or more by their culture and history as by their current senior leaders, and indeed the latter are probably more chosen by the former, than the latter produce or design the former. (Burgoyne 2009: 10)

Another school of thought suggests that contemporary university organizations are becoming the same as global forces and the effects of international league tables encourage universities to emulate each other (Enders 2009). Neoinstitutional theory maintains that organizations are influenced by their environment and that coercion, normative forces, and the desire to mimic other successful organizations lead toward similar organizational forms and cultures in a process called isomorphism (DiMaggio and Powell 1991; Dimaggio 2001). This perspective holds that universities can, in fact, change, but they generally change in similar ways.

What, then, does the future hold for university organization and management? In 2004, the Organization for Economic Co-operation and Development (OECD 2006) outlined four scenarios for the future of higher education worldwide. The first, "Open networking," envisioned voluntary collaboration between institutions across different national systems, which in time could lead to greater harmonization of the kind sought by the European Higher Education Area and its Bologna process (Neave 2003). The open-networking scenario emphasized both teaching and research as well as open access to knowledge funded by the public purse. The second OECD scenario, "Serving local communities," saw universities focused mainly on local needs, with public funding and a mission oriented toward teaching and lifelong learning as well as research in the arts and social sciences (either regionally or nationally directed). In this scenario most scientific research was done outside the university, though it was still publicly funded. In the third scenario, "New public responsibility," universities were still partially publicly funded, but market forces and financial incentives were increasingly important. In this scenario, higher-education institutions were private and legally autonomous, with students paying fees while businesses and other sponsors funded research; moreover, this scenario predicted a stark differentiation of missions between institutions, with some specializing in research and others in teaching. In the fourth scenario, "Higher Education, Inc.," there was fierce global competition between universities to provide education and research, with a rigid separation between those that focused on one or the other. A business approach cast students as "customers," although governments still funded research in areas of national though not commercial interest.

These four scenarios may be useful to some, but to leaders who are preparing to change their institutional structures or cultures, they provide little guidance. The four scenarios cannot be neatly separated in administratively sensible ways. How, then, do leaders acquire ideas about how their universities might be organized? One way to imagine the organizational future of the twenty-first-century university might be to stop thinking of universities as *either* "global" *or* "national" (Organization for Economic Co-operation and Development 2006) and to start thinking of universities as organizations that operate at multiple levels simultaneously. We have moved on from the days when universities were simply institutions designed to transmit or nurture national cultures (Delanty 2001), but the increasingly global orientation of higher education does not mean that universities face a stark choice between being world-class (Salmi 2009; Deem et al. 2009) or belonging to a residual category of also-ran institutions. As the work of Anthony Welch in this volume shows, not only does this dichotomy condemn most universities in the developing world (and more than a few in the developed world) to third-class status, but it also ignores the many ways in which higher-education institutions now collaborate. As Glen Jones has noted, a single institution can be both globally oriented *and* locally and nationally focused (Jones 2007). Indeed, as Ka Ho Mok's chapter in this volume demonstrates, all universities are embedded in networks of national, regional, and international contexts (Epstein 2007), whether they like it or not. Some call the university a *glonacal* institution—a neologism referring to the involvement of global, national, and local dimensions in a single institution (Marginson and Rhoades 2002).

The global positioning of higher education and the race for scarce resources within higher-education systems add to competitive pressures, as does the ranking of universities on a range of scales from the national to the international (Hazelkorn 2009; Stensaker and Kehm 2009). Given this diversity, university leaders must find flexible organizational forms suited to twenty-first-century conditions. University reform in the future may entail collaboration, mergers, strategic alliances, or some combination of these approaches. Each of these options seeks to alleviate competition between institutions, but each has both advantages and disadvantages. Collaboration can involve institutions that are not direct competitors, while mergers can enable the incorporation of competitors without threatening a leader's position, but such tactics can also lead to overextension. Mergers, by creating larger and more comprehensive organizations (which, in theory, may be better able to compete, Harman and Harman 2003), are attractive in some ways but may be expensive and time-consuming and may threaten organizational hierarchies, cultures, and values. Strategic alliances can involve national or global partners (Beerkens 2004) and have the added advantage of leaving each organization's internal structure untouched, but it is hard to get an entire university engaged in the activities of partner organizations, and alliances may be effective in dealing with only certain kinds of competition. None of these options is perfect by itself, but leaders who experiment with a range of strategies—learning not only from others around the world but also from history—might find new organizational forms that transcend the OECD's all-too-limited scenarios and create new opportunities for their institutions.

BIBLIOGRAPHY

Archer, L. (2007). "Diversity, Equality and Higher Education: A Critical Reflection on the Ab/uses of Equity Discourse within Widening Participation." *Teaching in Higher Education* 12(5): 635–653.

Baldridge, V. J. (1970). "Images of the Future and Organizational Change: The Case of New York University." Retrieved December 2009, from http://www.eric.ed.gov:80/ERICDocs/data/ericdocs2sql/content_storage_01/0000019b/80/38/43/e7.pdf.

Barnett, R. (1999). *Realizing the University in an Age of Supercomplexity.* Buckingham: Society for Research into Higher Education and Open University Press 2000.

Becher, T. and P. Trowler (2001). *Academic Tribes and Territories: Intellectual Enquiry and the Cultures of Disciplines.* Milton Keynes: Society for Research into Higher Education and Open University Press.

Beerkens, E. (2004). *Global Opportunities and Institutional Embeddedness. Higher Education Consortia in Europe and Southeast Asia.* Enschede, Center for Higher Education Policy Studies, University of Twente.

Bensimon, E. M. (1995). "Total Quality Management in the Academy: A Rebellious Reading." *Harvard Educational Review*(4, Winter): 593–611.

Bok, D. (2004). *Universities in the Marketplace: The Commercialization of Higher Education.* Princeton: Princeton University Press.

Bolden, R., G. Petrov, and J. Gosling (2008). "Developing Collective Leadership in Higher Education." London, Leadership Foundation for Higher Education. Retrieved January 2010, from https://www.lfhe.ac.U.K./protected_login_form.html?item=bolden.pdf.

Boulton, G. and C. Lucas. (2008). "What Are Universities For?" Retrieved November 2008, from http://www.leru.org/?cGFnZT00.

Breakwell, G. and M. Y. Tytherleigh (2008). "The Characteristics, Roles and Selection of Vice Chancellors—Final Report." London, Leadership Foundation for Higher Education. Retrieved January 2010, from https://www.lfhe.ac.U.K./protected_login_form.html?item=breakwellreport.pdf.

Brew, A. (2006). *Research and Teaching: Beyond the Divide.* Basingstoke: Palgrave Macmillan.

Bryman, A. (2007). "Effective Leadership in Higher Education." London, Leadership Foundation for Higher Education. Retrieved January 2010, from https://www.lfhe.ac.U.K./protected/brymanfinal.pdf.

Burgoyne, J., S. Williams, and J. Mackness (2009). "Baseline Study of Leadership Development in Higher Education." London. Retrieved January 2010, from https://www.lfhe.ac.U.K./protected_login_form.html.

Castells, M. (1997). *The Information Age: Economy, Society and Culture, Vol. 1, The Rise of the Network Society.* Malden, MA, and Oxford: Blackwell.

Cheng, M. (2009). *Changing Academics: Quality Audit and Its Perceived Impact.* Saarbrücken, Germany: VDM Verlag.

Ciancanelli, P. (2007). "Re/producing Universities: Knowledge Dissemination, Market Power and the Global Knowledge Commons." *Geographies of Knowledge, Geometries of Power: Framing the Future of Higher Education in the 21st Century; World Year Book of Education 2008.* Ed. D. Epstein, R. Boden, R. Deem, F. Rizvi, and S. Wright. New York: Routledge Falmer: 67–84.

Clark, B. (1998). *Creating Entrepreneurial Universities: Organizational Pathways of Transformation.* New York and Amsterdam: Elsevier.

Clarke, J. and J. Newman (1997). *The Managerial State: Power, Politics and Ideology in the Remaking of Social Welfare.* London: Sage.

Cohen, M. D., J. G. March, and J. P. Olsen (1988). "A Garbage Can Model of Organizational Choice." *Decisions and Organizations.* Ed. J. G. March. Oxford: Blackwell.

Conole, G. and M. Oliver, Eds. (2007). *Contemporary Perspectives in E-learning Research: Themes, Methods and Impact on Practice.* London: Routledge.

Deem, R. (2001). "Globalization, New Managerialism, Academic Capitalism and Entrepreneurialism in Universities; Is the Local Dimension Still Important?" *Comparative Education* 37(1): 7–20.

——— (2003). "Managing to Exclude? Manager-Academic and Staff Communities in Contemporary U.K. Universities." *International Perspectives on Higher Education Research: Access and Inclusion.* Ed. M. Tight. Amsterdam. London: Elsevier Science JAI: 103–125.

——— (2007a). "Managing a Meritocracy or an Equitable Organization? Senior Managers' and Employees' Views about Equal Opportunities Policies in U.K. Universities." *Journal of Education Policy* 22(6): 615–636.

——— (2007b). "The Knowledge Worker in the Divided University." *Knowledge, Higher Education and the New Managerialism: The Changing Management of U.K. Universities.* Ed. R. Deem, S. Hillyard, and M. Reed. Oxford: Oxford University Press: 67–100.

———. (2008). "Producing and Re/producing the European University in the 21st Century: Research Perspectives on the Shifting Purposes of Higher Education." *Higher Education Policy* 21(4): 439–456.

——— (2009). "Leading and Managing Contemporary U.K. Universities: Do Excellence and Meritocracy Still Prevail over Diversity?" *Higher Education Policy* 29(1): 3–17.

——— (2010). "Herding the Academic Cats: The Challenges of 'Managing' Academic Research in the Contemporary U.K. University." *Perspectives* 14(2): 37–43.

Deem, R. and K. J. Brehony (2005). "Management as Ideology: The Case of 'New Managerialism' in Higher Education." *Oxford Review of Education* 31(2): 213–231.

Deem, R. and L. Lucas (2006). "Learning about Research: Exploring the Learning & Teaching/Research Relationship amongst Educational Practitioners Studying in Higher Education." *Teaching in Higher Education* 11(1): 1–18.

Deem, R. and L. Morley (2006). "Diversity in the Academy? Staff and Senior Manager Perceptions of Equality Policies in Six Contemporary U.K. Higher-Education Institutions." *Policy Futures* 4(2): 185–202.

Deem, R. and R. N. Johnson (2003) "Risking the University? Learning to Be a Manager-Academic in U.K. Universities." *Sociological Research on Line* 8.

Deem, R., K. H. Mok, and L. Lucas (2008). "Transforming Higher Education in Whose Image? Exploring the Concept of the 'World-Class' University in Europe and Asia." *Higher Education Policy* 21(1): 83–97.

Deem, R., L. Lucas, and K. H. Mok (2009). "The 'World-Class' University in Europe and East Asia: Dynamics and Consequences of Global Higher Education Reform." *University Rankings, Diversity, and the New Landscape of Higher Education.* Ed. B. Stensaker and B. Kehm. Rotterdam: Sense.

Deem, R., L. Morley, and A. Tlili (2005). "Negotiating Equity in HEIs: A Case-Study Analysis of Policies and Staff Experiences." Retrieved May 2005, from http://www.hefce.ac.U.K./pubs/rdreports/2005 /rd10_05/.

Deem, R., S. Hillyard, and M. Reed (2007). *Knowledge, Higher Education and the New Managerialism: The Changing Management of U.K. Universities.* Oxford: Oxford University Press.

Deem, R., O. Fulton, R. Johnson, S. Hillyard, M. Reed et al. (2001). "New Managerialism and the Management of U.K. Universities." End of Award Report. Swindon.

Delanty, G. (2001). *Challenging Knowledge: The University in the Knowledge Society.* Buckingham: Open University Press.

Dimaggio, P. (2001). *The Twenty First Century Firm.* Princeton: Princeton University Press.

DiMaggio, P. and W. Powell, Eds. (1991). *The New Institutionalism in Organizational Analysis.* Chicago: University of Chicago Press.

Enders, J. (2009). "Global University Rankings and the Academic Reputation Race." *Global Rankings and League Tables in Higher Education: Promising, Perilous or Perverse.* Bath. SRHE South West Higher Education Research Network. Retrieved November 13, from http://www.srhe.ac.U.K./downloads/swrn-131109a.pdf.

Epstein, D., R. Boden, R. Deem, F. Rizvi, and S. Wright, Eds. (2007). *Geographies of Knowledge, Geometries of Power: Framing the Future of Higher Education in the 21st Century; World Year Book of Education 2008.* New York: Routledge Falmer.

Exworthy, M. and S. Halford, Eds. (1999). *Professionals and the New Managerialism in the Public Sector.* Buckingham: Open University Press.

Fraser, N. (2000). "Rethinking Recognition." *New Left Review* (3, May–June): 107–120.

Fraser, N. and A. Honneth (1998). *Redistribution or Recognition?: A Political-Philosophical Exchange.* London: Verso.

Fuller, S. (2007). "University Leadership in the Twenty-First Century: The Case For Academic Caesarism." *Geographies of Knowledge, Geometries of Power: Framing the Future of Higher Education in the 21st Century; World Year Book of Education 2008.* Ed. D. Epstein, R. Boden, R. Deem, F. Rizvi, and S. Wright. New York: Routledge Falmer: 50–66.

Garrison, D. R., T. Anderson, and R. Garrison (2003). *E-Learning in the 21st Century: A Framework for Research and Practice.* New York: Routledge.

Gosling, D. and A. Hannan (2007). "Responses to a Policy Initiative: The Case of Centers for Excellence in Teaching and Learning." *Studies in Higher Education* 32(5): 633–646.

Gumport, P. (2000). "Academic Restructuring: Organizational Change and Institutional Imperatives." *Higher Education* 39(1): 67–91.

Hannan, A. and H. Silver (2000). *Innovating in Higher Education.* Buckingham: Open University Press.

Harman, G. and K. Harman (2003). "Institutional Mergers in Higher Education: Lessons from International Experience." *Tertiary Education and Management* 9(1): 29–44.

Harris, S. (2007). *The Governance of Education in Neo-liberal Times.* London: Continuum.

Hattie, J. and H. W. Marsh (1996). "The Relationship between Research and Teaching: A Meta-analysis." *Review of Educational Research* 66: 507–542.

Hazelkorn, E. (2009) "Rankings and the Battle for World-Class Excellence: Institutional Strategies and Policy Choices." *Higher Education Management and Policy* 21(1): 47–68.

———(2011). *Rankings and the Reshaping of Higher Education: The Battle for World-Class Excellence.* Basingstoke: Palgrave.

Henkel, M. (2000). *Academic Identities and Policy Change in Higher Education.* London: Jessica Kingsley.

Hoare, Q. and G. Nowell-Smith, Eds. (1971). *Antonio Gramsci: Selections from Prison Notebooks.* London: Lawrence and Wishart.

Jenkins, A., M. Healey, and R. Zetter. (2007). "Linking Teaching and Research in Disciplines and Departments." Retrieved April 2008, from http://www.heacademy.ac.U.K./assets/York/documents/Linking TeachingAndResearch_April07.pdf.

Jenkins, A., T. Blackman, R. Lindsay, and R. Paton-Saltzberg (1998). "Teaching and Research: Student Perspectives and Policy Implications." *Studies in Higher Education* 23(2): 127–142.

Johnson, R. and R. Deem (2003). "Talking of Students: Tensions and Contradictions for the Manager-Academic and the University in Contemporary Higher Education." *Higher Education* 46(3): 289–314.

Jones, G. (2007). *Can Provincial Universities Be Global Institutions? Rethinking the Institution as the Unit of Analysis in the Study of Globalization and Higher Education?* Unpublished paper presented to the "Critical Perspective on Realizing the Global University," Worldwide University Network Conference, November 14, Thistle Hotel, Marble Arch, London.

Keenoy, T. and M. Reed (2008). "Managing Modernization: Introducing Performance Management in British Universities." *European Universities in Transition: Issues, Models and Cases.* Ed. C. Mazza, P. Quattrone, and A. Riccaboni. Cheltenham, UK; Northampton, MA: Edward Elgar: 188–205.

Kehm, B. and U. Lanzendorf, Eds. (2006). *Reforming University Governance: Changing Conditions for Research in Four European Countries.* Bonn: Lemmens/Verlag.

King, R. (2009). *Governing Universities Globally: Organizations, Regulation and Rankings.* Cheltenham: Edward Elgar.

Kwiek, M. (2003). "The Social Functions of the University in the Context of the Changing State/Market Relations." *Globalization and Competition in Higher Education.* Ed. J. de Groofe and G. Lauwers. Antwerp: Wolf Legal.

——— (2005). "The University and the State in a Global Age: Renegotiating the Traditional Social Contract?" *European Educational Research Journal* 4(4): 324–342.

——— (2006). *The University and the State.* Frankfurt and New York: Peter Lang.

——— (2007). "The University and the Welfare State in Transition: Changing Public Services in a Wider Context." *Geographies of Knowledge, Geometries of Power: Framing the Future of Higher Education in the 21st Century; World Year Book of Education 2008.* Ed. D. Epstein, R. Boden, R. Deem, F. Rizvi, and S. Wright. New York: Routledge Falmer: 32–49.

Laing, S. (2009). "Why University Public Engagement?" Retrieved January 2010, from http://www.publicengagement.ac.U.K./what-public -engagement/stuart-laing.

Leisyte, L., H. F. de Boer, and J. Enders (2006). "England: The Prototype of the 'Evaluative State.' " *Reforming University Governance: Changing Conditions for Research in Four European Countries.* Ed. B. Kehm and U. Lanzendorf. Bonn: Lemmens: 21–58.

Lucas, L. (2006). *The Research Game in Academic Life.* Maidenhead: Open University Press and the Society for Research into Higher Education.

Lucas, L. and N. Turner. (2007). "Early Career Academics and Their Experiences of Linking Research and Teaching: A Collaborative U.K./Canadian Project." Retrieved June 2008, from http://escalate .ac.U.K./4061.

Lyotard, J. F. (1984). *The Postmodern Condition: A Report on Knowledge.* Manchester: Manchester University Press.

Manuel, A. (2008). "From Old Boys Network to Virtual Network: A Study of Internet Technology Use amongst U.K. Academics, and the Extent to which It Is Disrupting the Gendered Academic Research Culture. *Graduate School of Education.* Bristol, UK: University of Bristol. Unpublished PhD thesis.

March, J. G. and J. P. Olsen (1989). *Rediscovering Institutions: The Organizational Basis of Politics.* New York: Free Press.

——— (1989). *Discovering Institutions.* New York: Free Press.

Marginson, S. (2007). "The Public/Private Divide in Higher Education: A Global Revision." *Higher Education* 53(3): 307–333.

Marginson, S. and G. Rhoades (2002). "Beyond National States, Markets and Systems of Higher Education: A Glonacal Agency Heuristic." *Higher Education* 43(3): 282–309.

Marginson, S. and M. Considine (2000). *Enterprise University in Australia. Governance, Strategy and Reinvention.* Cambridge: Cambridge University Press.

Marshall, S., Ed. (2007). *Strategic Leadership of Change in Higher Education: What's New?* London: Routledge.

Martin, B. and J. Wajcman (2004). "Markets, Contingency and Preferences: Contemporary Managers' Narrative Identities." *Sociological Review* 52(2): 239–263.

Meyer, J. W. and B. Rowan (1977). "Institutionalised Organizations: Formal Structure as Myth and Ceremony." *American Journal of Sociology* 83: 340–363.

Middlehurst, R. (1993). *Leading Academics.* Buckingham: Open University Press.

Moberly, W. (1949). *The Crisis in the University.* London: SCM Press.

Naidoo, R. (2003). "Repositioning Higher Education as a Global Commodity: Opportunities and Challenges for Future Sociology of Education Work." *British Journal of Sociology of Education* 24(2): 249–259.

——— (2004). "Commodifying Learning: Pitfalls and Possibilities." *Reflections on Higher Education* 13: 50–61.

Naidoo, R. and I. Jamieson (2005). "Empowering Participants or Corroding Learning? Towards a Research Agenda on the Impact of Student Consumerism in Higher Education." *Journal of Education Policy* 20(3): 267–281.

Neave, G. (2003). "The Bologna Declaration: Some of the Historic Dilemmas Posed by the Reconstruction of the Community in Europe's Systems of Higher Education." *Educational Policy* 17(1): 141–164.

Nedeva, M. (2007). "New Tricks and Old Dogs? The 'Third Mission' and the Re-production of the University." *Geographies of Knowledge, Geometries of Power: Framing the Future of Higher Education in the 21st Century; World Year Book of Education 2008.* Ed. D. Epstein, R. Boden, R. Deem, F. Rizvi, and S. Wright. New York: Routledge Falmer: 85–103.

Newman, J. H. (1852). *The Idea of the University.* Notre Dame: Notre Dame University Press.

Nyborg, P. (2003). "Higher Education as a Public Good and a Public Responsibility." *Higher Education in Europe* 28(3): 355–359.

Organization for Economic Co-operation and Development (2006). "Four Future Scenarios for Higher Education." Paris. Retrieved January 2010, from http://www.oecd.org/document/8/0,3343,en_2649_S35845581_37031944_1_1_1_1,00.html.

Palfreyman, D. and T. Tapper, Eds. (2009). *Structuring Mass Higher Education: The Role of Elite Institutions.* New York: Routledge.

Peters, M. (2007). "Reimagining the University in the Global Era." Retrieved September 2007, from http://recordings.wun.ac.U.K./id/2007/id20070525/index.html.

Readings, B. (1996). *The University in Ruins.* Cambridge, MA: Harvard University Press.

Robertson, J. and C. H. Bond (2005). "The Research-Teaching Relation—A View from the Edge." *Higher Education* 50(3): 509–535.

Salmi, J. (2009). *The Challenge of Establishing World-Class Universities.* Washington: World Bank.

Sastry, T. and B. Bekhradnia (2006). *Using Metrics to Allocate Research Funds.* Oxford: Higher Education Policy Institute.

Savin-Baden, M. (2008). *Learning Spaces: Creating Opportunities for Knowledge Creation in Academic Life.* Maidenhead: Open University Press.

Scase, R. and R. Goffee (1989). *Reluctant Managers: Their Work and Lifestyles.* London: Unwin Hyman.

Shah, S. and J. Brennan (2000). "Quality Assessment and Institutional Change: Experiences from 14 Countries." *Higher Education* 40(3): 331–349.

Shattock, M. L. (2006). *Managing Good Governance in Higher Education.* Maidenhead: Open University Press.

Slaughter, S. and G. Leslie (1997). *Academic Capitalism.* Baltimore: Johns Hopkins University Press.

——— (2001). "Expanding and Elaborating the Concept of Academic Capitalism." *Organization* 8(2): 154–161.

Sporn, B. (1996). "Managing University Culture: An Analysis of the Relationship between Institutional Culture and Management Approaches." *Higher Education* 32: 41–61.

——— (1999). *Adaptive University Structures: An Analysis of Adaptation to Socio-economic Environments of US and European Universities.* London: Jessica Kingsley.

Stensaker, B. and B. Kehm, Eds. (2009). *University Rankings, Diversity, and the New Landscape of Higher Education.* Rotterdam: Sense.

Strathern, M. (2000). *Audit Cultures: Anthropological Studies in Accountability, Ethics and the Academy.* London: Routledge.

Taylor, J. (2006). ""Big Is Beautiful." Organizational Change in Universities in the United Kingdom: New Models of Institutional Management and the Changing Role of Academic Staff." *Higher Education in Europe* 31(3): 251–273.

Taylor, R. (2009). "Benchmarking Higher Education Internal Communications and the Development of Best Practice Standards, to Enhance Institutional Effectiveness, Leadership, Management, and Staff Relations." Bristol, Higher Education Funding Council. Retrieved January 2010, from http://www.hefce.ac.U.K./lgm/build/lgmfund/projects/show.asp?id=136&cat=11.

Trainor, R. (2010). "Review of R Zemsky's Making Reform Work: The Case for Transforming American Higher Education." *Times Higher Education* (January 14–20): 46–47.

Von Humboldt, W. (1970). "University Reform in Germany: Reports and Documents: Reprint of 'On the Spirit and the Organizational Framework of Intellectual Institutions in Berlin.'" *Minerva* 8: 242–250.

von Tunzelmann, N. and E. K. Mbula (2003). "Changes in Research Assessment Practices in Other Countries since 1999: Final Report." Bristol. Retrieved March 2008, from http://www.ra-review.ac.U.K./reports/.

Wallace, M., R. Deem, J. Morrison, and M. Reed (2009). "Developing Organization Leaders as Change Agents in the Public Services." End of Award Report. Cardiff.

Wang, Y. (2007). "China's Higher Education on a Overpass of 4 Fold Enrollment Expansion." Retrieved September 2007, from http://recordings.wun.ac.U.K./id/2007/id20070430/index.html.

Wei, I. (2007). "The University of Paris in the Thirteenth Century and the Institutionalization of Scholarly Ideals." Retrieved January 2010, from http://recordings.wun.ac.U.K./id/2007/.

Weingart, P. (2005). "Impact of Bibliometrics upon the Science System: Inadvertent Consequences?" *Scientometrics* 62(1): 117–131.

Whitchurch, C. (2008). "Shifting Identities and Blurring Boundaries: The Emergence of Third Space." *Higher Education Quarterly* 62(4): 377–396.

———(2009). "The Rise of the Blended Professional in Higher Education: A Comparison between the U.K., Australia and the United States." *Higher Education* 59(3): 407–418.

Zemsky, R. (2009). *Making Reform Work: The Case for Transforming American Higher Education.* New Jersey: Rutgers University Press.

PART III

Academic Roles and the Purposes of Universities

CHAPTER 5

Medieval Universities and Aspirations to Universal Significance

Ian P. Wei

INTRODUCTION

This chapter focuses on the emergence of the University of Paris in the late twelfth century and its aspirations to universal significance in the thirteenth century. Geographically the world of Parisian masters and students was much more limited than ours, and their concerns were largely limited to Christendom, so the university was not "global" in our sense. On the other hand, they aimed to save souls and thus shape events in the afterlife, so in spiritual-temporal terms their mission was more universal than that of most university scholars today. In part this chapter will show that the problems faced by universities enjoying or aspiring to global status are not as new as often supposed. I will conclude the chapter by seeking to deploy the medieval University of Paris as a heuristic device by means of which we may be able to reflect usefully on the opportunities presented to universities by globalization today.

AIMS AND ASPIRATIONS

A number of striking images were frequently used to express the way in which the University of Paris was understood to have significance for the whole of the Christian world. James of Vitry studied and taught in Paris and enjoyed a distinguished career in the Church.

His considerable literary output included his *Historia Occidentalis,* written probably in the early 1220s. To look back to around 1200, Paris was already an international center for education, but simply having students from all over Western Europe was not a recipe for success:

> their diversity of origin gave rise to mutual hostility, envy, and detraction, and they rudely hurled a multitude of insults and slanders at each other, saying that the English drank too much and had tails, the French were arrogant, comfort-loving, and effeminate, the Germans were hot-tempered and coarse in their pleasures, the Normans silly and boastful, the Poitevins treacherous and friends of Fortune. They saw the Burgundians as brutish and stupid, and condemned the Bretons as lightweight and frivolous... They called the Lombards greedy, malicious, and cowardly; the Romans seditious, violent, and ungrateful; the Sicilians overbearing and cruel; the Brabants bloodthirsty, arsonists, marauders, and rapists; the Flemings self-indulgent, extravagant, devoted to feasting, and soft as butter. And as a result of abuse of this kind, they would often progress from words to blows.

Fortunately, with the development of the university, matters had improved:

> now, transformed by the hand of the Most High, who makes the desert bloom and turns a wilderness into the garden of the Lord, it has become a faithful and glorious town, the city of the great King, like a paradise of pleasure and a garden of delights filled with all kinds of fruit, breathing the sweetness of its scent over the whole earth, while from it the great Father, as if from his treasury, offers both ancient and new gifts. For this city, like a garden spring and a well of living waters, irrigates the surface of the whole earth, offering fine bread and delicacies to kings, and nourishment sweeter than honeycombs to the whole church of God.[1]

This rich passage condenses and interweaves many themes of significance in the early history of the university, not least the fusion of city and university (a theme of ongoing interest today, notably among those concerned with the role universities play in cities that claim to be "global knowledge hubs"). In this passage, we should also note in particular the play on words whereby Paris (*Parisius*) and Paradise (*Paradisus*) are conflated; the image of water flowing out from Paris to give life to the whole earth; and food being produced for the entire church.[2] To give just one more example, this last image crops up again in a sermon preached by Eudes of Châteauroux, a master of theology later in the thirteenth century:

> Your city is the mill in which all God's wheat is ground for the nour-ishment of the entire world; it is ground, I say by the lectures and the discussions of the masters. Your city is the oven, and the kitchen, in which the entire world's bread is baked and this world's food is prepared.[3]

Such imagery conveyed how men with a Paris education saw their university—and the teaching and learning that went on there—in the greater scheme of things.

These grand images reflected a very particular vision of the univer-sity and its purpose. Its functions and responsibilities were essentially pastoral, bound up with the church's mission to save souls. This vision was articulated repeatedly by masters of theology when they discussed what they were supposed to be doing. In 1269, for example, Thomas Aquinas, the Dominican master of theology, tackled an issue that was put to many masters in one form or another. How could they justify remaining at the university rather than working directly to save souls? Aquinas was asked whether someone was bound to give up studying theology to pursue the salvation of souls, even if he were fit to teach others. Using an image derived from Aristotle, he responded by com-paring the master of theology with an architect. The ordinary priests who had direct responsibility for the cure of souls were like manual laborers, Aquinas explained, but in any construction, the architect who arranged the construction was more important than a manual worker who followed instructions. Thus in the construction of build-ings the architect was more highly paid than the manual workers who hewed planks and cut stone. In the work of spiritual construc-tion, those who were directly concerned with the cure of souls, for example, by administering the sacraments, were like manual workers. However, both bishops, who arranged how these priests should carry out their duties, and doctors of theology, who investigated the means of salvation and taught them to others, were like architects. It was, therefore, better to teach sacred doctrine, and more meritorious if done with good intention, than to be concerned with the salvation of individuals.

It was also better—in matters pertaining to salvation—to instruct those who could benefit both themselves and others rather than sim-ple folk who could benefit only themselves. To this point Aquinas added just one qualification: in certain cases of necessity both bishops and doctors would have to lay aside their office and attend directly to the salvation of souls. This was not, however, the ordinary state of affairs. Normally the masters, too exalted to attend directly to the cure of souls, were responsible for those who did. Like bishops they had a definite status within a hierarchy. But whereas bishops ruled, the masters carried out a process of inquiry that resulted in teaching. Operating at a higher level of understanding, they passed on the fruits of their learning and thus played a crucial role in ensuring right order within the Church.[4] All masters held the same view of themselves. They benefitted the whole Church by teaching others, elucidating the truth, removing doubt and error, defending the faith against heretics, and teaching others how to preach, teach, and save souls throughout society. They were at the top of a hierarchy of knowledge, and their job was to direct ordinary priests and preachers. This directing role gave them a status comparable to that of bishops in this life, and meant that they would have special status in heaven alongside martyrs and virgins.[5] (This notion of academics' special role is echoed in the chapter by Xu Xiaozhou and Xue Shan in this volume.)

This vision was deployed not only for the edification of university audiences, but also in public when the university negotiated its relations with major external powers, especially the papacy. Moreover, this vision of academics' special role was used to justify formal grants of key privileges. Most significantly, in 1231 Pope Gregory IX issued the bull *Parens scientiarum* when he restored order after an argument, involving a tavern bill, had led to escalating violence. The death of several students at the hands of men acting on behalf of royal authority had prompted the departure of the majority of students and masters to pursue their studies in other cities in Western Europe. *Parens scientiarum* brought the students back to Paris. It recognized academics' legal status as a corporation, allowed the members of the university to make and enforce their own rules, acknowledged their right to strike, and regulated some essential aspects of university life (e.g., customs associated with dress and funerary rites). The opening of the bull, although frequently ignored, merits particular attention:

Paris, parent of sciences, like another *Cariath Sepher, city of letters* [Joshua 15.15; Judges 1.11], and precious, shines forth. It is great indeed but concerning itself raises hopes for greater things that are pleasing to those who teach and those who learn, where, surely as if in wisdom's special workshop, *there is a mine for silver, and a place for gold which they refine* [Job 28.1], from which those prudent in mystical eloquence, stamping *ornaments of gold, studded with silver* [Song of

Songs 1.10], and making necklaces elaborately, adorn and make beautiful the bride of Christ with precious stones, or rather stones beyond price. There *iron is taken out of the earth* [Job 28.2], because when its earthly fragility is solidified by firmness, from it is made the breastplate of faith, the sword of the spirit, and other armour of Christian soldiery, potent against the aerial powers. And *copper is smelted from the ore* [Job 28.2], because while stony hearts burn, blown on by the fervour of the Holy Spirit, they take fire and are made to proclaim the praises of Christ with resonant preaching.[6]

This is a very rich text, with embedded quotations from the Bible, and echoing Gregory the Great's *Moralia in Job*.[7] The final line is critical: the university served the Church by transforming men into preachers. This was a huge programmatic statement. This was the vision, the idea, of the university.

KNOWLEDGE AND ITS COMMUNICATION

Was this vision of the university, with its expression of common interests, transformative powers, and pastoral responsibilities, actually realized? In some ways it was, most notably with regard to knowledge and its communication. University scholars produced theories of knowledge that embraced all forms of knowledge, placed theology at the top of a hierarchy, and stressed the overriding importance of moral theology. They by no means agreed with each other, and the fights could be bitter, especially when they had to take account of newly discovered and translated Aristotelian texts, but there was an underlying consensus that it was possible to know some types of truth, that there was a hierarchy in play, and that the production of knowledge should serve a moral purpose. Many theoretical discussions could be cited here, but the fundamental point was made with engaging good humor in a sermon preached by a master of theology, Ranulphe de la Houblonnière, in 1273. A poor Paris student fell in love with a Parisian lady. He told her that he loved her so much that he could not sleep or study, and that he wanted her. She pointed out that she was of much higher social standing, but gave him advice that offered hope: "I tell you what you should do...Learn so much that you become a master, and then it would be more honorable for me to do as you wish." He studied so hard that he was a master within four or five years. When he went to her with the news, she asked in what science he had achieved this status and he said that he was a master of arts. She explained that everyone thought that masters of arts were idiots, and that he needed to learn more. She suggested that he go and study medicine and become a master, and then he would have an excuse to come to her house. He duly became a master of medicine and returned, but she pointed out that her husband and family were healthy so he could not keep visiting. Her advice now was to become a lawyer: they had legal problems all the time, so he would have an excuse to visit. He became a master of law and returned, but it was still not enough: lawyers were tricky characters and it would look bad for her if he kept calling. Once again she had advice: he should become a master of theology, and because they were all good men, he would be able to come to her without suspicion. He, therefore, became a master of theology and returned. "Just one thing," she said, "go and look in those theology books of which you are a master, and see if it says anywhere that I should break my marriage vow for you. If you can find that, I'm yours." He read and read, and the more he read the more he realized that his love was false. Finally he went and told her that he was now a good clerk and she was free of him. This exemplary story, presumably told to an audience from all faculties in the university, captures the hierarchy of knowledge topped by theology and its morally transformative power.[8]

Theologians also claimed to make moral judgments about all aspects of human behavior, because sin was always possible—even likely—and they communicated their views through disputations, preaching, and confession. They theorized and refined these techniques of communication and spent a great deal of time and effort putting them into practice. Preaching in particular was an integral part of the life of the university. Students and masters were expected both to hear and to give sermons, and this expectation was embedded in the regulations and routines of the university as an institution. There were no classes in preaching as such, but a close relationship between study and preaching was taken for granted. All members of all faculties were obliged to attend university sermons, while both masters and bachelors in the faculty of theology were required to preach them. Preaching, therefore, bound the university together as a community. It also provided a point of direct contact between university men and the rest of society.

Masters regularly preached not only to students and each other, but also to a much wider audience, especially in Paris. Many of their sermons were preached *ad populam*, or "to the people," in the churches of Paris. These sermons for lay people were delivered in French, but written down in Latin from which they could be translated subsequently into any vernacular language. This was important because, in addition to communicating directly by preaching themselves, Parisian scholars had a profound influence on preaching across Western Europe. In part this was a matter of former students and indeed masters leaving Paris and preaching as part of whatever role they went on to play in the Church. But even for those who never went to Paris at all, a whole host of preaching aids was produced in Paris. Countless books and manuals on the art of preaching taught students the theory of preaching. Collections of model sermons provided basic plans, while *Florilegia* and collections of *exempla* gave quick access to the raw material that could be used within them. Books of distinctions listed words used in the Bible and explained the different meanings that they could have, often illustrating each meaning with a biblical passage. The production of preaching aids and the development of preaching techniques were by no means exclusive to Paris, but it was without doubt a key center for the education of preachers and for the production and diffusion of preaching aids. So, from the late twelfth century, Paris was regarded as a source from which moral teaching was spread through sermons to Christendom as a whole.[9]

The vision of the University of Paris as an internationally significant center for education was also realized in so far as men came to study and teach in Paris from all over Western Europe and then left to pursue academic careers or work in secular or ecclesiastical bureaucracies on an equally wide scale. This was relatively easy because in many respects learned men shared a common intellectual culture. There was a common language for scholarship: Latin. Perhaps English has a similar status now, but Latin did not put some scholars at a disadvantage as any language is bound to do now. There was a very similar curriculum in all arts faculties that all students followed before moving on to higher faculties, so scholars in all disciplines and all universities shared a substantial body of basic knowledge and fundamental methods of analysis. Teaching and research methods were also the same in all universities and all subjects. The lecture (*lectio*) involved reading and interpreting an authoritative text. The disputation (*disputatio*) required masters and students to engage in structured debate leading to the resolution of questions. Perhaps global information technologies today are generating similar "student experiences" in all academic disciplines and in all countries, but the differences between disciplines and intellectual traditions in different countries are surely much greater now than in the middle ages. There was also a high degree of mobility among medieval scholars, with many universities granting "the right to teach anywhere" (*ius ubique docendi*) as part of the teaching license that signaled the attainment of magisterial status. (The dynamics and implications of academic mobility are a central concern in the chapter by Glen Jones and Bryan Gopaul in this volume.)

COMMUNITIES WITHIN COMMUNITIES

While the idea—or ideal—of the university as an institution unified by a sense of pastoral mission was in some ways realized, there were also some very obvious ways in which this vision of the university was not realized. It was by no means the case that everyone went to university because they wanted to be turned into preachers. Many were attracted to the university because of the job opportunities that they expected or hoped to be on offer as a result. Masters had extremely good career prospects in the Church, many becoming prelates and others taking up positions in cathedral chapters. The French and English kings also employed increasing numbers of men who could claim the title of "master," with the English kings using them in far greater numbers for most of the thirteenth century. It is much harder to track the careers of those who did not become masters, but there is little doubt that many of them staffed the growing bureaucracies of ecclesiastical and secular government. There was constant criticism of students who were driven by worldly ambition, but to no avail. Such ambitions drew many to study in Paris.[10]

Furthermore, the university was in many respects a dysfunctional community, a complex community of communities offering masters and students a range of sometimes competing identities. The masters of arts divided themselves into four nations, with arts students gaining affiliation with a particular nation through association with their masters. Exactly when and how this system took root is not known: the earliest reference to the nations dates from 1222 and there is firm evidence for a well-developed system by 1249, but their composition and structure continued to evolve in the course of the thirteenth and early fourteenth centuries. The four nations were France, Picardy, Normandy, and England. Each was a very rough and somewhat arbitrary geographical grouping. Thus, by the early fourteenth century, the French nation consisted of masters not only from the Ile de France but also from the south of France, Spain, Italy, Greece, and the East. The masters of the Picard nation came from the north of France and the Low Countries. The Norman nation was made up of masters from Normandy and Brittany. The English nation included not only English masters but also masters from Germany and elsewhere in Northern and Eastern Europe. Each nation was a distinct and largely autonomous corporation, with its own assembly, seal, statutes, financial arrangements, records, and elected officials. Each nation elected a proctor who summoned and chaired the assembly and carried out key administrative and disciplinary functions. The system was highly democratic in that proctors were entirely subject to their assemblies and held office for no more than a month or six weeks.

Together the nations constituted the faculty of arts whose rector was elected by the proctors or four other representatives chosen by the nations. The rector's period of office was also limited to a month or six weeks until it was extended to three months in 1266. The nations were responsible for organizing the teaching in the arts faculty. They maintained the schools in which the arts students were taught, mostly on the Rue du Fouarre, or "street of straw," so named because of the straw on which the students sat. They allocated teaching space to the masters, collected fees from the students, and organized payment of the masters. Students were not, however, obliged to attend the schools of their own nation. Many other aspects of life also revolved around the nations. Each nation employed messengers, termed *nuntii volantes* or "flying messengers," who traveled between Paris and the lands from which the scholars came, bearing letters, property, and money. Eventually they also established arrangements with bankers and merchants in Paris, called *nuntii maiores* or "greater messengers," who provided banking services for the masters and students of the nation, arranging the transfer of funds from their families in the territories of the nation, changing money, and making loans.

The nations also provided the focus for the religious life of its members. The nations celebrated their own patron saints. By the fourteenth century, and probably earlier, the nations made payments to their masters for attending masses and fined them if they failed to turn up. Unsurprisingly many masters and students felt an overwhelming sense of loyalty to their nation. This loyalty could lead to tensions between nations. Throughout the thirteenth century there were conflicts between the nations, some of them extremely violent. They were usually caused by arguments about which nation a particular master should join, disputes over the election of the rector, or the French nation's resentment that it had no more power than each of the other nations even though it had many more members. Thus, while all belonged to the university, the university's members were not a perfectly unified body. They had both common *and* competing interests and identities.[11]

Matters were further complicated by the faculty structure. The faculty of arts developed at the same time as the nations of which it was composed. Its status as a legal corporation with an elected rector at its head was well established by the middle of the thirteenth century. The masters teaching theology, canon law, and medicine remained informal groupings until the second half of the century when they too produced written statutes, acquired seals, and elected officers, including deans to preside over them. It is impossible to offer statistical analysis of the university in the thirteenth century for lack of evidence; there are, for example, no matriculation records. Nevertheless it is clear that the faculty of arts was far larger than the others. Taking students and masters together, it has been estimated that the faculty of arts made up about two-thirds of the university. As far as masters were concerned, there were probably never more than 10–16 in any one of the higher faculties at any one time, whereas there were probably well over a hundred arts masters. Perhaps because the faculty of arts was so much larger, and perhaps also because the other faculties developed so much later, the rector, the elected head of the faculty of arts, came increasingly to act as the head of the university as a whole. By the end of the thirteenth century, all four faculties were well established as independent corporations. There was, however, a measure of interpenetration. Many students and bachelors in the higher faculties were also masters of arts, and until they became masters in these higher faculties, they remained members of their nations in the faculty of arts, at once subject to their jurisdiction and active participants in their governmental processes. Furthermore, students in the faculty of arts had to take an oath of obedience before they could become bachelors. In the developed form of this oath, they had to swear obedience to the rector, whatever their future position might be. Many of the secular masters in the higher faculties, as well as many of the students and bachelors, were, therefore, bound by oath to the rector of the arts faculty. The federal structure of the university—with four faculties under a common head—was most strikingly revealed at its general assembly or congregation. It was composed of all the regent masters, chaired by the rector. When a matter required discussion, each nation of the faculty of arts and each of the higher faculties considered the matter separately. Their views were reported by their proctors or deans. The four nations and the three higher faculties cast one vote each, and the decision was carried by the majority of these seven votes.[12]

Within and sometimes cutting across the structure of faculties and nations were a growing number of colleges. The earliest were charitable foundations, developed from or modelled on hospitals, and providing little more than basic accommodation and a small financial grant for a limited number of poor scholars. The first, which became known as the Collège des Dix-Huit, was set up in 1180 by an Englishman, Jocius of London, on his way back from a pilgrimage to Jerusalem. He visited the Hospital of the Blessed Mary of Paris and saw within it a room customarily occupied by poor clerks. Acting on the advice of the dean and chancellor of Paris, he purchased the room for the accommodation of 18 scholars who would also receive a monthly payment from the alms given to the hospital. In return, the scholars were obliged only to participate in the funerary rituals of those who died in the house and to say nightly prayers. Other colleges were soon established. Some of them admitted only scholars studying a particular subject. Thus the Collège de Sorbonne, founded around 1257 by the theologian Robert of Sorbon with the active support of Louis IX, provided initially for 16 theology students, 4 from each nation, and later for a total of 36.

Other colleges admitted scholars only from a particular region. The College of the Treasurer, for example, was founded in 1268 to house and support 12 students of theology and 12 of the arts, all to be "chosen, when the need arises, by the two archdeacons of Grand-Caux and Petit-Caux," and all to originate "from Grand-Caux and Petit-Caux, if in those two places they find sufficient and fit persons, or if not in the two Caux, at least from the whole diocese of Rouen."[13] Some of these later colleges were highly complex institutions. The Sorbonne in particular regulated the lives of its members in great detail and required them all to participate in its internal management by holding various offices in turn. It also gave a great deal of support to their studies, providing an excellent library and even running special classes for extra revision and practice. The overwhelming majority of students rented houses in groups, boarded with masters, or lodged with townspeople, but for a few the colleges provided essential material support and in some cases even dominated their domestic and scholarly routines.[14] (The gradual differentiation and hierarchization of Parisian colleges—which could lead to differential opportunities for students—presages some of the effects of institutional differentiation that Glen Jones and Bryan Gopaul examine in their chapter.)

The university was not, therefore, a single community; rather there were communities within communities, and communities overlapping with each other. There were also communities that straddled the university's conceptual boundaries, most obviously and contentiously the friars. The friars included some of the university's most outstanding theologians, but also threatened the means by which the emerging university was asserting its autonomy. Both the Franciscan and the Dominican orders expanded dramatically in the first two decades of the thirteenth century, espousing voluntary poverty and undertaking a universal preaching mission. Right from the start, the Dominicans valued learning and set out to establish themselves in Paris and Bologna. They developed a hierarchical system of schools within the order, with the best students ending up at one of their top schools. Unlike Dominic, Francis had not himself set much store in formal learning, and the Franciscans were much slower to establish a system of education. Before long, however, they too were active as scholars in Paris. Neither order permitted its members to study or teach in the faculty of arts; they came to Paris to study theology. The rest of the university made them welcome, and friars were taught by secular masters of theology. The Dominicans received the house of St. Jacques and associated rights partly from Jean de Barastre, a secular master of theology who had been asked to teach in their school by Pope Honorius III, and partly from the university as a whole. The Franciscans set up a new convent, the Grand Couvent des Cordeliers, with financial assistance from the king.

The friars were not, however, fully tied into the emerging structure of the university. Unless a friar had been a master of arts before converting, for example, he had not taken the oath to obey the statutes of the university that masters of arts took upon inception. As the university's structure emerged, and as the university acted to assert its privileges, such anomalies began to matter. A critical point was reached when the university went on strike in 1229: the friars refused to suspend their studies, and even opened their schools to secular students who wished to continue their studies in Paris. Moreover, Roland of Cremona was granted the first Dominican chair in theology. After the masters and students returned in 1231, the Dominicans kept their chair and the mendicant schools remained open to secular students. Tension mounted thereafter not only because the friars clearly could not be relied upon to support a strike, but also because their success was damaging the careers of the secular masters. The friars were attracting growing numbers of students, thus reducing the income received by the secular masters of theology. Moreover, by converting secular masters of theology, the friars gained more chairs. (Here again, the chapter by Glen Jones and Bryan Gopaul resonates with the past, showing the relationship between academic mobility and the construction of professional hierarchies.)

Tensions between the friars and secular masters only grew. In 1231, the year the students returned to Paris, Alexander of Hales entered the Franciscan order to become the first Franciscan master of theology at Paris. Around the same time John of Saint Giles dramatically took the habit of the Dominicans in the middle of a sermon, thus creating a second Dominican chair of theology. It is not known exactly how professorial succession functioned, but it was clearly accepted that when a chair fell vacant, it passed to a master from the same order. If a secular master converted while continuing to hold his chair, he reduced the number of chairs available for secular scholars, thus damaging their career opportunities. Tensions between the secular members of the university and the friars flared up on many future occasions. It was impossible to escape from the problems caused by the friars and members of other religious orders who wished to be part of the university, and yet to retain their identity as members of wider religious communities.[15]

Individuals within the university were also members of groups that existed primarily *outside* the university, as they were constantly reminded by their need for financial support. The cost of university education was high, and probably increased from the middle of the thirteenth century. Many scholars depended on their families for money and material assistance. Most were from lesser noble families or the wealthy urban classes. Great noble families rarely sent their sons to university until much later. Few from the peasantry or the poorer urban classes could find the means to attend university, and even fewer could stay at university for long enough to become masters in the higher faculties, though there were some striking exceptions. Model letters reflect the way in which scholars found it necessary to seek assistance from their parents, siblings, and clerical uncles. Another source of income was the holding of ecclesiastical benefices. A scholar might be permitted to employ another cleric to do the work while he himself was nonresident because he was at university. He paid less than the income he received, and kept the difference for himself. It is not known how many students and masters were funded in this way, but successive popes strongly encouraged the practice. Many scholars, therefore, held offices in churches outside Paris and, despite their nonresidence, were drawn into the local politics of the communities of which they were now members.

Financial support was also provided by wealthy patrons. Royal backing could be very generous. While Henry III of England directed most of his educational patronage to Oxford, he nevertheless gave money to several Parisian students. At the end of the thirteenth century, Philip IV of France made systematic payments to scholars at Paris, as well as to two colleges, and it may be that this practice had begun earlier in the century. Other patrons included nobles, high-ranking churchmen, prominent townspeople, and rich academics. Sometimes they simply funded individuals for a period of time. On occasion, however, especially in their wills, they established "flying scholarships," or *bursae volantes*. Income from property or invested capital was used to provide grants to scholars, termed "flying scholarships" because the holder did not have to live in a specific college. Usually, however, certain conditions had to be met: these might include coming from a particular area, attending a specific university, studying a particular subject, being studious, or being poor. (For a discussion of a modern scholarship program with similar constraints, see, again, the chapter by Jones and Gopaul.) Financial management and responsibility for selecting holders was generally placed in the hands of the founder's family or representatives of an ecclesiastical institution. While patrons may have been primarily motivated by charity, the recipients of their generosity were bound to feel informal ties of obligation and to be drawn into the political, regional, or ecclesiastical networks through which patronage operated (in this way, the system of patronage bears some resemblance to the complexities of external financial support described in the final section of this volume, in the chapters by John Taylor and Peter Maassen).[16] In short, being a member of the university could mean very different things to different men, and the university environment was sometimes highly volatile.

The grand vision was contested in one final respect. The theologians' view of their own position at the top of a hierarchy of learning giving them universal authority did not always play well with members of the other faculties or with Church leaders outside the university. Lawyers tended to think that canon law existed to deal with practical matters and that they should exercise power through the Church courts. Prelates did not expect to defer to masters of theology when running their dioceses. Cardinal Benedict Gaetani, the future Pope Boniface VIII, was both a lawyer and a prelate, and in 1290 at the Council of Paris he had had enough of theologians disagreeing with papal policy on the friars:

> These masters imagine that we consider them learned whereas we think them more stupid than the stupid because they have filled not only Paris but the whole world with this noxious doctrine.[17]

Not everyone accepted the theologians' claims that their pastoral mission superseded all others.

CONCLUDING THOUGHTS

So, in the end, did the vision, the idea, of the university matter? I would argue that it did. First, it offered a set of values in which many university men, including those in leadership roles, sincerely believed, which many actively sought to implement, and which everyone understood and generally respected, even if they had other priorities. It was genuinely meaningful within the university. Second, it was publicly elaborated when secular and religious authorities gave their backing to the university, *Parens scientiarum* being only the most striking example. Those who supported the university either believed in its pastoral mission, or had to be seen to believe in it in order to preserve their own standing. It, therefore, offered a discourse through which to negotiate effectively with those who held power outside the university.

At this point, I want to ask a different type of question. Are there any ways in which a case study from the past can serve as a heuristic device to help us understand the present? It would be naive to suggest that there are direct lessons to be learned, but perhaps, having examined the past, we can see the present in a fresh light. Perhaps in particular we can identify absence, we can recognize what is not there. I have argued that the University of Paris in the thirteenth century deployed a discourse that expressed ideals genuinely held by many and recognized as meaningful by all within the university, and effective in negotiation with those who were powerful outside the university. I would suggest that, in the United Kingdom at least, we lack an effective discourse that expresses a shared vision of what universities are for, and allows us to negotiate successfully for support, above all for funding, from outside the university. The lack of an idea or vision holding the university together from within is not new. Clark Kerr's observation in 1963, when discussing "the idea of a multiversity," that the modern university can be thought of as "a series of individual faculty entrepreneurs held together by a common grievance over parking," is well known.[18] Yet as Xu Xiaozhou and Xue Shan note in their chapter in this volume, the problem starts inside the university. We do not agree on what we are trying to do collectively; no idea or vision holds the university together. That in itself creates problems for decision making within the university—on what grounds might a decision be considered legitimate? When, however, the university negotiates with external powers, the absence becomes critical. The university has no discourse to present from within and necessarily accepts the terms of negotiation supplied from outside.

This is to negotiate at a disadvantage, to put it mildly. Consequently, in the United Kingdom and elsewhere, as so many of the chapters in this book point out, the key terms of negotiation come from the world of finance and business. Concern for the generation of material wealth comes to the fore. As universities seek to present themselves as meeting the relevant criteria, those who conduct negotiations on the university's behalf require everyone within the university to use an appropriate language and conceptual framework, and to shape their activities to fit this alien discourse.

Does globalization offer the foundation for an idea of the university, a discourse that unites and inspires the academic community and finds sufficient acceptance outside the university to permit effective negotiation between the university and others? It depends. If globalization just means a transnational framework for competition and the striking of bargains, with, for example, universities competing to outrank each other in international ranking systems, then it will just compound the existing problems in ways set out in other chapters. There are, however, opportunities here. Globalization can bring ideas about international understanding and mutual respect into play, as demonstrated elsewhere in this book. It can give universities opportunities to break free of or step outside local and national frameworks. And there is perhaps a vacuum to be filled: university leaders and national governments want to have global universities, they are willing to commit resources to global projects, but they do not always seem to know what global academic activity should look like. Those who work in universities should tell them, and not wait to be told.

Notes

1. *The Historia Occidentalis of Jacques de Vitry: A Critical Edition*, ed. J. F. Hinnebusch (Fribourg: Fribourg University Press, 1972), pp. 90–93; translated by Bella Millett at http://www.soton.ac.uk /-enm/vitry.htm.
2. See S. C. Ferruolo, "Parisius-Paradisus: the city, its schools, and the origins of the University of Paris," in T. Bender (ed.), *The University and the City: From Medieval Origins to the Present* (Oxford: Oxford University Press, 1988), pp. 22–43.
3. As quoted by E. Marmursztejn, "A normative power in the making: theological *quodlibeta* and the authority of the masters at Paris at the end of the thirteenth century," in C. Schabel (ed.), *Theological Quodlibeta in the Middle Ages: The Thirteenth Century* (Leiden: Brill, 2006): 345–402 at 345.

4. Quodlibet I.14. *S. Thomae Aquinatis Doctoris Angelici quaestiones quodlibetales*, ed. R. Spiazzi (Turin: Marietti, 1956), pp. 13–14. See Marmursztejn, "A normative power," pp. 358–359; E. Marmursztejn, *L'autorité des maîtres: scolastique, normes et société au xiiie siècle* (Paris: Les Belles Lettres, 2007), pp. 49–54; I. P. Wei, "The self-image of the masters of theology at the university of Paris in the late thirteenth and early fourteenth centuries," *Journal of Ecclesiastical History* 46 (1995): 398–431 at 409–410.

5. Wei, "The self-image of the masters," pp. 398–431.

6. *Chartularium Universitatis Parisiensis*, ed. H. Denifle and E. Chatelain, 4 vols. (Paris: Delalain, 1889–1897), vol. 1, no. 79, pp. 136–139.

7. See I. P. Wei, "From twelfth-century schools to thirteenth-century universities: the disappearance of biographical and autobiographical representations of scholars," *Speculum* 86 (2011): 42–78 at 73–8.

8. N. Bériou, *La prédication de Ranulphe de la Houblonnière: sermons aux clercs et aux simples gens à Paris au XIIIe siècle*, 2 vols. (Paris: Etudes augustiniennes, 1987), vol. 1, pp. 114–115.

9. On preaching, see J. W. Baldwin, *Masters, Princes and Merchants: The Social Views of Peter the Chanter and his Circle*, 2 vols. (Princeton: Princeton University Press, 1970); N. Bériou, "La prédication au béguinage de Paris pendant l'année liturgique 1272–1273," *Recherches Augustiniennes* 13 (1978): 105–229; N. Bériou, *L'avènement des maîtres de la parole. La prédication à Paris au XIIIe siècle*, 2 vols. (Paris: Institut d'études augustiniennes, 1998); D. d'Avray, *The Preaching of the Friars: Sermons Diffused from Paris before 1300* (Oxford: Clarendon Press, 1985); M. M. Mulchahey, *"First the Bow is Bent": Dominican Education before 1350* (Toronto: Pontifical Institute of Mediaeval Studies, 1998); P. B. Roberts, "Sermons and preaching in/and the medieval university," in R. B. Begley and J. W. Koterski (eds.), *Medieval Education* (New York: Fordham University Press, 2005), pp. 83–98; R. H. and M. H. Rouse, *Preachers, Florilegia and Sermons: Studies on the Manipulus Florum of Thomas of Ireland* (Toronto: Pontifical Institute of Mediaeval Studies, 1979); R. H. Rouse and M. A. Rouse, *"Statim invenire*: schools, preachers, and new attitudes to the page," in R. L. Benson and G. Constable (eds.), *Renaissance and Renewal in the Twelfth Century* (Cambridge, MA: Harvard University Press, 1982), pp. 201–225.

10. R. Avi-Yonah, "Career trends of Parisian masters of theology, 1200–1320," *History of Universities* 6 (1986–1987): 47–64; J. W. Baldwin, *"Studium et Regnum*: the penetration of university personnel into French and English administration at the turn of the twelfth and thirteenth centuries," *Revue des études islamiques* 44 (1976): 199–215; J. W. Baldwin, "Masters at Paris from 1179 to 1215: a social perspective," in Benson and Constable (eds.), *Renaissance and Renewal*, pp. 138–172; W. J. Courtenay, *Teaching Careers at*

the University of Paris in the Thirteenth and Fourteenth Centuries (Notre Dame, IN: United States Subcommission for the History of Universities, University of Notre Dame, 1988); G. Leff, *Paris and Oxford Universities in the Thirteenth and Fourteenth Centuries: An Institutional and Intellectual History* (New York: Wiley, 1968), pp. 6–8.

11. A. B. Cobban, *The Medieval Universities: Their Development and Organization* (London: Methuen, 1975), pp. 87–90; A. Gieysztot, "Management and resources," in H. de Ridder-Symoens (ed.), *A History of the University in Europe, Volume I: Universities in the Middle Ages* (Cambridge: Cambridge University Press, 1992), pp. 108–143 at 114–116; P. Kibre, *The Nations in the Mediaeval Universities* (Cambridge, MA: Mediaeval Academy of America, 1948), pp. 14–28, 65–115; Leff, *Paris and Oxford Universities*, pp. 51–60; O. Pedersen, *The First Universities: Studium Generale and the Origins of University Education in Europe* (Cambridge: Cambridge University Press, 1997), pp. 194–195; H. Rashdall, *The Universities of Europe in the Middle Ages*, revised and ed. F. M. Powicke and A. B. Emden, 3 vols. (1936; repr. Oxford: Clarendon Press, 1997), vol. 1, pp. 311–320, 408, 414–415, 420–421; H. de Ridder-Symoens, "Mobility," in Ridder-Symoens (ed.), *Universities in the Middle Ages*, pp. 280–304 at 282–285; R. C. Schwinges, "Student education, student life," in Ridder-Symoens (ed.), *Universities in the Middle Ages*, pp. 195–243 at 211.

12. J. A. Brundage, *The Medieval Origins of the Legal Profession: Canonists, Civilians, and Courts* (Chicago: University of Chicago Press, 2008), pp. 246–247; Cobban, *Medieval Universities*, pp. 84–86; Gieysztor, "Management and resources," in Ridder-Symoens (ed.), *Universities in the Middle Ages*, pp. 109–113; Leff, *Paris and Oxford Universities*, pp. 52, 60–67; Pedersen, *The First Universities*, pp. 191–194, 196–198, 200–204; Rashdall, *Universities*, vol. 1, 321–334, 408–414; N. Siraisi, "The faculty of medicine," in Ridder-Symoens (ed.), *Universities in the Middle Ages*, pp. 360–387 at 367–368; Verger, "Patterns," in Ridder-Symoens (ed.), *Universities in the Middle Ages*, pp. 38, 52.

13. L. Thorndike, *University Records and Life in the Middle Ages* (New York: Columbia University Press, 1944), Document no. 36, p. 76.

14. A. B. Cobban, "The role of colleges in the medieval universities of northern Europe, with special reference to France and England," *Bulletin of the John Rylands University Library of Manchester* 71 (1989): 49–70 at 51–53; Gieysztor, "Management and resources," in Ridder-Symoens (ed.), *Universities in the Middle Ages*, pp. 116–119; P. Glorieux, *Les Origines du Collège de Sorbonne* (Notre Dame, IN: Mediaeval Institute, University of Notre Dame, 1959), pp. 17–23; Pedersen, *The First Universities*, pp. 226–229; Rashdall, *Universities*,

vol. 1, pp. 497–511; Schwinges, "Student education, student life," in Ridder-Symoens (ed.), *Universities in the Middle Ages*, p. 214.

15. Cobban, *Medieval Universities*, pp. 91–94; Kibre, *Scholarly Privileges*, pp. 103–118; Leff, *Paris and Oxford Universities*, pp. 34–47; P. R. McKeon, "The status of the university of Paris as *Parens Scientiarum*: an episode in the development of its autonomy," *Speculum* 39 (1964): 651–675; Mulchahey, *"First the bow is bent,"* pp. 362–364; Pedersen, *The First Universities*, pp. 173–182; Rashdall, *Universities*, vol. 1, pp. 370–397; B. Roest, *A History of Franciscan Education (c. 1210–1517)* (Leiden: Brill, 2000), pp. 1–21, 53–58; A. G. Traver, "Rewriting history? The Parisian secular masters' *Apologia* of 1254," *History of Universities* 15 (1997–1999): 9–45.

16. J. W. Baldwin, "Masters at Paris from 1179 to 1215: a social perspective," in Benson and Constable (eds.), *Renaissance and Renewal*, pp. 138–172 at 150–151; J. Dunbabin, "Meeting the costs of university education in northern France, c. 1240–c. 1340," *History of Universities* 10 (1991): 1–27; C. H. Haskins, "The life of mediaeval students as illustrated by their letters," in *Studies in Mediaeval Culture* (Oxford: Clarendon Press, 1929), pp. 1–35, as revised and expanded from *American Historical Review* 3 (1898): pp. 203–229; Leff, *Paris and Oxford Universities*, pp. 67–68; J. Paquet, "Coût des études, pauvreté et labeur: fonctions et métiers d'étudiants au moyenâge," *History of Universities* 2 (1982): 15–52; Pedersen, *The First Universities*, pp. 216–221; F. Pegues, "Royal support of students in the thirteenth century," *Speculum* 31 (1956): 454–462; F. Pegues, "Ecclesiastical provisions for the support of students in the thirteenth century," *Church History* 26 (1957): 307–318; Schwinges, "Student education, student life," in Ridder-Symoens (ed.), *Universities in the Middle Ages*, pp. 240–241; P. Trio, "Financing of university students in the middle ages: a new orientation," *History of Universities* 4 (1984): 1–24; J. Verger, "Teachers," in Ridder-Symoens (ed.), *Universities in the Middle Ages*, pp. 144–168 at 151.

17. H. Finke (ed.), "Das Pariser Nationalkonzil vom Jahre 1290. Ein Beitrag zur Geschichte Bonifaz VIII. und der Pariser Universität," *Römische Quartalschrift für christliche Alterthumskunde und für Kirchengeschichte* (Rome, 1895): pp. 178–182.

18. C. Kerr, *The Uses of the University*, 5th edition (Cambridge, MA: Harvard University Press, 2001), p. 15.

CHAPTER 6

The Changing Role of the Academic: Historical and Comparative Perspectives

Xu Xiaozhou and Xue Shan

INTRODUCTION

In the postindustrial era, universities have accepted more and more responsibility for the development of a "knowledge economy." At the same time, with the process of globalization, the external environment of the university has changed, and these changes have, in turn, affected the *internal* organization of academic life. What can we learn from the evolution of academic roles over time? How have academic roles been defined? How have scholars balanced different roles while also fulfilling their core academic duties? How should we value the diverse roles of academics in the modern university? These are the questions discussed in this chapter.

ACADEMIC ROLES

The roles of academics have been debated for a very long time. Most discussions of academic roles focus on teaching, research, and service to society. Some maintain that teaching, research, and service are independent of each other; others emphasize the integration of these roles and regard teaching, research, and service as different parts of a whole. Those adopting the first perspective point to a negative relationship, or trade-off, between teaching and research, a relationship represented in terms of a Scarcity Model, a Differential Personality Model, or a Divergent Reward System Model. Those espousing the integration of teaching, research, and service point to a more positive relationship, or complementarity, between these roles, often represented by the Conventional Wisdom Model or the "G" Model. Still others find little relationship at all—neither positive nor negative—between teaching and research. They draw on the Different Enterprises Model, the Unrelated Personality Model, or a Bureaucratic Funding Model.[1]

Among those who see a positive relationship between teaching and research, Ernest Boyer has advanced an especially prominent theory. Boyer (1990) hoped to correct an overemphasis on "research" in academic evaluation systems. Based on his analysis of academic work, he stated that academic work was not a single activity but rather included four interrelated components: discovery, integration, application, and teaching.[2] Building a theoretical framework based on these activities, he proposed that evaluations of academic work should not be limited to research but should consider all four components.[3] Boyer advocated a comprehensive definition of academic work that placed teaching itself within the scope of research (e.g., he cast the publication of research as a kind of teaching via the dissemination of knowledge). Boyer's theory triggered a wide range of discussions in the academic world and played a guiding role in the improvement of academic evaluation systems.[4] Yet, while his work may have reconciled conflicts between teaching, research, and service in *theory*, it did little to resolve these conflicts in practice.

This chapter argues that we need to reexamine academic roles not only in theory, with static models, but also from a more dynamic perspective, with the help of long-term historical and comparative analysis. Since the roles of academics—and the relationships between their different roles—are constantly evolving, it is difficult to understand their current situation without understanding the past. In this chapter, we do not intend to explore the different roles of academics at the micro level; rather, we intend to investigate the evolution of academic roles at a macro-historical level and to provide comparative references for understanding these roles in a changing global context.

HISTORICAL AND COMPARATIVE PERSPECTIVES ON ACADEMIC ROLES

Knowledge Transmitter: From the Elite to the Mass

Since the origin of the university, academics have been regarded as skilled transmitters of knowledge. Indeed, the idea of a close association of teachers and students—the purpose of which was the acquisition and transmission of knowledge—was regarded as the earliest manifestation of "the university" as such.[5] As Ian Wei explains in his chapter in this volume, the medieval university had explicit stipulations with respect to teaching practice. The degree itself verified that a student had completed the training necessary to become a teacher.[6] In a sense, the medieval university was like an advanced teacher-training institution. Soon, however, universities composed of teachers and students gave rise to a class of "intellectuals" with political significance for both civil and ecclesiastical authorities. The university thus gained the approval of the ruling classes, who assured its survival and continued development. In this way, teaching aimed at the cultivation of talent formed an early contractual relationship (or what Peter Maassen's chapter in this volume calls a special "pact") between the university and society. This contractual relationship became more entrenched over time and enabled the university to grow and prosper.

Many academics in the medieval university worked as both teachers and priests. They imparted knowledge of theology, law, medicine, and philosophy in order to develop scholars qualified to disseminate beliefs and suppress heresy. The contents of university education shifted over time as the influence of Renaissance humanism—and, later, the scientific revolution—reshaped the scope as well as the "methods" of knowledge acquisition and transmission. While the university was, in many ways, an intellectually conservative institution, it was not immune to change. With the rise of technological innovation during the industrial revolution, the university established closer ties with the industrial world, and the production of technical talent became a major aim of university-based knowledge transmission (see, for example, John Taylor's chapter in this volume). This development continued apace. Starting in the twentieth century, a new international commercial framework and new patterns of global competition have led to new interpretations of the role of academics in knowledge transmission. Since the 1960s, human-capital theory has emphasized the pivotal role of talent in international competition and has highlighted the goal of talent cultivation in the university. Today, knowledge transmission is about not only knowledge itself, but also the ability to acquire and process vast quantities of information.

The targets of this information are, of course, students, but the number as well as the status of students in the university has changed over time. In the medieval university, students faced few formal

entrance barriers, but starting in the fifteenth century, academic life
became increasingly aristocratic. The cost of obtaining degrees rose
considerably, and impoverished students faced obstacles both in access
and in the choice of studies that were open to them. The university
became an organization for training the gentry and high-level government officials.[7] This restriction of access continued through the
eighteenth century. In the wake of the industrial revolution, however,
with the expansion of science and technology, it became evident that
the supply of workers completing secondary education was insufficient
to support rapid industrial development. To train qualified workers,
the doors of the university started to open to the lower classes, and
enrollments, often in newly founded institutions, gradually increased
(again, see John Taylor's chapter). By the mid-twentieth century,
higher education in the developed world entered a phase known as

Table 6.1 Higher-education enrollment rate in selected industrialized
countries, 1995–2007

	1995	2000	2001	2002	2003	2004	2005	2006	2007
Australia	m	59	65	77	68	70	82	84	86
Germany	26	30	32	35	36	37	36	35	34
Italy	m	39	44	50	54	55	56	55	53
Japan	31	40	41	42	43	42	44	45	46
Korea	41	45	46	46	47	49	51	59	61
United Kingdom	m	47	46	48	48	52	51	57	55
United States	m	43	42	64	63	63	64	64	65
Average of OECD	37	47	48	52	53	53	55	56	56

Source: Education at a Glance 2009: OECD Indicators.

Table 6.2 Higher-education enrollments in China, 1999–2008

Year	Enrollment	School attendance	Gross rate
1999	159.68	879.16	10.5
2000	220.61	1230	12.5
2001	268.68	1300	13.3
2002	320.5	1600	15
2003	382.17	1900	17
2004	447.34	2100	19
2005	504	2300	21
2006	540	2500	22
2007	570	2700	23
2008	607.7	2900	23.3

Source: Yearbook of China Educational Statistics, 2000–2008.

"massification." Whereas in 1800, less than 3 percent of the college-age cohort attended universities, by 2007, the average enrollment rate in OECD countries reached 56 percent of the age cohort (table 6.1).[8] China, by comparison, started to expand its higher-education system in 1999 and moved into a massification stage in 2002. By 2008, the gross enrollment rate of higher education in China had reached a remarkable 23.3 percent (table 6.2). With more and more students, the question became this: how could academics in the modern university ensure the efficiency and quality of knowledge transmission and the cultivation of talent?

Knowledge Producer: From the Theoretical to the Practical

In the modern university, the role of academics as knowledge transmitters goes hand in hand with the role of academics as knowledge producers. Teaching goes hand in hand with research. It has not always been so. Medieval academics, influenced by Greek metaphysics, pursued theoretical knowledge in philosophy and theology, while other knowledge—technical, commercial, and political—was generally excluded from the university. "Practical" knowledge, including knowledge of architecture, mechanics, agriculture, and so on, remained largely outside the university's purview. Although some forms of knowledge exploration occurred in the medieval university, the production of "new" ideas was not taken as the main task of academics. As late as the eighteenth century, some German theoreticians felt that universities and professors had no obligation to pursue new discoveries (a task left to scientific societies); rather, the most important responsibility of a professor was to be a good teacher. Even as the publication of papers became a professional obligation, these publications were intended to enhance the university's prestige more than they were intended to produce new ideas per se.

It was not until the early nineteenth century—after Germany was defeated in the Napoleonic Wars—that European leaders looked to universities to advance research for the sake of economic development as well as the revival of cultural nationalism. The University of Berlin, founded by the neohumanist Wilhelm von Humboldt in 1810, integrated scientific research and knowledge production into the mission of the new university. The University of Berlin embraced a new spirit of academic freedom by stressing that the university should enjoy both religious and political autonomy for the sake of unencumbered knowledge production. Humboldt and other academics hoped to minimize the pressures of short-term economic and political interests and focus instead on long-term intellectual development.

Although the early University of Berlin encompassed only philosophy and the humanities as research fields and did not at first admit technical or practical studies (these pursuits continued to take place in other institutions, notably learned societies), the idea of autonomous scholarship and academic freedom laid a foundation for the "modern" university. The birth of the University of Berlin brought a new age in which the identity of the modern scholar was (allegedly) free of any narrow focus on short-term practical benefits. To guarantee academic freedom and protect scholars' role as knowledge producers, professors in German universities were given the status of high government officials, appointed and paid by the state and entitled to authority and respect, as well as space in which to conduct their work. Indeed, after World War II, the new German constitution reinstated the guarantee of academic autonomy and reconfirmed the lifelong official status of professors to safeguard their freedom of research and teaching.

Today, not only in Europe but around the world, the university's role in knowledge production has received unprecedented attention. Governments and business enterprises have shown great enthusiasm for supporting research. Yet, at the same time, the principles of academic autonomy have been redefined. External interest groups—chiefly from industry, but also from government—have essentially hired academics to do research by providing financial support. From 1960 to 1967, funding provided for basic science research in the United States grew from US$2 billion to US$5 billion, increasing 15 percent a year.[9] Achievements in basic research brought massive economic benefits to the United States. A report from AEDC in 1999 noted that basic research had played the key role in the American economic growth in the twentieth century. Similarly, a report on "The economic impact of Boston's eight research universities on the metropolitan Boston area" noted that Boston's universities had received 264 patents, signed 250 commercial licensing agreements, and helped to create 41 start-up companies in the year 2000 alone. Of the 50 early-stage start-up companies in the Boston area that attracted the most outside investment, nearly half were engaged in the commercialization of technology first developed at one of the city's eight universities or were founded by faculty members or graduates who got their start in a university incubator.[10] While these university-industry partnerships have yielded many benefits, new funding relationships have redefined the social contract (or pact) between the university and society. Academics have exchanged some of their autonomy for the goal of meeting the demands of external funders.

In China, as in the United States, university funding from government and industry has increased exponentially in recent years. From 1998 to 2007, research support from the Chinese government and the business community increased sixfold (see table 6.4). With this support have come yearly increases in the number of Chinese monographs and published papers (see figures 6.1 and 6.2). Besides the increase in the quantity of publications, the quality of publications has also progressed. University academics have claimed a greater share of China's research prizes (prizes that previously went to scholars working in national research institutes). During the period from 1985 to 2007, there were 457 university-based winners (or 52.4 percent) of the National Prize for Natural Sciences, 1,130 university-based winners (or 35.9 percent) of the National Prize for Technological Inventions, and 2,775 university-based winners (or 29.4 percent) of the National Prize for Progress in Science and Technology.[11]

Table 6.3 Chinese universities awarding more than 100 patents continuously (2003–2006)

Higher-education institutions	2003	2004	2005	2006
Fudan University	272	156	300	357
Shanghai Jaiotong University	396	287	782	867
Tsinghua University	504	471	779	731
Zhejiang University	430	277	713	914

Source: Data collected by the project "The Evaluation of the University Creativity" in Zhejiang University.

Table 6.4 Research support from government and business enterprises in China (1998–2007)

	1998	1999	2000	2001	2002	2003	2004	2006	2007
Government	41.1	49.2	97.5	109.8	137.3	164.8	210.6	287.8	345.4
Business Enterprise	36.8	53.2	55.5	72.5	89.6	112.6	148.6	197.4	219.2
Total	77.9	102.4	153	182.3	226.9	277.4	359.2	485.2	564.6

Source: China Statistical Yearbook on Science and Technology, 2008.

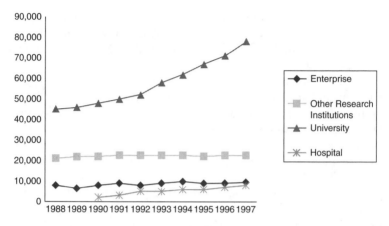

Figure 6.1 Domestic publications at all kinds of research institutions (1988–1997)

Source: Report on the Development of Science and Technology in China, 1999.

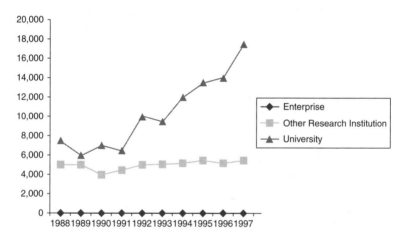

Figure 6.2 International publications at all kinds of research institutions (1988–1997)

Source: Report on the Development of Science and Technology in China, 1999.

Over the same period, there has also been an increase in the number of commercial patents awarded to Chinese universities (see figures 6.3 and 6.4). The number of the patents awarded to universities has increased dramatically, from 1,850 in 2001 to 12,043 in 2006. In just three years—between 2003 and 2006—the number of patents rose from 430 to 914 at Zhejiang University, from 396 to

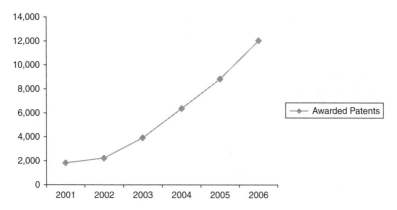

Figure 6.3 The number of patents awarded to universities in China (2001–2006)

Source: Yearbook of China Educational Statistics 2002–2007.

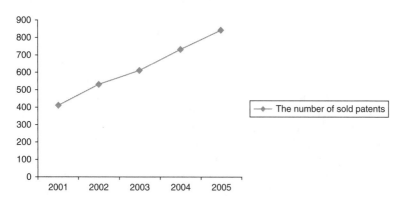

Figure 6.4 The number of sell patents awarded to Chinese universities (2001–2005)

Source: Yearbook of China Educational Statistics 2002–2006.

867 at Shanghai Jaio Tong University, and from 504 to 731 at Tsinghua University (see table 6.3).

These trends reflect a broader trend in the role of academics toward satisfying external interests. University-business partnerships confirm the role of academics as knowledge producers, but knowledge produced for patents is less often based on the individual interests of academics or the motive of pursuing universal or profound knowledge. Rather, the short-term interests of external funders have become the most important factor driving academics' choice of research projects.

Service Provider: From the Government
to the Public

This growing emphasis on publications and patents reflects a new conception of the role of academics. Besides their roles as knowledge transmitters (teachers) and knowledge producers (researchers), academics have also played a role of service to society. Although in the Middle Ages service to society was generally understood in terms of religion, academics served both civil and ecclesiastical authorities to a great extent. To cite just one example, during the Great Schism and Concilliar Movement (1378–1449), academics in the domains of theology and law made significant contributions to the debate with their learned opinions. Monarchs of the time relied upon academics to serve as judges in secular courts and diplomats in foreign affairs.[12] In early modern Europe, academics working in both government and the church shared their work at conferences, assisted in foreign affairs, oversaw the transcription of new books, and wrote treatises on religion, politics, and education. The role of service was not so much a duty as the willing contribution of academics as individuals.

Today, of course, the service function of academics has expanded dramatically. It encompasses everything from giving advice on economic development to providing technical assistance to business and industry to offering community medical care to supporting local initiatives in the fine arts, education, and so on. In modern society, the public has much higher expectations of the university to serve diverse needs. According to data from the National Center for Education Statistics, university expenditures on public service in the United States have shown substantial growth over time (see figure 6.5). This increase reflects not only the attention given to service but also the growing revenues that universities obtain from services offered to the public. Figure 6.6 illustrates this rise in public-service revenues.

A similar emphasis on public-service responsibilities is taking place in China, where academics not only provide practical research and technical instruction for business enterprises but also continuing education for the public and policy consultation and reports for government agencies at both the local and national level. Academics' role as a "brains trust" has been brought to new prominence as a result. Under the principle of service, Chinese academics, like their counterparts around the world, have become service providers to the

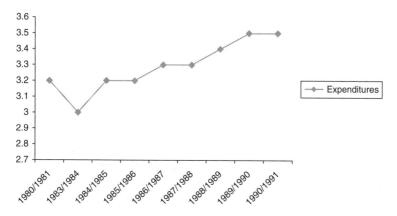

Figure 6.5   Expenditures on public service in US universities (1980–1990)
Source: Digest of Education Statistics 1993; National Center for Education Statistics, United States.

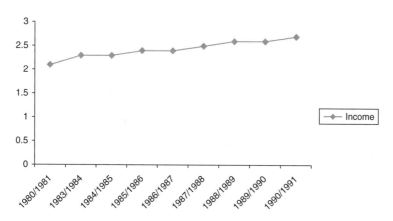

Figure 6.6   Income from public teaching in US universities (1980–1990)
Source: Digest of Education Statistics 1993; National Center for Education Statistics, United States.

general public, through the production and transmission of specialized knowledge. At the same time, the rapid expansion and differentiation of academic roles has created a dilemma: how to balance these roles? While the balance between teaching, research, and service to society is always changing, some aspects of the modern university reveal emerging—and perhaps troubling—trends.

Changing Academic Roles in the Modern University

Neglected Teaching

Transmitting knowledge and training talent through teaching are the most enduring and perhaps the most important roles of academics. Yet, as the demands of knowledge production increase, academics' teaching role has weakened. Research in the United States has shown that, between 1979 and 1999, academics at all four-year postsecondary educational institutions spent more time on activities associated with research and publication. Academics in research universities reported a drop in the amount of time spent teaching, and academics in nonresearch universities, while not reducing their time in the classroom, reported that some of the extra time they devoted to research came from limiting their involvement with students. Indeed, across all institutional types, there has been a decrease in the amount of time faculty spend advising and counseling students, and in research universities, comprehensive universities and liberal arts colleges, the decrease was statistically significant.[13] According to the Scarcity Theory, given a limited availability of time and energy, more time spent on one activity means less time spent on others. This tendency to replace teaching with research reflects changes in university-funding priorities. As shown in figure 6.7, expenditures on research have increased in the

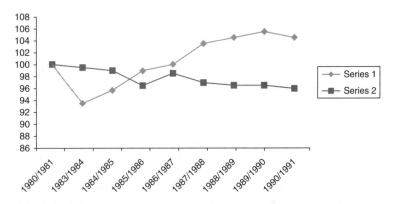

Figure 6.7 Expenditures on teaching and research in US universities (1980–1990)

Source: Digest of Education Statistics 1993; National Center for Education Statistics, United States.

United States since the 1980s, while expenditures on teaching have decreased. With a student population growing year by year, the per-pupil share of the budget spent on teaching has decreased. As Cardinal John Henry Newman stated in his classic work *The Idea of the University*, "If the goal of university is discovery in science and philosophy, I do not understand why the university should enroll the students." Newman insisted that the most important purpose of the university as an *educational* institution was cultivating students' talents. Only in this way could the university really distinguish itself from other research and social-service institutions. A modern society characterized by the explosion of knowledge, rapid economic development, and increasing international competition imposes new requirements for the cultivation of talent. As transmitters of knowledge, academics must find new ways to accommodate individual learning needs and must meet society's demands for talent. Modern universities, however, have deemphasized teaching at just the moment when excellent teaching is most urgently needed.

Commercialized Research

In the current university environment, the role of academics as teachers may be weakening in favor of research, but academics' role as researchers is also changing in significant—and perhaps unsettling—ways. In today's knowledge-based economy, knowledge itself is considered an important factor in economic development. The transformation of knowledge and technical know-how is playing a more vital role in enhancing the productive forces of economic growth. To deal with fierce competition in the context of economic globalization, governments, private agencies, and business enterprises have all turned to universities, especially research universities, for the production of knowledge that can be transformed into profit. To stimulate commercial knowledge production, university funders are no longer donors but buyers. As funders seek to "purchase" knowledge from individual scholars or research teams, universities "bid" for lucrative research contracts, a process that has engendered an increasingly commercialized culture in university-based research.

This commercialized culture requires academics to become "research entrepreneurs" who are able to attract outside funding to support their work. Slaughter and Leslie have dubbed this phenomenon "academic capitalism."[14] The competitive environment resulting from academic capitalism has, slowly but surely, changed the university from an institution that provides protection to academics to an institution that opens academics to intensely competitive pressures. In this context, academics tend to regard research as a free-market economic activity, and they quickly lose their loyalty to the university as such (a dilemma that may extend to university managers, according to Rosemary Deem's chapter in this volume). Under pressure to advance their own interests and pad their own income, scholars may become less inclined to focus on teaching as they devote more time to organizing cooperative research ventures and communicating with government, industry, and university patent officers. Over time, the increasingly commercialized culture of research affects the university's commitment to seeking broader knowledge. In today's universities, research directions are no longer based chiefly on the interests of academics but rather on market forces. This shift may have a negative influence on the entire process of knowledge production as it brings narrow utilitarian (and often fickle) motives to academic inquiry.

FACTORS INFLUENCING ACADEMIC ROLES TODAY

Social Expectations

It could be inferred from the analysis above that the university is no longer an "ivory tower"—or perhaps that it never was. Between the university and society there has always been a kind of contractual relationship (or pact), based on the perception of mutual benefits. By the terms of this pact, the university cultivates scholars and provides research while society offers a supportive and protective environment for academics and students. This contractual relationship between the university and society, which has varied across historical periods, reflects the changing expectations placed on universities under different cultural, political, and economic circumstances. For example, to win help from academics and the talents they cultivate, the medieval church and various monarchs granted charters to associations of academics and students and gave them both economic and legal privileges. Later, in the nineteenth century, to promote nationalist sentiments after the Napoleonic Wars, Germany turned to academics to advise the state and guide its development. Today, under the pressures of global competition, nation-states have increasingly lost patience with knowledge aimed at long-term benefits and have tended to ask academics to serve the short-term interests of society.

Governments as well as businesses increasingly regard research in terms of its profit potential, and they see knowledge itself as a commodity available for trade (not, as Rosemary Deem's chapter suggests, as a universal good produced for humanity as a whole). Of course, this view of knowledge in service to economic growth is not entirely new, but it has become considerably more pronounced in the past half-century or so. Various policies have come to support the commercialization of university-based research. For example, since the mid-1990s, the United Kingdom has fostered a commercial dimension in academic research (a dimension with a long history, as John Taylor's chapter in this volume shows). A UK government White Paper in 1987 held that research should take the prospect of commercial development as a goal.[15] A later paper in 1993 urged institutions of higher education to make direct contributions to the creation of wealth through research.[16] In 2004, the British HM Treasury Science and Innovation Investment Framework stressed "an economic imperative to make sure that scientific knowledge is used by business to create wealth."[17] Meanwhile, since the early 1980s, the US government has promulgated a series of policies to encourage competition in research and to give intellectual property rights to universities for government-funded projects. As shown in the table 6.5, restricted funds and contracts from all levels of government and all kinds of donors increased dramatically in the United States in the 1980s while unrestricted funds decreased (restricted funds carry the expectation that funders will be allowed to direct academic research projects to serve their own needs). The increase in restricted funds has made external funders far more influential in the setting of university research priorities.

According to the Resources Dependency Theory, universities' dependence on external financial support not only determines research directions but also entitles funders to greater authority within the university. Gradually, academics—even those pursuing well-funded research—lose their autonomy. As academics endeavor to meet the requirements of external funders by engaging in restricted research, they devote less time and energy to teaching or pursuing research with more long-term objectives. These shifts follow logically from academics increasing reliance on external financial support.[18] (See Peter Maassen's chapter in this volume for the implications of such resource dependency on universities in sub-Saharan Africa.)

Table 6.5 The types of financial support of US university (1980–1990)

Supporter	Types	1980/1981	1983/1984	1984/1985	1985/1986	1986/1987	1987/1988	1988/1989	1989/1990	1990/1991
Federal government	Restricted	9.2	7.1	7.1	7.2	7.1	7	7	7	7
	Unrestricted	1.7	1.6	1.6	1.7	1.7	1.7	1.7	1.7	1.7
State government	Restricted	1.2	1.1	1.2	1.3	1.6	1.7	1.9	1.9	1.9
	Unrestricted	0.1	0.1	0.1	0.2	0.2	0.2	0.3	0.3	0.2
Local government	Restricted	0.4	0.4	0.4	0.3	0.4	0.4	0.4	0.4	0.4
	Unrestricted	*	0.1	0.1	0.1	0.1	0.1	0.1	0.1	0.1
Private gifts, grants, and contracts	Restricted	3	3.2	3.2	3.3	3.4	3.5	3.6	3.7	3.8
	Unrestricted	1.8	2	2.1	2.1	2.1	1.9	1.9	1.9	1.8
Endowment income	Restricted	0.9	1	0.9	1	1.1	1.1	1.1	1.1	1.2
	Unrestricted	1.2	1.2	1.3	1.3	1.1	1.1	1.2	1.2	1

Source: Digest of Education Statistics, 1993, National Center for Education Statistics, United States.

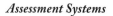

Assessment Systems

Of course, the existence and development of universities has always relied on some measure of external support. Yet, traditionally, the university has also served as a buffer between academics and external interests. This separation—and the oft-criticized notion of an "ivory tower"—forms part of the unique spirit of the university. The *balance* between this spiritual tradition and societal needs lies at the heart of the university itself, and academics' success in achieving this balance constitutes, in a sense, the foundation of the "evaluation system" that governs the university. From the medieval to early modern era, academics' role as teachers was viewed as the main factor in the "evaluation" of universities. Some institutions even stated explicitly that academics who won respect through writing (or "research") were unlikely to attract students, while academics who gained prestige through excellence in teaching attracted large crowds.

Over time, however, as knowledge production gained more attention, research rather than teaching came to be regarded as the basic currency of prestige in the academic world. Research achievements played an increasingly prominent and powerful role in academic recruitment and promotion. Even British universities famous for their emphasis on teaching tended to pay more attention to research achievements. Similarly, in modern Germany, the qualifications for full professorships focused mainly on research ability and productivity. In the United States, it was reported that, in 1982, publications ranked second behind teaching among criteria for faculty recruitment, but by 1992, publications ranked first. A survey in 2008 with data from 130 deans or directors showed that tenure and promotion decisions in the United States were made on the basis of research in 45.4 percent of all academic programs and 55.5 percent of academic units with doctoral programs.[19]

In China, research ability and achievements have become the primary criteria for professorial recruitment. At the prestigious Peking University, for example, the standards for faculty promotion are: profound theoretical knowledge, encyclopedic specialized expertise, a rigorous attitude toward academic work, the ability to be an academic leader, outstanding national and international prestige, landmark research achievements, and, finally, teaching ability. Peking University has explicit standards concerning faculty candidates' research productivity, the amount of research funds that academics secure, and the number of prizes awarded for research achievements. Obviously, then, academics must produce more research if they want to be promoted.

The evaluation system for recruitment and promotion has shifted over time from an emphasis on teaching to an emphasis on research. This evaluation and reward system, which forms the microenvironment of academic work and determines academics' professional fate, exerts a powerful influence on academic roles.

Individual Needs

Academics, like nonacademics, have needs not only for professional survival (and success) but also for professional fulfillment. From medieval to early modern times, before the idea of an academic "profession" existed, teaching was regarded by many academics as a step on the ladder to official positions. Teaching was not necessarily a career in itself; many academics left the university after 10–15 years to work in the church. Gradually, though, with the organizational maturity of universities, academics made their careers in the university. They formed professional communities with more hierarchical structures; they formed professional associations (often organized around research journals); they divided themselves into various disciplines and subdisciplines and sought prestige within these networks. Meanwhile, within the university itself, academics at different levels of the institution played different roles and had different levels of authority (as well as different salaries and degrees of intellectual and civil freedom). For example, full professors in German universities came to have extremely high levels of professional authority while academics in more intermediate positions had less security, both in terms of career options and in terms of the independence of their scholarly work. Given these hierarchies, the pursuit of career development became a driving force in the definition of academic roles (see the chapter by Jones and Gopaul in this volume for more on this topic).

In the modern university, the commercialization of scholarship has to some extent given academics a chance to obtain more material benefits through research. At the same time, however, the pursuit of material benefits has affected other aspects of academic life. The ethos of academic work demands that scholars maintain a degree of separation from external interest groups so they can resist outside enticements and even, when necessary, criticize the direction of social development. Especially in matters of intellectual freedom and institutional autonomy, the work of scholarship differentiates academics from other members of society and requires a degree of detachment and disinterestedness. Indeed, it is precisely this sense of disinterestedness—this reputation for "objectivity"—that has traditionally entitled academics to public reverence and respect (at least according to the model outlined by Kant, Weber, Jaspers, and others). In this way, academics play a unique role that cannot easily be played by other social groups. In a crucial sense, the ethos of scholarly work forms the standard of value by which the balance of academics roles—teaching, research, and service to society—must be assessed.

Conclusions

In many ways, the social acceptance of the university is not the result of a single role but rather the diversity of roles played by the entire academic community. No academic can play all these roles all the time, and the diverse roles of academics are not static. The roles of academics in teaching, research, and service to society have evolved over the centuries, and the prioritization of these roles has varied widely across time. Today's university must accept the diversity of academic responsibilities, recognize the importance of each role, and protect each role in its evaluation systems. It is wise to maintain a pluralistic evaluation system to account for the diversity of academic roles, especially with respect to balancing teaching and research.

Even still, the diversification of academic roles has given rise to tensions and conflicts. How to balance the roles has become a major problem, both in theory and in practice. Given the ever-changing dynamics and shifting historical contexts that shape academic roles, it is difficult to use fixed criteria to measure the relative importance of each role or to describe all their interrelationships. After all, the diversity of roles did not result from the independent choices of academics themselves but formed through academics' interaction with changing social expectations and university systems. Our understanding of these roles should not, therefore, be static. A dynamic and historically informed balance of roles is the only realistic way to maintain the flexibility needed to meet the demands of society and fulfill the university's "social contract" (or pact), which, in the end, is the key to the university's vitality, durability, and legitimacy.

To achieve a dynamic balance of academic roles, the university must consider not only the material but also the spiritual aspects of academic work. In the modern university, academics and the knowledge they produce have come to be seen increasingly in commercial terms. Society has been cast as the "consumer" of knowledge, which can be bought, packaged, delivered, and measured by money. Academics, in turn, have been cast as the "exporters" of knowledge rather than "experts" with unique contributions to make to social development.

This hypercommercialized outlook has sapped the free and independent spirit of the university. The result, according to Tony Becher and Paul Trowler, is that "people's attitude toward the university will be more like [their attitude] to other organizations and [they will] treat professionals more like other laborers."[20]

Academics cannot ignore social expectations, but it is worth considering whether catering to the short-term needs of society is their most useful role. Decades ago, Burton Clark noted that, given the enormous complexity of modern social development, various sectors in society were likely set up their own scientific research institutions. When this happened, he noted, "the monopoly of university in the scientific research will become out of date."[21] Perhaps so, but in comparison with other research institutions, universities play a truly unique role. The value of the university lies in its capacity to lead social development based on rational judgments, academic freedom, and an independent spirit rather than a narrow devotion to immediate social needs. Without this independence, or objectivity, the value of the university will disappear. To say that universities must move beyond their ivory tower does not mean that academics do not need the ivory tower at all; on the contrary, the academic spirit must always be nurtured in a warm home. Given the inevitable pressures and temptations of modern society, protecting and preserving the academic spirit requires courage, wisdom, judgment, and, ultimately, reverence for the enduring responsibility of knowledge transmission and production. These special traits, and the academics who embody them, distinguish the university from other social institutions.

Notes

1. John Hattie and H. W. Marsh, "The Relationship between Research and Teaching: A Meta-analysis." *Review of Educational Research* 66(4) (1996): 507–542
2. E. L. Boyer, "Scholarship Reconsidered." The Carnegie Foundation for the Advancement of Teaching, 1990
3. E. L. Boyer, "From Scholarship Reconsidered to Scholarship Assessed." *Quest* 48 (1996): 129–139.
4. Jan Karlsson, *Service as Collaboration an Integrated Process in Teaching and Research. Teaching in Higher Education* 12(2) (2007): 281–287.
5. H. H. Charles, *The Rise of Universities.* Trans. Mei Yizheng. Shanghai: Sanlian Press, 2007,4 (in Chinese).
6. Ibid.

7. H. De Ridder Symoens, *A History of the University in Europe*, Volume II *Universities in Early Modern Europe (1500–1800)*. Trans. He Guoqing, Wang Baoxing, Qu Shujie, Zhang Tingshu, Zhang Wei, and Jin Chuanbao. Baoding: Hebei University Press, 2007, 327–328, 338 (in Chinese).

8. OECD Indicators, "Education at a Glance 2009." http://www.oecd.org/document/24/0,3343,en_2649_39263238_43586328_1_1_1_1,00.html

9. Donald Kennedy, *Academic Duty*. Trans. Yan Fengqiao. Beijing: Xinhua Press, 2002, 37 (in Chinese).

10. "Engines of Economic Growth: The Economic Impact of Boston's Eight Research Universities on the Metropolitan Boston Area." http://www.bc.edu/offices/comaf/economic/engines.html

11. Ministry of Education of P. R. China, "National Commission of P. R. China for UNESCO." *Country Report on Higher Education Reform and Development in China* (7) (2009): 4.

12. John C. Scot, "The Mission of the University: Medieval to Postmodern Transformations." *Journal of Higher Education* 77(1) (2006): 1–39.

13. Jeffrey F. Milem, Joseph B. Berger, and Eric L. Dey, "Faculty Time Allocation a Study of Change over Twenty Years." *Journal of Higher Education* 71(4) (2000): 454–475.

14. Sheila Slaughter and Larry L. Leslie, *Academic Capitalism: Politics, Policies, and the Academic Capitalism*. Trans. Liang Xiao and Li Li. Beijing: Peking University Press, 2008, 37 (in Chinese).

15. Ibid.

16. Ibid.

17. Paul Clark, "The Commercial of University Research and Economic Productivity." *Higher Education Management and Policy* 19(1) (2007): 133–144.

18. Slaughter and Leslie, *Academic Capitalism*, 62.

19. Robert G. Green, "Tenure and Promotion Decisions the Importance of Teaching, Scholarship and Service." *Journal of Social Work Education* 44(2) (2008): 117–127.

20. Tony Becher and Paul R. Trowler, *Academic Tribes and Territories*. Trans. Tang Yueqin, Pu Maohua, Chen Hongjie. Beijing: Peking University Press, 2008, 10 (in Chinese).

21. Burton R. Clark, *Places of Inquiry: Research and Advanced Education in the Modern University*. Trans. Wang Chengxu. Hangzhou: Zhejiang Education Press, 2001, 226 (in Chinese).

PART IV

Shifting Patterns of Graduate and Undergraduate Education

CHAPTER 7

Toward General Education in the Global University: The Chinese Model

Chen Hongjie, Shen Wenqin, and
Cai Leiluo

INTRODUCTION

Before the eighteenth century, most students in Western universities received an undergraduate education based on the liberal arts, with an emphasis on logic, rhetoric, and grammar rooted in classical texts. Chinese higher education in this period was similarly based on Confucian classics. After the eighteenth century, however, higher education in Europe became more and more specialized owing to two forces: the rise of new technologies and the steady professionalization of modern science. The formation of modern disciplines during the nineteenth century further contributed to the rise of academic specialization worldwide. Higher education in China and the Soviet Union from the 1950s to the 1970s had the most specialized education systems.

Although some American universities—especially the University of Chicago and Columbia University—proclaimed and practiced the idea of general education in the early twentieth century, the pattern of undergraduate education worldwide was, for the most part, specialized until the mid-twentieth century. However, the pattern of higher education in the second half of the twentieth century gradually changed from "specialized" back to "general," as seen in various reforms in

American universities, such as Harvard's curriculum reforms in the 1940s and again in the 1970s. This trend toward general education is also evident in the Bologna Process in Europe and in recent curricular reforms in many Chinese universities, such as Peking University, Fudan University, and Sun Yat-Sen University. Undergraduate education in both research universities and comprehensive universities has been shifting back toward generalization. Three forces seem to be driving this return to general education. First, the conditions of mass higher education have required universities to offer general and comprehensive education to an ever-growing number of young students. Second, the rapid expansion of knowledge has blurred the boundaries between specialized academic disciplines, leading to a desire for broad knowledge and "interdisciplinary" work. Third, internal divisions within universities have moved specialized education to the postgraduate level, especially the doctoral level, making room at the undergraduate level for a more general (or "liberal arts") curriculum.

In different historical periods, higher education has had different goals and knowledge bases. In agricultural societies, higher education was typically aimed at cultivating intellectual elites by offering general knowledge and intellectual skills. In industrial societies, higher education pursued greater professionalization with a greater emphasis on specialized knowledge. In the postindustrial or "knowledge society" of the past few decades, higher education has moved away from specialized education toward general education, especially at the undergraduate level in elite institutions. This chapter uses China as an example to illustrate a worldwide trend toward generalism in higher education.

THE TRADITION AND CRISIS OF GENERAL EDUCATION

Higher learning in China has a long tradition. In the fifth century BCE, when Confucius (BCE 551–479) lived, various masters ran schools, imparting advanced knowledge. For instance, Confucius was said to have as many as 3,000 followers. Afterward, higher-education institutions came into being in China. In the fourth century BCE, the emperor of Qi State founded a scholarly academy—Ji Xia Xue Gong[1]—which lasted for more than 100 years. In 124 BCE, the ruler of the Han dynasty established a nationwide educational institution, Tai Xue,[2] which became the most revered public academic establishment in China. Around the tenth century CE, just before the first universities took shape in Europe, the private academy Shu Yuan[3] was set up in China. With government support, it was the main institution of the Chinese higher-education system for the next 1,000 years. For nearly 2,000 years, Chinese higher education was confined to Confucian classics. Traditionally, it sought to bring up well-rounded people with a thorough knowledge of the Confucian classics and well-developed composition skills. The curriculum excluded all specialized or practical knowledge. A famous Confucian saying held that "An educated man is not an instrument." Zhu Xi, a well-known scholar during the Song dynasty, explained that an instrument could have only one specific function, but an educated man was not merely an expert in one specific field; he was a person with broad knowledge and moral integrity who could accomplish a wide variety of tasks.

During the mid-to-late nineteenth century, when China failed to compete with Western military powers (e.g., in the Opium Wars), traditional concepts of general knowledge and the pattern of general education became a source of major concern. Many people attributed China's failures to Confucian education. Critics summarized its disadvantages in two ways. First, they noted, practical knowledge involving natural science and technology was not represented in the Confucian classics. Second, traditional education lacked a way to teach and learn specialized knowledge. Reformers, therefore, called for new ways of organizing and transmitting knowledge in institutions of higher education.

In a critique of traditional, or general, Chinese higher education, the German missionary Ernst Faber stressed the importance of specialized studies. In his work *On Education*, published in 1875, Faber wrote: "Knowledge itself should be classified. Such occupations as scholars, farmers, workers, [and] businessmen require special knowledge in their respective aspects. Specialized knowledge is so profound that only those specializing in the field can grasp it." Subsequently, more and more Chinese intellectuals came to accept Faber's view. For example, the famous reformer Kang Youwei commented in his work *On Great Harmony* that "The more civilized the society, the [greater the division of labor], and the more specific knowledge will be needed." He also stated that "when the great harmony comes, labor will be divided and different people will hold special knowledge." Another famous scholar, Wang Guowei, also elaborated on the idea of specialized education. "Nowadays," he wrote, "it is a world of specialization. All knowledge and professions have their own skills and require specialized training. Once a man takes up his job, he will do it for his whole life. When a man conducts research in one field, he could hardly do so in others at the same time. A man can only be engaged in one job at a time, just like one cannot make a carpenter do metalworking or an arrow manufacturer make armor."

In the wake of their exposure to Western education, contemporary Chinese intellectuals came to see many disadvantages in traditional general education and subscribed to the classification and specialization of knowledge as well as the pursuit of modern professionalization. Yet, what they saw as a distinction between Chinese and Western education was principally a distinction between traditional and modern, between general and specialized, models of higher education.

THE TRIUMPH OF SPECIALIZED EDUCATION

For centuries of Western history, the training of leaders and professional elites relied mainly on liberal education. Thus, general knowledge and general education were predominant in higher education. Phrases such as *eleutheria epistemon* in Greek, *artes liberals* in Latin, *liberal education* in English, *Allgemeine Bildung* in German, and *culture générale* in French all indicate a tradition of general or liberal education in Western culture.

But in modern times, especially since the eighteenth century, practical and specialized knowledge became more prominent. On the one hand, French higher education underwent significant reform in the eighteenth century under the influence of the Enlightenment. As a result of these reforms, traditional models of training in French universities were abolished and replaced with more specialized training. The *grand écoles*—special and practical institutions of higher education—took the stage. In the meantime, with the advent of industrialization in Europe, technical knowledge began to gain more importance; mechanical skills transformed into specialized technology and entered into the organizational structure of higher education. In 1747, the first college of engineering—the *École nationale des ponts et chaussées*, or the National Institute of Bridges and Roads—was founded, followed by specialized institutes of agriculture and mines in both France and Germany.

Meanwhile, the modern disciplinary system gradually came into being. In German universities in particular, the specialization of knowledge led to the formation of modern disciplines, and the basis of the modern knowledge system took shape. At the end of the eighteenth century, modern disciplines such as physics and chemistry began to form, which promoted greater specialization in the natural sciences. History and philology also became disciplines during the same period. In short, specialization became a prominent feature of higher-education institutions. As world-systems theorist Immanuel Wallerstein observed, the formation of disciplines and the greater specialization of knowledge marked a knowledge revolution during the nineteenth century.[4]

During the twentieth century, higher education in the Soviet Union and China embraced these changes. Meeting the requirements of a planned economy, specialized education attained its full development in these two national systems. Chinese higher-education institutions were restructured in 1952 and 1953. One purpose of these reforms was to develop specialized institutes, especially engineering institutes (i.e., polytechnic institutes) and training colleges for scientific specialists. Thereafter, programs in these institutes and in comprehensive universities became highly specialized in China.

There were two results of the 1950s reconstruction in China. First, while the specialized institutes prospered, the total number of comprehensive universities was reduced from 49 to 21. Engineering institutes increased from 14 to 33, and agriculture and forestry colleges increased from 11 to 25. Corresponding departments across the universities and colleges were also restructured. Second, the underlying principle of higher education came to focus on specialization. For example, majors—or intensive training in particular subjects to prepare students for specialized professions—were established according to the needs of national development.[5] Each major had a fixed program to train engineers or specialists in certain fields.[6] In this way, specialized institutes and specialized training became a key feature of Chinese higher education, reflecting the demands of the Chinese state in an era of rapid industrialization.

GENERALIZATION IN UNDERGRADUATE EDUCATION: A GLOBAL TREND

After the triumph of specialized education, Germany, France, Sweden, Japan, and China all adopted this model. Even in Britain, where liberal education had a long and illustrious history, universities ceased offering compulsory general studies for undergraduates. In both Germany and France, general training was assumed to be offered in secondary education, while in Sweden, students, once enrolled in universities, commenced their professional training as doctors, engineers, or teachers without any required general courses. Meanwhile, in Japan, universities accepted specialized and professionalized education under the influence of European and American models even before World War II.[7]

While specialized education expanded across the world, general education kept its position in select American universities. At the beginning of the twentieth century, general education was institutionalized and reinforced in the United States by the efforts of Woodrow Wilson at Princeton, Abbott Lowell Lawrence at Harvard, John Erskine and later Mark Van Doren at Columbia, Robert Maynard Hutchins at the University of Chicago, and others. In these institutions, liberal education became an essential part of the undergraduate curriculum. In the United States as a whole, liberal education came to represent a cornerstone of the curriculum, representing upward of 30 percent of undergraduate course credits.[8]

The reasons for the institutionalization of general education in the United States are complicated, but two points are worth mentioning. First, compared with Germany and France, high-school study in America is regarded as less academic, so universities offered general education to make up for the shortcomings of high schools. Second, America is a multicultural country, and general education is presumed to help shape a common cultural identity and enhance national cohesion. Hence, the history of Western culture has received great attention in American general-education courses. This emphasis on a "common culture" has been especially pronounced at times when national cohesion has been in doubt (e.g., during and after periods of significant immigration or war).

The American model of general education originated from the United States' peculiar cultural and educational background, but the influence of this model has spread throughout the world. Since the 1980s, Mainland China, Hong Kong, Japan, Hungary, Russia, Poland, South Korea, South Africa, and Sweden have all introduced general-education programs inspired by the American model.[9] For instance, Lunds University in Sweden introduced a core curriculum under the influence of the Henry Rosovsky Report issued by Harvard (which, in turn, was influenced by the report of the Task Force on Higher Education and Society, coauthored by Rosovsky and David Bloom with support from the World Bank and UNESCO).[10] Meanwhile, throughout Europe, the Bologna Process, started in 1999, has had a great impact on undergraduate training in the direction of general education. In Berlin in 2003, education ministers from European countries agreed that, in universities that offered higher levels of training, general education should be offered to all undergraduates.[11]

The Reform of General Education in China

In the past ten years, the model of specialized training has faced increasing criticism in China. Today, unlike the 1950s, 1960s, and 1970s, it is harder to set specific goals to meet the needs of the changing labor market or students' desire for employment; universities must constantly adjust their objectives to meet changing demands. As economic dependence on knowledge increases, more and more agencies are beginning to undertake the roles once monopolized by universities in education, training, and scientific research. At the same time, the boundaries between disciplines are less definite. With the advance of science and technology and the increasing need for interdisciplinary training, the margins between disciplines have eroded. In this context, universities have pushed specialized education to higher levels of the overall structure; specialized knowledge is now reserved for master's or doctoral students.

All of these changes have led to a resurgence of interest in general education in China. In the 1980s and especially the 1990s, general education reform took off. Indeed, since the 1990s, general education has become a key issue in Chinese higher-education reform. In the past two decades, the number of majors fell from over 1,000 to 250 as reformers sought to expand the basic foundations of knowledge in the curriculum and increase students' adaptability to diverse employment opportunities. Meanwhile, in the late 1990s, a wave of amalgamation and institutional consolidation swept across higher education in China, during which previously specialized institutes and colleges were converted into comprehensive universities, either by establishing new majors or merging with one another. Many of the leading universities in China, including Peking University, Tsinghua University, Fudan University, and Sun Yat-Sen University, began to launch general-education programs to improve students' capacity for critical thought and broad analysis.

Three waves of general-education reform have occurred in China over the past 20 years. The first was launched by Peking University. In the early 1980s, Peking University began to offer elective courses for its undergraduates in different majors and common courses for all. At the same time, the university devised a credit system that required each bachelor's degree candidate to complete 32–44 credits in common, or general, courses. In addition, the university required all students specializing in the humanities or social sciences to take at least one course in the natural sciences, and students in the natural sciences had to take at least one course in the humanities or social sciences. The purpose of these reforms was to carry all undergraduates beyond narrowly specialized training. In 1988, Peking University declared that the basic principles of its undergraduate education program were to "strengthen foundations, confront overspecialization, teach according to the student's ability, [and] train students with different goals." Subsequently, Hong Kong and Taiwan implemented general-education reform (e.g., Tsinghua University in Taiwan founded a Center for General Education).

The second wave of general-education reform started in the mid-1990s. In 1993, Ernest Boyer's work *College: The Undergraduate Experience in America* was translated into Chinese. Boyer's work gave Chinese educators a better idea of the principles behind the American approach to general education. In the following years, general education became a topic of increasing education research. In 1996, Peking University implemented newly revised undergraduate programs. The new curriculum was classified into three levels: common courses for all students, elective courses in specialized fields or colleges, and required courses in each students' major. Each level comprised one third of the credit system. Three years later, in 1999, Peking University put forward a strategy of providing general education in the junior year and a broadly specialized education in the senior year. The university introduced general-education courses in five fields: mathematics and natural science, social science, philosophy and psychology, history and languages, and literature and fine arts. Each student was required to complete 16 credits in common courses with at least 2 in each field. By the late 1990s, general education—largely borrowed from the American model—was a well-known concept and widely accepted by Chinese higher-education policymakers.

The third wave of general education started in 2000. It had two main features. First, universities began to set up special institutions to reinforce general education. Peking University initiated its Yuanpei Program in 2001, and Fudan University established Fudan College, an institution to implement general education and manage the teaching of first- and second-year undergraduates. Similar institutions arose one after another, including Yaming College at Nanjing University in 2006, Yuanpei College at Peking University in 2007, and the Liberal Arts College at Sun Yan-Sen University in 2009. Institutes of technology have not established special institutions for the purpose of general education, but they have set up committees to promote this agenda. Shanghai Jiaotong University, for example, established a General Education Directing Committee in 2007, composed of a chairman, two vice chairmen, and a committee responsible for the management and planning of general education at the university. Second, general education since 2000 has increased its scope in China's higher-education system. In the first two periods, general education was adopted by only a few elite universities. As time went on and the idea of general education became more widely accepted, more and more universities have implemented general-education reform. General education has also been promoted in some specialized institutes of technology and engineering. For example, the prominent Beijing Institute of Technology requires all undergraduates in Science and Engineering to take general-education courses worth at least six credits. Shanghai Jiaotong University passed a regulation concerning Elected General Education Courses in 2007, stipulating that each department must specify at least one or two courses as commonly required for undergraduates. Comprehensive universities traditionally occupied a leading position in offering high quality programs in social science and humanities, such as Peking University and Fudan University, have taken further steps in general-education reform, and it is conceivable that general-education reforms will be intensified in both types of institutions.

CONCLUSION

The reform of general education in China has been advanced in accordance with a global trend toward the generalization of undergraduate training. At the same time, the Chinese case suggests that a distinctly American model of general education has spread around the world. Its influence can be seen in all aspects in Chinese reform. For example, teachers from Peking University went to America to investigate before they initiated their general-education reforms in the 1980s and 1990s. The name of the Liberal Arts College at Sun Yat-Sen University was obviously inspired by the US model. Yet, the idea of general education and its programs have not encountered great opposition in China because the all-around education that was favored in China for centuries has much in common with general education. Indeed, the Chinese people began to look for their own model of general education *before* the American model was generally known.

Compared with traditional demands on the university—including the needs of the labor market—the "customers" and "partners" of universities nowadays are more difficult to define. Hence, universities have no choice but to enable students to master various disciplines and develop transferable skills in order to equip themselves with a broad foundation of knowledge. For this reason, general learning at the undergraduate level has become a trend in Chinese comprehensive universities and some institutes of science and engineering. We predict that this trend will continue in the future and that more universities in China will offer general-education courses. Slowly but surely, a Chinese model of general education is coming into being.

When analyzing the uniqueness of Western society, Max Weber pointed out that specialized education and professional experts were unique phenomena in the West. He wrote: "A variety of universities or similar institutions [such as the modern] university or academy of science have existed in other places (e.g., China, the Islamic world), but the rationalized and systematic activities of scientific profession, that is, the trained experts and their dominant positions in the entire civilization, exist only in the West."[12] Weber said the key goal in other civilizations was to bring up "cultivated men," but in the modern West, the goal was to train "professional experts." According to Weber, specialized expertise was one of the fundamental cornerstones of modern Western civilization. As we can see today, professional experts and specialized models of training are the products of industrial civilization, no matter where it unfolds. With the arrival of a postindustrial or knowledge-based society, the idea of training experts and professionals seems to be changing. A renewed emphasis on generalization could be regarded as a sign of a new era in global higher education.

NOTES

1. Ji Xia Xue Gong literally means the Academy at the Gate of Ji. It is the most famous scholarly academy in early China. Scholars came from great distances to lodge in the academy, with the most important scholar holding the rank of Great Prefect. Notable scholars with different schools of thought worked at the academy.
2. Tai Xue literally means Greatest Study or Learning. It marks the establishment of the first nationwide public school system in China, with Tai Xue located in the capital of Chang'an and local schools established in the local provinces and in the main cities of the smaller counties. Tai Xue taught Confucianism and Chinese literature among other things for the high-level civil service.
3. Shu Yuan literally means Academies of Classical Learning. They were private establishments. Unlike national academy and local schools, they were usually built away from cities or towns, providing a quiet environment where scholars could engage in studies and contemplation without restrictions and distractions.

4. Immanuel Wallerstein, ed., *Open the Social Sciences*. Beijing: Sanlian, p. 8.
5. Each major has a definite program fixed by the state according to the needs of national development. All courses within a major are required; there is no choice.
6. Zeng Shaolun, "The Problem of Setting-Up 'Majors' in Higher Education Institution," *People's Education*, 9 (1952). 6–9.
7. Yutaka Otsuka, "Some Thoughts on Liberal Arts Education in Japanese Universities in the Era of Globalization," *Comparative Education Review*, 1 (2009): 1–6.
8. Steven Brint, "General Education Models: Continuity and Change in the US Undergraduate Curriculum, 1975–2000," *Journal of Higher Education*, 80 (6) (November/December 2009): 605–642.
9. Susan H. Gillespie, "Opening Minds: The International Liberal Education Movement," *World Policy Journal*, 18 (4) (Winter 2001–2002): 79–89.
10. Sven-Eric Liedman, "In Search of Isis: General Education in Germany and Sweden," in *The European and American University since 1800: Historical and Sociological Essays*. Cambridge: Cambridge University Press, pp. 74–108.
11. Barbara M. Kehm, "The Road to Doctorate: Between Elite Selection and Scale Expansion," *Peking University Education Review*, 2 (2009): 2–11.
12. Max Weber, *Wirtschaft und Gesellschaft*. Tuebingen: Mohr, 1972, p. 578.

CHAPTER 8

Doctoral Education and the Global University: Student Mobility, Hierarchy, and Canadian Government Policy

Glen A. Jones and Bryan Gopaul

INTRODUCTION

This chapter focuses on (1) the changing role of doctoral education (and the doctoral student) in the context of the global university and (2) the role of government funding policies in these changes. The repositioning of the research university as a central institution within the "knowledge economy," the increasing use of research outputs as the primary inputs to global rankings, and the complex pressures associated with globalization all suggest major changes in the role and positioning of doctoral education in major research universities. These changes include the rise of Mode 2 knowledge— that is, knowledge produced in collaboration with parties outside the university—in the context of doctoral research, the increased commodification of knowledge and education, and a shift in emphasis toward doctoral programs in science and technology. Our analysis of recent policies and trends in Canadian higher education suggests that there are national nuances to these global trends. Doctoral education continues to be defined in national terms, and, given the heavy dependence of doctoral programs on research funds, these programs are influenced by national research policies and funding priorities. We begin this chapter with a historical review of federal government policies related to doctoral education in Canada. We then review the literature on the changing nature of doctoral education and focus on two key issues that emerge from this literature: the changing nature of doctoral-student mobility and the increasing role of institutional hierarchy in doctoral education.

DOCTORAL EDUCATION AND CANADIAN HIGHER-EDUCATION POLICY

Garth Williams (2005) opened his thoughtful analysis of doctoral education in Canada with a quotation from Michael Lazaridis, founder and president of Research-in-Motion, the company that makes the Blackberry mobile phone. Speaking of the graduates of elite doctoral programs, Lazaridis (2004) remarked:

> Armed with cutting edge technology from around the world, the latest tools, the latest techniques and processes learned from their work under the very best researchers, they graduate with much fanfare and go on to build the industry, institutions and society of our country. (8)

Research-in-Motion, like its chief product, is a former poster child for the importance (and possibilities) of research and innovation in Canada. Research innovation, in turn, is presumed to rest, at least in part, on the strength of Canada's doctoral research programs. Indeed, Williams framed his analysis of doctoral education in terms of its contributions to economic development; for Williams, doctoral graduates were Canada's "best hope for new discoveries and deeper understanding" and for "a proud place in the international intellectual community" (1).

As Williams notes, the presumption that doctoral training is a key component of the innovation infrastructure required for economic development is a relatively recent phenomenon in Canada, tracing back only to the 1980s. Canada's first doctoral degree was awarded by the University of Toronto in 1900, and McGill awarded its first doctoral degree in 1909. While the number of universities offering graduate programs gradually expanded, these two universities were responsible for more than half of all Canadian doctoral degrees awarded before World War II (McKillop 1994). The postwar expansion of higher education, funded largely through direct grants to universities from the federal government, focused at first on the expansion of access to undergraduate education. Given the small number of doctoral students in Canadian universities, the majority of new professors hired to teach a rapidly expanding undergraduate population came from the United States, the United Kingdom, and France (Williams 2005).

Funding and coordinating the expansion of higher education raised a series of jurisdictional issues between Canada's federal and provincial governments. While the initial postwar expansion was funded directly by the federal government of Canada, the provinces asserted their constitutional role in education under the British North America Act of 1867 and held that direct operating grants from the federal government to support enrollment growth interferred in an area of provincial responsibility. Subsequently, in the late 1960s, higher-education policy shifted, becoming the primary responsibility of the provinces. The federal government's financial support for university operating costs took the form of conditional transfers to the provinces, replaced in the late 1970s by unconditional transfers. In addition to providing money to the provinces to support higher education, the federal government also came to assume a greater role in policy arenas regarded as areas of shared responsibility (such as student financial assistance) or as areas in which federal involvement was justified by other constitutional responsibilities (e.g., support for training and apprenticeship programing, supporting bilingualism). Without a national ministry of education or higher education, Canada's higher-education sector became a patchwork of initiatives designed to work around provincial territorial concerns while addressing national interests (Jones 1996b).

One of the policy areas in which federal involvement was regarded as legitimate was research. The National Research Council, created in 1916, was a modest response to the realization of the important role that research universities had played in the economic and military development of Germany. The council worked closely with university researchers, supported university-based research initiatives, and provided scholarships for advanced study. Over time the National Research Council became repositioned as a national research entity, and the responsibility for funding university research was assigned to arms-length granting councils, which, by the 1970s, had become the Medical Research Council (later to become the Canadian Institutes for Health Research), the Natural Sciences and Engineering Research Council, and the Social Sciences and Humanities Research Council (Cameron 1997). These three granting councils were increasingly linked to discussions of doctoral education both because of their overall role in supporting the direct costs of university research (which included the employment of doctoral students and their contribution to projects led by university professors) and because of their direct role in supporting future generations of researchers through masters, doctoral, and postdoctoral scholarship/fellowship programs.

Three policy issues underscored the federal government's support for the expansion of doctoral education. The first was a national response to an increasingly global infatuation with investing in science and technology, initially reinforced by the politics of Sputnik and the cold war, but, by the early 1980s, almost entirely rationalized by the argument that knowledge creation in the university sector, and technology transfer to industry, were components of a broader national strategy for economic development. The second policy issue was a labor shortage: the expansion of higher education in previous decades led to a huge demand for graduates from doctoral programs to fill university faculty positions, prompting the granting councils to support increasing graduate enrollment through scholarship and research grant programs. Thereafter, the number of doctoral graduates in Canada increased from 306 in 1960, to 1,680 in 1970, to 3,660 in 2001 (Williams 2005).

The third policy shaping government support for doctoral education was cultural in nature. A new sense of nationalism emerged during Canada's 1967 centennial year, but a number of studies and books reported that Canadian schools were largely relying on American textbooks (Hodgets 1968) and that Canadian universities were increasingly staffed by foreign-trained professors who were now responsible for teaching Canadian undergraduates about Canadian history and culture (Cormier 2004; Mathews and Steele 1969). The policy response to this surge of nationalism was a new set of programs to ensure that a stronger foundation was provided for scholarship focusing on Canadian social sciences and humanities, and for teaching this new knowledge in Canada's schools and undergraduate classrooms (Symons 1975). In many respects the Canadianization movement in the higher-education sector paralleled the increasing economic and cultural nationalism associated with the Trudeau government. Trudeau's liberal government supported new initiatives to boost a floundering Canadian publishing industry, to encourage playing Canadian music on Canadian radio, and to find a balance that would allow a Canadian television and film industry to survive in the face of increasing American domination of cultural industries. Publication programs emerged within the federal granting councils to support Canadian journals, and Canadian immigration and employment policies forced universities to employ Canadians unless there were no qualified Canadian applicants, a shift in policy that served to stifle a subtle preference for credentials from elite foreign institutions (unless the credentials were earned by a Canadian). As Claude Bissell (1977), president of the University of Toronto, noted,

> In our colonial heart of hearts, we believed that advanced degrees from Harvard, Stanford, Michigan, and California glowed more brightly than advanced degrees from McGill, Toronto, Alberta, and British Columbia. I think that attitude is changing and we now have confidence in what we can do ourselves. (1)

Government policy thus supported the expansion of graduate education and generally encouraged Canadian students to study in Canada. With few exceptions, Canada's national scholarship programs were available only to Canadians studying in Canada—a policy approach that was designed both to support Canadian doctoral studies and the research capacity of Canadian universities (Jones 2009). As Trilokekar (2007) has noted, while scholarships for international study sometimes emerged through bilateral foreign policy relationships, these scholarships were easy targets in federal budget cuts, and the big soft-power initiative to emerge during this period was the Canadian Studies Abroad program that supported the study of Canada by researchers in other jurisdictions, including the development of Canadian Studies programs and centers at foreign universities. Rather than supporting internationalization by funding Canadian students to learn about the world and attend "global" universities, the flagship program of the Academic Relations division of the Department of External Affairs was designed to encourage scholars at non-Canadian institutions to study and teach about Canada (Trilokekar 2009).

Canadian policy toward research and doctoral education shifted under the Mulroney conservative government of the 1980s as the country transitioned from economic nationalism toward free trade under the Canada-US, and later North American, Free Trade Agreement. There were slight reductions in federal support for investigator-initiated research projects but, at the same time, major new investments in initiatives designed to build a university research infrastructure in areas viewed as strategic within an increasingly competitive economic environment and, perhaps more importantly, programs designed to encourage private-sector investment in industry-based research and technology transfer between universities and industry (Fisher et al. 2006). While there were no significant increases in the support of doctoral students through scholarship programs, the role of training (and, therefore, funding) doctoral students within funded research programs was emphasized by the granting councils.

Professors competing for research funds from the Social Sciences and Humanities Research Council, for example, were explicitly asked to describe the role of graduate students and how their projects would contribute to research training.

With the election of the Chretien liberal government in 1993, the clear federal priority became dealing with the federal government's deficit. In this context, substantial reductions in unconditional transfers to the provinces became an expedient means of reducing expenditures. The mid-1990s saw a major reduction of federal government support for postsecondary education, and in most provinces most of these cuts were passed along to the institutions. At the turn of the millennium, with annual federal deficits now replaced by annual federal surpluses, the federal government began to reinvest in priority areas, but instead of recommitting to federal transfers, the Chretien government began to pursue an "innovation" agenda focusing on strengthening Canada's research infrastructure for the "new economy" (Fisher et al. 2006). Major new investments were made in increasing the country's research capacity, including the creation of 2,000 new Canada Research Chairs in an attempt to retain top talent and recruit leading foreign researchers. Meanwhile, the Canada Foundation for Innovation provided matching grants to support major research infrastructure projects.

The conservative government under Stephen Harper announced a number of innovative programs under a science and technology plan released in 2007 entitled *Mobilizing Science and Technology to Canada's Advantage*. The plan focused on developing Canada's entrepreneurial advantage, knowledge advantage, and people advantage, and it was under the third category that the federal government positioned a number of major scholarship enhancements for doctoral students. While continuing to support doctoral scholarships operated by the three granting councils, the government announced a major expansion of Canada Graduate Scholarships tenable only at Canadian universities and the creation of a new elite scholarship program entitled the Vanier Canada Graduate Scholarship. Doctoral students holding a Canada Graduate Scholarship could also apply for a Michael Smith Foreign Study Supplement to support international research visits under the supervision of a university professor.

Federal government policies concerning doctoral education have shifted over the past century, but federal funding programs have consistently viewed doctoral education in two distinct ways. The first is to view doctoral education as an individual activity pursued by meritorious candidates: fellowship and scholarship programs administered by the granting councils (much like the modest scholarships provided by the National Research Council following World War I) are highly competitive programs designed to encourage and support excellent students to pursue doctoral programs in Canada. The second is to view doctoral education as research training under the apprenticeship of a professor: research grant programs supporting faculty-initiated research projects are evaluated, at least in part, on their potential to provide research training for graduate students. In the first approach the government supports meritorious students who can choose the institution they would like to attend (with the most prestigious scholarships focusing on Canadian universities), while in the second the government supports meritorious research projects (with the past performance of the researcher or research team as a key factor in making awards) with the understanding that at least some component of the research funding will be used to support graduate students who will learn through their involvement in a research project.

Mobility

Issues of mobility and hierarchy are key themes emerging from the analysis of doctoral education, and these themes serve to illustrate some interesting aspects of government policies focusing on doctoral education in Canada. An analysis of the 2008 scholarship competition administered by the Social Sciences and Humanities Research Council of Canada (SSHRC) illustrates the ways in which scholarships are used to support a national research infrastructure in Canada.[1] In the traditional doctoral-student competition, which supports students choosing to study at Canadian or foreign institutions, a total of 675 doctoral scholarships were awarded. Ninety-three of these awards (14 percent) were taken up at foreign universities. The vast majority of these 93 students pursued degrees in American (61 or 66 percent) and British (26 or 28 percent) universities. Only six students (6 percent) were studying in universities outside Canada, the United States, and the United Kingdom. Interestingly, this distribution maps onto global trends such that the United States, United Kingdom, Germany, and France attract 70 percent of all academically mobile students (Akers, Bill, and Guther 2007). With a few exceptions, students attending foreign universities choose to enroll in highly ranked "global" universities; the three most frequently listed institutions were Oxford, Cambridge, and the University of California at Berkeley.

The more elite graduate scholarships funded by the government of Canada, however, are offered under the Canada Graduate Scholarships program. The Social Sciences and Humanities Research Council of Canada (SSHRC) awarded 1,300 CGS graduate scholarships to masters students, and 430 elite scholarships to doctoral students. Under the terms of these awards, all recipients must pursue their degrees at Canadian universities. In a comprehensive review of SSHRC doctoral award holders in the social sciences and humanities, Knight and Madden (2008) found similar patterns discouraging student mobility. For instance, the authors contended that most of the scholarships available to doctoral students do not explicitly encourage mobility; they argued that increased flexibility of these policies to allow for both short-term and long-term study abroad was essential to expanding international mobility opportunities for doctoral students (ibid.).

International student mobility, therefore, has not been a key component of federal government policy related to doctoral education. For the most part, concerns about losing top Canadian doctoral students through "brain drain" has underscored Canadian policy in this area. There is some government support for students to study in other countries under certain conditions, but the most prestigious national scholarships require students to study at Canadian universities. A small number of government initiatives support international study to specific institutions and/or destinations, though, of the country-specific awards, most are to Commonwealth countries or to the United States, thereby patterning doctoral-student mobility in particular ways (Knight and Madden 2008). Student mobility in the Canadian context primarily takes the form of providing students with the financial support necessary to move within Canada to attend Canadian institutions, therefore reinforcing a national institutional hierarchy and providing modest levels of support so that Canadian students attending Canadian institutions can have the opportunity to obtain some research experience at foreign institutions as a component of a Canadian university program.

It is interesting to note that, while Canada's funding policies are designed to encourage top Canadian students to study at home, Canada has been a major beneficiary of an increasingly international academic labor market. A majority of individuals holding doctorates in Canada were born *outside* the country (54 percent in 2001), compared with 46 percent in Australia (in 2001), 26 percent in the United States (2003 data), and 12 percent in Germany (2004 data) (Auriol 2007). Of all doctorate holders employed in Canada, approximately 37 percent are categorized as teaching professionals in Canada's colleges or universities (in 2001), compared with 33 percent of all doctorate holders in the United States (in 2003), or 13 percent in Germany (in 2004). Compared with the United States, fewer doctorate holders in Canada are employed in "other professions" categories, including business professionals (ibid.). Thus, compared with the United States, a larger percentage of individuals with doctorates in Canada were born outside the country and are employed in the higher-education sector.

Canadian doctoral students are encouraged under federal government funding mechanisms to study in Canada as part of national policies designed to encourage the development of highly skilled human resources, but this emphasis on keeping Canadian students in Canada takes place in a context where the majority of doctorate holders were born outside Canada—a nationalistic approach to doctoral education in the context of a country that has been (and continues to be) a major beneficiary of immigration and international labor flows.

Hierarchy

The Canadian university system that emerged from post–World War II massification was relatively homogeneous. The new universities created during this period were generally modeled on existing, publicly supported institutions. The private, denominational university sector largely disappeared from Canada as institutions either secularized to obtain public funding or federated with existing publicly funded secular institutions (Jones 1996b). Thereafter, Canadian universities shared a range of key characteristics, including their legal status as private, not-for-profit corporations, their provincial-government operating support, and their roughly similar governance arrangements. Most universities were comprehensive, offering some combination of undergraduate, graduate, and professional programs, and all had a research function. There was no formal attempt to differentiate institutions and no clear institutional hierarchy; rather, provincial governments treated degree-granting as a public monopoly and tightly controlled the creation of new universities. Generally speaking, universities treated each other as equals, at least in terms of the quality of their undergraduate programs. Given the assumption of roughly common standards, there was no pressure to create a national institutional accreditation system or a national quality framework for higher education (ibid.).

Two recent factors appear to be increasing the level of institutional differentiation and hierarchy within the Canadian university sector. The first type of differentiation occurs as a function of provincial government policies that have expanded the number and type of institutions with the authority to offer degrees. As Marshall (2008) has noted, the emergence of new universities, combined with the expansion of degree-granting in the community-college sector, is creating new institutional categories. The second type of differentiation is associated with the expansion of research funding and graduate education. While all Canadian universities have a research function, there have always been differences in the intensity of these research activities, and these differences have been exacerbated by nationally competitive funding mechanisms and the mammoth investments in research funding and infrastructure support that began to emerge in the mid-1990s (Shanahan and Jones 2007).

In the new research environment, a relatively small number of universities have been able to access a greater share of the expanding research funding pie. While this obviously has an impact on differentiation between institutions based on research support, it is also important to note that this differentiation is taking place within a system that, historically, has been nonhierarchical. For example, while a handful of Canadian universities are frequently listed in the top-100 universities in the world in global ranking systems, 22 Canadian universities (or roughly a third of the traditional public institutions) appear in the 2009 Shanghai Jiao Tong University ranking of the top-500 universities based on research activity. In other words, many Canadian universities have a relatively strong profile of research activity, but a small number are now competing among the very best institutions in the world (on a similar point, see both Ka Ho Mok's chapter on East Asian universities and Peter Maassen's discussion of Nordic universities' high placement in global higher-education rankings).

The development of hierarchical relationships within the Canadian university sector becomes especially clear when one focuses on doctoral education. While a large percentage of universities award doctoral degrees, the majority of doctoral students graduate from just five Canadian universities, and most Canadian doctoral students are enrolled in institutions in just three major urban centers: Toronto, Montreal, and Vancouver (Williams 2005). There is already a clear hierarchy of universities in terms of doctoral education, and one might argue that this hierarchy is being reinforced by federal government policies that have encouraged the best Canadian doctoral students to study at Canadian universities, and through research funding mechanisms that, while competitive, have tended to advantage a small number of institutions that already possess a strong research infrastructure, including large graduate programs. Canada is experiencing a gradual—but increasingly evident—hierarchicization of its doctoral education programs.

MOBILITY AND HIERARCHY IN CANADIAN DOCTORAL EDUCATION

How does Canada's experience with doctoral education fit the broader literature on this subject? Although scholarly interest in doctoral education has an extensive history (see Berleson 1960; Storr 1953, 1973), much of this literature has focused on non-Canadian institutions and has been written by non-Canadian researchers. In fact, considerable scholarship on doctoral education has been anchored in US, UK, and Australian contexts (McAlpine and Norton 2006; Neumann 2002; 2007; Parry 2007). The past two decades have seen a significant increase in scholarly attention to doctoral education, with influential studies of doctoral-student attrition (Golde 2000; Lovitts 2001), financial aid (Nettles and Millet 2006), supervisor relations (Baird 1990; Golde and Dore 2001), socialization (Austin 2002), and discipline (Golde 2000, 2004), as well as the overall structure of doctoral education (Tinto 1997), but this literature, too, has not had a particular emphasis on a Canadian context.

Recently, higher-education scholars have used the notion of globalization to call for more attention to doctoral education, including issues of doctoral-student mobility; heightened linkages between doctoral training and market forces; the growing emphasis on doctoral study related to science, technology, and engineering; the intensification of interdisciplinary research conducted by national as well as international teams of experts (Nerad and Heggelund, 2008), and other subjects. Nerad and Trzyna (2008) highlight eight implications of these globalization-related changes for doctoral education: (1) the commodification of knowledge; (2) the penetration of market logics into the university; (3) the rise of Mode 2 knowledge that emphasizes linkages between university and nonuniversity partners; (4) the phenomenon of brain drain; (5) the increasing use of English, even in non-English-speaking countries; (6) the increasing "standardization" of doctoral education; (7) the adoption of new audit systems to assure quality in doctoral education; and (8) the Bologna accords in Europe, which seek to encourage greater student mobility across borders.

Our aim here is to discuss how doctoral education is changing in light of a new discourse about "global" or "world-class" universities. To that end, we have focused on two themes that we believe encapsulate many of the implications of this new discourse: (1) mobility and (2) hierarchy. Mobility, here, involves a multilayered analysis that includes the mobility of both people and ideas, both students and knowledge. To connect mobility and knowledge is to draw attention to the permeability of both national and intellectual boundaries. The permeability of boundaries, in turn, connects to a sustained debate in the discourse surrounding doctoral education in world-class universities, namely, a debate about both *internationality* and *interdisciplinarity*. "Mobility" thus concerns the movement of students across the boundaries of nations and knowledge as they collaborate with fellow researchers and seek exposure to multiple disciplines. What does—or what should—doctoral education look, sound, and feel like in today's "global university"?

It would be impossible to answer this question fully in a short chapter, but surely one aspect of the mobility debate—that is, the debate over *where* and *how* both students and knowledge "move"—concerns the transition from Mode 1 to Mode 2 knowledge. Whereas Mode 1 knowledge describes traditional forms of university-based research determined by disciplinary forces and undertaken by scholars working in established fields, Mode 2 knowledge is inter-/transdisciplinary and is undertaken in a variety of nonuniversity settings, not by individuals but by problem-solving teams. Gibbons et al. (1994) characterize Mode 2 research activity as carried out in heterogeneously organized forms that are fundamentally transient and not institutionalized primarily within the university. In Mode 2 knowledge production, the emphasis falls on multidisciplinary approaches to scholarship, the migration of scholars toward alternative (nonuniversity) research sites, and the constant movement of people and ideas across and between sites (locally, regionally, and internationally).

Of course, the increasing role of nonuniversity actors in Mode 2 knowledge production affects not only the types of knowledge produced but also for whom—and for what purposes—such knowledge is generated. The rise in Mode 2 knowledge production leads to key questions not only about the internationality and interdisciplinarity of doctoral research but also about the commodification and commercialization of knowledge. Who sets the scholarly agenda for doctoral education, and who sets the criteria for assessing doctoral programs? The involvement of nonuniversity actors in doctoral education has cast doubt on the traditional validation of knowledge by academics and their disciplinary communities. In some instances peer-review processes are being replaced by other mechanisms for gauging the value of scholarly output and research competence. Specifically, the role of nonacademic industrial and governmental partners in doctoral education has led to heated debates about the rise of "academic capitalism" as both professors and students reform doctoral training programs to suit various external interests (Slaughter and Rhoades 2004). Inasmuch as Mode 2 knowledge can be bought, sold, traded, and otherwise commodified, so, too, presumably, can the doctoral education associated with this knowledge.

How has the shift from Mode 1 to Mode 2 knowledge production changed the employment trends of doctoral degree recipients? Evidence suggests that the involvement of nonacademic actors in doctoral education has reoriented not only the job choices of doctoral graduates but also their perceptions of academic life (Mendoza 2007). Recent doctoral degree recipients are increasingly "mobile" in ways that often lead them *out* of academic work. In some fields, the desire for a traditional professorial appointment upon completion of doctoral studies is becoming the exception, not the rule (Statistics Canada 2008). In the physical sciences and engineering, for example, doctoral students frequently pursue research careers with industrial and governmental partners, often facilitated by their exposure to nonuniversity networks during their doctoral studies (Mendoza 2007). This rise in nonprofessorial appointments is motivated in part by a perception of a more desirable work-life balance in the business world, as well as the sense that jobs in industry offer more professional autonomy as well as far greater financial compensation (Mendoza 2007; Statistics Canada 2008). Such views reflect the realities of a changing academic profession—a profession characterized by declining job security and decreasing pay. While the prevalence of these changes affect disciplines differently, institutional policy and practices may need to encourage greater attention to how these factors map on to the career preferences and trajectories of doctoral graduates.

A broadening field of employment options for doctoral degree holders has been aided by globalization. A globalized labor market has created new opportunities for academic as well as nonacademic hiring. Doctoral graduates are moving across countries and state jurisdictions in unprecedented numbers. This mobility, however, raises difficult questions about the returns on state investment in doctoral education. If graduates move away, can the state recoup its investment in their training? Canada's emphasis on keeping doctoral students at home reflects precisely this sort of calculation, but is this approach optimal in the long run? What can policymakers do to increase the chances that doctoral graduates will stay in Canada— and will distribute themselves in equitable ways across the country?

Upon graduation, doctoral degree holders frequently move to specific regions to pursue specific employment tracks, yet just as Canadian policies advantage the cities of Toronto, Montreal, and Vancouver, so too, on a global scale, doctoral mobility now concentrates talent in regions and in careers that reinforce historic inequities and patterns of economic stratification. (Indeed, while the increasing use of English in doctoral education facilitates geographic mobility in various ways—especially among elites—yet, on both a national and international level, the rise of English has reinforced enduring patterns of advantage and disadvantage.)

How can universities turn global mobility to their advantage? This question is becoming increasingly prominent among higher-education planners. University leaders around the world are looking for ways to increase the "global competence" of university graduates, and strategic university partnerships—including international partnerships in doctoral education—are one way to do so. Joint degree programs, branch campuses, and other ventures have created new opportunities (as well as incentives) for student mobility. Such initiatives, however, are not inexpensive. In most cases, elite universities have taken the lead in pursuing these programs in hopes of furthering their competitive advantage. Elite universities, for example, are key players in the Bologna Process, which provides a framework for doctoral education to be constructed and pursued in multiple institutions across nations. This highly coordinated endeavor results from an intense investment of time, energy, and resources to develop cooperative systems. Such efforts are not unique to Europe. Ka Ho Mok's chapter in this volume outlines similar strategies in East Asia, and Anthony Welch's chapter discusses related cross-national ventures that are playing out in Southeast Asia and Australia. All these efforts are designed to capitalize on the increasing geographic mobility of academics.

Geographic mobility is not, however, the only major theme shaping contemporary doctoral education. The second major theme is hierarchy. As doctoral degree seekers and degree holders move from place to place, they generate a hierarchy of universities. This hierarchy is the focus of Marginson's (2006) work on national/international competition in higher education as well as the literature on changes in the academic profession and in academic work (Marginson 2000; Shuster and Finkelstein 2006). Doctoral education is inextricably tied to these dynamics. Given the global imperative for research activity and the centrality of the university in "knowledge production," doctoral education sits at the interface of national policy and international competition. As Marginson (2006) explains, higher education is a positional good (Hirsch 1976). In other words, "elite degrees and other positional goods confer advantages on some only by denying them to others" (4). Noting the ways in which institutional prestige serves as a proxy for educational quality, Marginson shows how competition at both the national and international level creates educational "winners" and "losers." Take the case of international university rankings. Particular institutions possess, or rather are presumed to possess, high value as signified by their ranking, and these rankings, in turn, are assumed to affect the choices—and the movement—of students who seek high-value academic degrees. Mobility and hierarchy thus go hand in hand. As Marginson notes, the result "is not just an unequal distribution of social opportunities, but the isolation of many of the fruits of intellectual life in a handful of hard-to-enter institutions" (6).

The relationship between mobility, hierarchy, and global rankings involves not only particular notions of prestige (usually associated with research activity), but also powerful implications for doctoral students. Marginson (2006) frames the relationship between students and universities succinctly by suggesting that "positional markets in higher education are a matching game in which the hierarchy of students is synchronized with the hierarchy of universities; and the peak group in each hierarchy is steeped in the habits of sustaining the other" (6). This synchronicity has implications for current and prospective doctoral students inasmuch as the power dynamics that reinforce hierarchies of universities permeate doctoral education. This hierarchy is manifested in two distinct ways: (1) through aspects of academic work that position doctoral students as competent and desirable based on particular achievements; and (2) through the implicit and explicit conditions of academia that privilege certain groups and marginalize others. Doctoral education, as a system that operates within a global higher-education market, reflects the dynamics of institutional competition and prestige—dynamics that govern international university rankings.

The "globalization" of doctoral education reinforces institutional hierarchies and, indeed, extends this process from a national to an international level. Universities now seek to recruit the best doctoral students from around the world. Better students are presumed to produce better research, which, in turn, is presumed to boost a university's ranking. Research output is inextricably tied up with the status of universities. Marginson argues that "in elite universities, research status and degree status feed into each other" (5). In the context of doctoral education, status associated with research establishes the very conditions on which institutional rankings are built. Top rankings produce prestige, which, in turn, generates resources, which funds research, which attracts faculty, which brings in students, which ultimately leads to higher rankings, and so on. Thus, Marginson notes, "high research performing universities with stand-out faculty attract bright students," just as, in the same way, a "well-funded research infrastructure allows universities to deploy their best performing faculty so as to concentrate areas of strength and secure intellectual leadership at both national and global levels" (Marginson 2006: 5). Star faculty attract star students, who, in turn, bolster the proxies of "quality" used by the global rankings—the very rankings on which the university builds its reputation and its ability to attract star faculty and students.

While the pursuit of global prestige reveals the connection between mobility and hierarchy in doctoral education, many universities are unable to participate in this "race." Just as the process of globalization has produced a hierarchy of "winners" and "losers" in doctoral education, so too has globalization reinforced hierarchies within the academic profession as a whole. Schuster and Finklestein (2007) provide a three-part framework to outline hierarchies within the academic profession. They document changes in academic appointments, academic careers, and academic work. Global pressures and institutional diversification have resulted in a complex international academic labor market marked by an increased use of contingent (adjunct) part-time instructors (Rajagopal 2002; Muzzin 2008). Fundamental to any discussion of changes in the professoriate is the rapid increase in adjunct or contingent workers—both full- and part-time—worldwide. Schuster and Finkelstein (2007) observe that "the number and proportion of contingent [nonprobationary] full-time appointees has continued to expand, and thus it is likely that their proportion of all full-time faculty will cumulatively exceed one half in the foreseeable future" (4). While the number of part-time adjuncts has risen dramatically, the number of full-time contingent appointments has increased even faster. Both of these developments illustrate the changing nature of academic appointments in the context of globalization.

Along with these changes in academic appointments, Schuster and Finkelstein (2007) call attention to changes in the balance of teaching, research, and service among those engaged in academic work in American universities. They note that research falls primarily on the shoulders of traditional tenured or tenure-track faculty, while the teaching responsibilities fall on contingent faculty members.

This pattern occurs both within institutions and across institutional types, with research universities showing not only a larger number of tenured and tenure-track faculty but also a greater commitment to research while nonresearch universities have more contingent academic staff and devote more time to teaching. The paucity of representation among contingent faculty in university administration and governance also suggests that adjuncts have less status in their institutions. Moreover, Schuster and Finkelstein note that the bifurcation of faculty work between full- and part-time status has enduring effects. Drawing on data from 1998, they found that "among current part-time faculty in 1998, the vast majority reported only previous part-time work experience; and among current full-time faculty in 1998, previous experience is primarily full-time" (6). In a hierarchical and increasingly globalized system of doctoral education, graduates of highly ranked institutions more likely find their way into secure and well-paid academic (or nonacademic) employment while graduates of less highly ranked institutions often struggle to build stable careers.

Concluding Observations

The contours of doctoral education are changing in the context of globalization and the emergence of global institutions. As we have noted, these changes are complex and multifaceted, but two clear aspects of these changes stand out: (1) student mobility in the context of an increasingly international labor market; and (2) institutional hierarchy in an environment of global competition, rankings, and divergent research opportunities. Perhaps the most obvious observation is that universities, no matter how global they may be in orientation and research profile, continue to rely on government resources and are, therefore, heavily influenced by government policies, especially policies and mechanisms supporting research. In the case of Canada, these policies and funding mechanisms have consistently positioned doctoral education as a crucial component of national human resource development and the growth of Canada's broader research and development infrastructure. The emphasis in these policies has been to provide support for Canadian students to attend Canadian universities; there has been little emphasis on attracting international students or in supporting Canadian students to attend universities outside Canada.

In the Canadian context there is relatively little federal government support for international student mobility. Students who decide to pursue a doctoral degree outside the country cannot rely on federal support; they must either support themselves or rely on funding or employment income from their university abroad. The federal government in Canada has recently created a new competitive funding mechanism that will provide limited support for Canadian doctoral students to spend time at a foreign university as a component of their Canadian doctoral program, but this is the first national initiative to support international student mobility in doctoral education. Still, though, the federal government's most competitive doctoral scholarship programs and the emphasis on research training in competitive research grant programs are mechanisms that support student mobility only *within* Canada—an approach that has enabled a relatively small number of universities to attract the majority of doctoral candidates.

These policies have served to reinforce a hierarchy of Canadian universities in terms of research and doctoral education. Since the most prestigious Canadian scholarship programs focus on doctoral studies in Canadian universities, the programs encourage students to select the Canadian institutions they believe will offer the best program of study and the greatest research opportunities. Universities with a broad profile of funded research activities are obviously in the best position to attract and financially support doctoral students. Given this policy framework, the recruitment and funding of international doctoral students has become the responsibility of individual institutions. Canadian universities may be global in orientation and impact, but this global orientation has emerged in the context of a federal government policy framework that has focused on the "national" rather than "global" aspects of doctoral education. There has been surprisingly little research on doctoral education in Canada, and there is an obvious need to move beyond a focus on federal government policy to investigate doctoral education in provincial governments, institutional approaches to curriculum and funding, and emerging relationships between universities and industry. Perhaps most importantly, there is a need to understand the educational experience of doctoral students and how this experience is changing in the new "global" university.

Note

1. Our analysis is based on the annual report of SSHRC scholarship awards available at www.sshrc.ca. The figures used were based on an analysis of data downloaded on November 20, 2009.

BIBLIOGRAPHY

Ackers, L., B. Bill, and J. Guther (2007). *Doctoral Mobility in the Social Sciences. Draft Report to the NORFACE ERA-NETWORK.* Liverpool, UK: University of Liverpool.

Auriol, L. (2007). *Labor Market Characteristics and International Mobility of Doctorate Holders: Results from Seven Countries* (STI Working Paper 2007/2). Paris: OECD.

Austin, A. (2002). Preparing the Next Generation of Faculty: Graduate School as Socialization to the Academic Career. *Journal of Higher Education,* 73: 94–122.

Baird, L. L. (1990). The Melancholy of Anatomy: The Personal and Professional Development of Graduate and Professional School Students. In J. C. Smart (Ed.), *Higher Education: Handbook of Theory and Research,* vol. 6. New York: Agathon Press, pp. 361–392.

Berelson, B. (1960). *Graduate Education in the United States.* New York: McGraw-Hill.

Bissell, C. (1977). The Recovery of the Canadian Tradition in Higher Education. *Canadian Journal of Higher Education,* 7 (2): 1–10.

Bowen, W. and N. Rudenstine (1992). *In Pursuit of the PhD.* Princeton, NJ: Princeton University Press.

Cameron, D. M. (1997). The Federal Perspective. In G. A. Jones (Ed.), *Higher Education in Canada: Different Systems, Different Perspectives.* New York: Garland, pp. 9–29.

Cormier, J. J. (2004). *The Canadianization Movement: Emergence, Survival and Success.* Toronto: University of Toronto Press.

Fisher, D., K. Rubenson, J. Bernatchez, R. Clift, G. Jones, J. Lee, M. MacIvor, J. Meredith, T. Shanahan, and C. Trottier (2006). *Canadian Federal Policy and Post-secondary Education.* Vancouver, BC: Center for Policy Studies in Higher Education and Training, University of British Columbia.

Gibbons, M., C. Limoges, H. Nowotny, S. Schwartzman, P. Scott, and M. Trow (1994). *The New Production of Knowledge: The Dynamics of Science and Research in Contemporary Societies.* London, UK: Sage.

Golde, C. (2000). Should I Stay or Should I Go? Student Descriptors of the Doctoral Attrition Process. *Review of Higher Education,* 23 (2): 199–227.

Golde, C. (2004). The Survey of Doctoral Education and Career Preparation: The Importance of Disciplinary Contexts. In A. Austin and D. Wulff (Eds.), *Paths to the Professoriate: Strategies for Enriching the Preparation of Future Faculty.* Jossey-Bass: San Francisco, pp. 19–45.

Golde, C. and T. Dore (2001). *At Cross Purposes: What the Experiences of Today's Doctoral Students Reveal about Doctoral Education.* Report for the Pew Charitable Trusts.

Hirsch, F. (1976). *Social Limits to Growth.* Cambridge, MA: Harvard University Press.

Hodgets, A. B. (1968). *What Culture? What Heritage? A Study of Civic Education in Canada.* Toronto: Ontario Institute for Studies in Education.

Industry Canada. (2007). *Mobilizing Science and Technology to Canada's Advantage.* Ottawa: Industry Canada.

Jones, G. A. (1996a). Diversity within a Decentralized Higher Education System: The Case of Canada. In V. Lynn Meek, Leo Goedegebuure, OsmoKivinen, and RistoRinne (Eds.), *The Mockers and Mocked: Comparative Perspectives on Differentiation, Convergence and Diversity in Higher Education.* Oxford: Pergamon, pp. 79–94.

——— (1996b). Governments, Governance, and Canadian Universities. In John C. Smart (Ed.), *Higher Education: Handbook of Theory and Research,* vol. 11. New York: Agathon Press, pp. 337–371.

———(2009). Internationalization and Higher Education Policy in Canada: Three Challenges. In R. D. Trilokekar, G. A. Jones, and A. Shubert (Eds.), *Canada's Universities Go Global.* Toronto: James Lorimer and Company (CAUT Series), pp. 355–369.

Knight, J. and M. Madden (2008). *International Academic Mobility Experiences for Canadian Social Science and Humanities Doctoral Students* Ottawa: SSHRC (unpublished report).

Lazaridis, M. (2004). The Importance of Basic Research. *Research Money,* 18 (18): 8.

Lovitts, B. (2001). *Leaving the Ivory Tower.* New York: Rowman and Littlefield.

Marginson, S. (2000). Rethinking Academic Work in the Global Era. *Journal of Higher Education Policy and Management,* 22 (1): 23–35.

——— (2006). Dynamics of National and Global Competition in Higher Education. *Higher Education,* 52: 1–39.

Marshall, D. (2008). Differentiation by Degrees: System Design and the Changing Undergraduate Environment in Canada. *Canadian Journal of Higher Education,* 38 (3): 1–20.

Mathews, R. and J. Steele (1969). *The Struggle for Canadian Universities.* Toronto: New Press.

McAlpine, L. and J. Norton (2006). Reframing Our Approach to Doctoral Programs: A Learning Perspective. *Higher Education Research and Development,* 25 (1): 3–17.

McKillop, A. B. (1994). *Matters of the Mind: The Ontario University, 1791–1951.* Toronto: University of Toronto Press.

Mendoza, P. (2007). Academic Capitalism and Doctoral Student Socialization: A Case Study. *Journal of Higher Education,* 78 (1): 71–96.

Muzzin, L. (2008). How Fares Equity in an Era of Academic Capitalism? The Role of Contingent Faculty. In D. Fisher and A. Chan (Eds.), *The Exchange University: Corporatization of Academic Culture* (pp. 105–124). Vancouver, BC: UBC Press.

Nerad, M. and M. Heggelund (2008). *Toward a Global PhD? Forces and Forms in Doctoral Education Worldwide.* Seattle, WA: University of Washington Press.

Nerad, M. and T. Trzyna (2008). Conclusion. In M. Nerad and M. Heggelund (Eds.), *Toward a Global PhD? Forces and Forms in Doctoral Education Worldwide* (pp. 300–312). Seattle, WA: University of Washington Press.

Nettles, M. and C. Millett (2006). *Three Magic Letters: Getting to PhD.* Baltimore: Johns Hopkins University Press.

Neumann, R. (2002). Diversity, Doctoral Education and Policy. *Higher Education Research and Development,* 21 (2): 167–178.

——— (2007). Policy and Practice in Doctoral Education. *Studies in Higher Education,* 32 (4): 459–473.

Parry, S. (2007). *Disciplines and Doctorates.* Dordrecht, The Netherlands: Springer.

Rajagopal, I. (2002). *Hidden Academics: Contract Faculty in Canadian Universities.* Toronto: University of Toronto Press.

Schuster, J. and M. Finkelstein (2006). *The American Faculty: The Restructuring of Academic Work and Careers.* Baltimore, MD: Johns Hopkins University Press:

——— (2007). *On the Brink: Assessing the Status of the American Faculty.* UC Berkeley: Center for Studies in Higher Education. Retrieved from: http:// escholarship.org/uc/item/1ch73352

Shanahan, T. and Jones, G. A. (2007). Shifting Roles and Approaches: Government Coordination of Postsecondary Education in Canada from 1995 to 2006. *Higher Education Research and Development,* 26 (1) 31-43.

Slaughter, S. and G. Rhoades (2004). *Academic Capitalism and the New Economy.* Baltimore, MD: Johns Hopkins University Press.

Statistics Canada (2008). *Survey of Earned Doctorates (SED), 2005–2006.* Ottawa, ON: Statistics Canada, Data Liberation Initiative.

Storr, R. J. (1953). *The Beginnings of Graduate Education in America.* Chicago: University of Chicago Press.

——— (1973). *The Beginning of the Future.* New York: McGraw-Hill.

Symons, T. H. B. (1975). *To Know Ourselves: The Report of the Commission on Canadian Studies,* vols. 1 and 2. Ottawa: Association of Universities and Colleges of Canada.

Tinto, V. (1997). Toward a Theory of Doctoral Persistence. In M. Nerad, R. June, and D. Miller (Eds.), *Graduate Education in the United State.* New York: Garland, pp. 322–338.

Trilokekar, R. D. (2007). *Federalism, Foreign Policy, and the Internationalization of Canadian Higher Education: A Case Study of the Academic Relations Division, Department of Foreign Affairs and International Trade, Canada.* Unpublished PhD thesis. University of Toronto.

———. (2009). The Department of Foreign Affairs and International Trade, Canada: Providing Leadership in the Internationalization of Higher Education? In R. D. Trilokekear, G. A. Jones, and A. Shubert (Eds.), *Canada's Universities Go Global* (pp. 98–118). Toronto: James Lorimer.

Williams, G. (2005). *Doctoral Education in Canada.* Ottawa: Canadian Association for Graduate Studies.

PART V

Universities and External Funding

CHAPTER 9

What Can Modern Universities Learn from the Past? English Universities Working with Industry, 1870–1914

John Taylor

INTRODUCTION

Links between universities and business have been a key strand not only within institutional strategic development but also within government policy toward higher education for many years. Figures released in 2010 showed that universities in the United Kingdom delivered services to business and industry valued at £2.97 billion a year (HEFCE 2010a). Despite a difficult economic situation in the context of the 2008–2009 global financial crisis, the annual UK Higher Education-Business and Community Interaction (HE-BCI) Survey showed an increasing number of new enterprises established by staff in higher education and by new graduates, increasing levels of continuing professional development, increasing income to higher education from research grants and contracts (especially in the public sector and third sector), and increasing income from intellectual property. In response, the UK minister of state for universities and science stressed that "even in difficult times, universities and other higher-education institutions are using their knowledge, expertise, and facilities to contribute to the UK economy. In these difficult economic times we face, the whole nation stands to benefit." Meanwhile, the director of research and innovation at the Higher Education

Funding Council for England (HEFCE) offered some historical perspective on the relationship between universities and business, noting that HEFCE (2010b) grants reflected "the core purposes for which universities were originally created—to support the social and economic transformations of their communities."

For universities, links with business and industry are a source of opportunity and pride, and they play a central part in institutional development. In 2010, the University of Birmingham (2010) emphasized that, through its links with the commercial world, it "adds value to business and industry all over the world by sharing the knowledge and expertise of our staff and students." Similarly, the University of Exeter, in its strategic plan for the period from 2007 to 2011, asserted that "We have an established reputation for working collaboratively with business, industry and government. We will act as a catalyst for partnerships, which deliver innovative solutions to real world problems and bring economic development to our region." The strategic plan went on to state that, going forward, Exeter (2007) "will strengthen our connections with employers, taking very active steps both within and outside our degree programs to ensure that our students have the skills they need for employment and for growing the economy."

These are just two examples of the importance that UK universities attach to links with business and industry. Such links span all types of institutions, old and new, broadly based and specialist, research-intensive and more teaching-oriented. These links embrace a wide range of activities, including teaching, research, and knowledge exchange; they are at the heart of the modern UK university in the twenty-first century. However, these links are not new. Sometimes, when reading the internal deliberations of individual universities or current policy documents from government, one gets the impression that the relationship between universities and business and industry is somehow a new problem, requiring a radical new response. Yet, links with industry and business have long been central to the development of universities. As the following analysis will show, these relationships were very important at the end of the nineteenth century and in the lead-up to World War I. After considering the current issues facing UK higher education, this chapter looks back to the links between universities and business in the period 1870–1914. In these links can be found the general themes that characterized the work of UK universities before World War I and some historical lessons that universities today might learn from their predecessors a century or more ago.

CURRENT DEBATES AND ISSUES

The present interest of the UK government in links between universities and business reflects a desire to strengthen international competitiveness within the world economy and a push to stimulate economic development at a local and regional level. In the context of increasing global competition, universities are both the provider of skilled workers within a knowledge economy and the source of significant innovation in products and processes. In theoretical terms, the interaction between universities, government, and industry may be understood as a Triple Helix (Etzkowitz 2008). Also important (as Glen Jones and Bryan Gopaul note in their chapter in this volume) are arguments regarding the apparent movement from traditional forms of research (Mode 1), based on curiosity and individual scholarship, to new forms of research (Mode 2) driven by external stakeholders, typically applied in nature, and often undertaken through partnerships and teams (Gibbons et al. 1994). In policy terms, the UK government white paper "Releasing Our Potential," issued in 1993, stressed the role of the sciences in wealth creation and was followed by a series of relatively low-level attempts to encourage more applied research and innovation in universities, such as the Realising Our Potential Awards (ROPAs), new procedures in the Engineering and Physical Sciences Research Council (EPSRC), and the encouragement of new Master of Research (MRes) programs. However, as universities began to fear the intrusion of government into research, with a focus on short-term activity, tensions began to emerge. In 1995, Sir Mark Richmond, previously vice-chancellor of the University of Manchester, warned that the White Paper was "already proving to be a charter for micromanagement by Government" (THES, February 3, 1995).

In 1998, a further White Paper titled "Our Competitive Future" (DTI 1998) emphasized the role of universities in knowledge creation and drew attention to the need for creative partnerships between universities and business. Then, in 1999, the government's Competitive Indicators identified room for improvement in these partnerships. "Only a small number of enterprises cite higher education institutions as important sources of information for innovation," one report stated. "An improvement in this indicator for the UK would include better utilisation of the U.K.'s science base." The Competitive Indicators report added that "The performance of university technology licensing offices, which encourage interchange and collaboration between universities and business, suggests that there is significant variation around the country." Noting the emergence of "industrial clusters based around universities," especially those in Cambridge, Oxford, Warwick, and Guildford, the report urged more universities to pursue such clusters. It stated: "the fact that there are differences between institutions regarding the extent of spin-outs suggests that the UK is not making the most of the commercial potential of its world-class academic research. Universities and business can learn from the experience of those higher education institutions with strong track records in commercial exploitation." In the end, it stressed that more needed to be done "to get the best out of our universities and the UK science base, for example through developing university-industry links and promoting networks and clusters" (DTI 1999).

After this flurry of activity, various initiatives followed to strengthen links between universities and business and industry. The University Challenge Seed Fund was established in 1998 to support the commercialization of research. Another fund, for Higher Education Reach-Out to Business and the Community (HEROBAC), was set up, followed by its successor, the Higher Education Innovation Fund (HEIF), to encourage links between universities and business. HEIF4, covering the period 2008–2011, will allocate £150 million per year to universities to support their business activities. Overall, the period since the 1990s has witnessed a shifting emphasis within UK universities as they have restructured in response to the emerging government agenda. New offices have arisen to coordinate and stimulate commercial activity, technology transfer, and regional links. In this context, links with business and industry have become a focus of university strategy. Shattock (2003) writes that "these pressures have profoundly changed the task of managing universities and have greatly extended the boundaries of university strategy and the scope of university operations."

In April 2008, the UK government issued a key strategy document: "Higher Education at Work—High Skills: High Value." This report, prepared following wide consultation with universities and employers, emphasized the importance of higher education in meeting national needs for high-level skills. In his foreword to the report, the minister of state stressed that "High-level skills—the skills associated with higher education—are good for the individuals who acquire them and good for the economy. They help individuals unlock their talent and aspire to change their life for the better. They help businesses and public services innovate and prosper. They help towns and cities thrive by creating jobs, helping businesses become more competitive and driving economic regeneration. High level skills add value for all of us" (UK Government 2008: 3). The report argued for a "culture shift" among higher-education providers and employers. It held that "universities need to help organisations through knowledge exchange as well as by supplying skilled graduates and postgraduates and by providing high level skills learning for those already in the workforce.... We wish all those involved in higher education—as stakeholders, learners and providers—to engage with this challenge and to help us develop a powerful consensus for change. This is an economic imperative" (UK Government 2008: 4).

Later, in December 2008, the Higher Education Funding Councils for England, Scotland, and Wales published the results of a survey of university-industry links in the United Kingdom undertaken by the University of Manchester. The report concluded that "There has been a spectacular growth in recent years across the United Kingdom in the scale, number and variety of linkages between higher education and industry. These linkages are manifested in research collaborations, provision of consultancy services, market transactions in the commercialisation of research, and industry's growing involvement as an interactive user of all types of teaching and training" (HEFCE 2008: 3). Despite these gains, the report highlighted "the need for closer involvement with their local and regional economies" as a key priority for universities and asserted that higher-education institutions were "making increased efforts to meet industry's needs for training" (4).

Also in 2008, the Council for Industry and Higher Education (CIHE) and the Center for Business Research (CBR) at the University of Cambridge published a joint report entitled "Universities, Business and Knowledge Exchange." This report took a broad view of links between universities and business, finding that a narrow focus on science, technology, engineering, and mathematics (the so-called STEM fields) had overlooked other areas of the university that were ripe for developing partnerships. It noted: "In recent years there has been an increasing focus on the role universities play in the economy and impact they make in promoting innovation and raising international competitiveness. But until recently there has been a prescriptive view of university-business interaction with a narrow focus on technology transfer. Although technology transfer may be important, it is also necessary to focus on the more diverse and varied impacts of business-university knowledge exchange relations.... The current policy agenda increasingly recognizes that the transfer of technology from the research base, a focus on science technology, engineering and mathematics (STEM) graduates, support for technology transfer offices in universities and the use of instruments (such as tax credits) that seek to encourage R&D is too narrow. This study reinforces recent moves to encourage a wider view on how universities and businesses together influence innovation and business performance" (CIHE 2008: 45). Stressing a range of possible collaborations between universities, businesses, and industries, the report concluded that "individual universities, and the academics within them, play different and varied roles in national and regional economies: the university's strengths, where it is located, and the business structure in which it is embedded, are all important and interdependent" (45).

Here then are some of the issues currently occupying the minds of university leaders and higher-education policymakers. Yet, awareness of the importance of links between higher education and business and industry is not new. What might we learn from the experiences of UK universities with business and industry a century or more ago?

UNIVERSITIES AND BUSINESS: A HISTORICAL PERSPECTIVE

Links between universities and business and industry were at the heart of the new universities that emerged toward the end of the nineteenth century. In 1870, in England, universities existed only in Oxford, Cambridge, Durham, and London (University College and King's College). A diverse collection of technical and medical colleges also existed. In Scotland, by contrast, four universities had been in existence for many centuries: Aberdeen, Edinburgh, Glasgow, and St. Andrews. This situation, however, was about to change. Over the next four decades, a massive expansion in higher education occurred in England. Sanderson estimates that the number of day students in English universities and university colleges increased from 770 in 1880 to 4,298 in 1913; a further increase occurred in the number of degree-seeking students (Sanderson 1972: 96). This expansion was driven largely by the needs of business and industry.

The establishment of Yorkshire College, later to evolve into the University of Leeds, is a good example. Following an open meeting in Leeds in 1869, a committee was formed "to investigate, consider and propose the best means to be adopted for the establishment of a Yorkshire College of Science." The committee stated in 1872 that "The Yorkshire College of Science is intended to supply an urgent and recognized want, viz., instruction in those sciences which are applicable to the Industrial Arts, especially those which may be classed under Engineering, Manufacture, Agriculture, Mining and Metallurgy. It is designed for the use of persons who will afterwards be engaged in those trades as foremen, managers or employers; and also for the training of teachers of technical science." The report went on to explain the university's plans to educate a cadre of well-trained industrial scientists as well as teachers of industrial science. "The chief work of the College should be the supply of the highest standard of instruction in Chemistry, Mining and Metallurgy, and Civil and Mechanical Engineering to students who have matriculated after an examination, and who are over the age of sixteen years. The College should also provide for the education of teachers to be employed in the ordinary science schools and classes of Yorkshire. In addition thereto evening classes should be formed in the College and in the principal towns for young men engaged in daily labour, on the same system as the evening classes at Owens College, Manchester, and Kings College, London." Two years later, in 1874, Yorkshire College opened.

The new universities and university colleges emerging in the second half of the nineteenth century were intimately connected with local business and industry. Their whole *raison d'être* was to meet the needs of business, and it was local business that was principally responsible for raising the funds to meet the costs of these new institutions. The first stage in their development was to raise a capital sum, normally through bequests, donations, and annual subscriptions. Owens College in Manchester led the way. John Owens, a wealthy Manchester merchant, died in 1846 and left a bequest of £100,000 to set up a college "to teach such learning and sciences as were usual in universities." Owens College opened in 1851, but, for 20 years, its growth was slow. According to one observer, the college, "having no precedents to follow,... tried to adopt the liberal arts education of the ancient universities rather than matching its education to the needs of the city." However, in the late 1860s, encouraged by the economic boom of the period and stimulated by the efforts of Henry Roscoe, a chemist, and Thomas Ashton, a cotton manufacturer—both of whom had been students in Heidelberg in Germany—a capital fund of over £200,000 was raised. Owens College thereafter moved to new premises in 1873.

The importance of local business was clearly evident from the occupations of those subscribing between £300 and £1,000 in the Owens College capital campaign. The first life governors of the college included 17 men from business and four men from the professions (Sanderson 1972: 62–63). A list of donor occupations identified 27 cotton merchants or manufacturers, 4 engineers, 4 calico printers, 3 gentry, 1 tea dealer, 1 publisher, 1 wire manufacturer, 1 blockmaker,

1 banker, 1 drysalter, 1 card manufacturer, and 1 warehouseman. Clearly, men from business and industry were closely involved in the establishment and funding of the new college.

A similar picture of industry aid emerged in Liverpool. Led by the Rathbone family, prominent merchants in the city, and the Muspratts, leaders in the chemical industry, £100,000 was raised to establish a University College, incorporated in 1881. Over the next three decades, funding from business and industry continued to flow into the college. In 1888, Sir Henry Tate (from the family that founded Tate and Lyle, sugar refiners) gave £16,000 for the library, and in 1889, Sir Andrew Walker, a local brewer, funded the engineering laboratories. Further support came to the institution both as part of the federal Victoria University (with Owens College and Yorkshire College) and, from 1903, as an independent University of Liverpool. In part, these business owners were motivated by philanthropic aims; in part, they were motivated by civic pride. However, the funding also represented sound business decisions, based on the added value the university could offer to manufacturing and trade. Thus, when ship owners T. Fenwick Harrison, J. W. Hughes, and Heath Harrison gave £35,000 to the University of Liverpool for new engineering laboratories in 1910, they noted that "as ship owners who use three thousand tons of coal a year they see the advantages to be derived from the internal combustion engine so far as ships are concerned" (Sanderson 1972: 65). Not surprisingly, research and development on ships' engines became a noted specialization of the Liverpool laboratories; for the ship owners, this was a business investment, intended to provide a competitive advantage—not unlike the objectives of the UK government a century later.

Industry funding also brought with it greater participation within university governance. These donors were clearly active in running the new university. For example, Henry Stephenson, the wealthy owner of a company of typefounders in Sheffield, was one of 18 trustees of the new Firth College in Sheffield. A major benefactor of the new college that opened in 1880, Henry Stephenson was also "one of the most important members of the governing bodies, and gave generously of his time, seldom missing even the dullest and seemingly least important committee meetings. To the affairs of the client institutions he brought an unusual clarity of thought and a massive common sense that welcomed every practicable development but withered fanciful or half-baked schemes" (Chapman 1955: 19).

Teaching in the new universities reflected the needs and expectations of their sponsors in business and industry. From the start,

Yorkshire College aimed to meet these expectations. In 1874–1875, both day courses and evening courses were offered, reflecting the schedules of the regions' chief industries. It was noted that "the majority of... students were persons connected with the management of collieries, iron works and machine shops in and around Leeds, Bradford and Wakefield." Leeds and West Yorkshire were major centers of textile manufacturing. In 1874–1875, the first year of Yorkshire College, the department of textile industries registered 7 day students and 20 evening students. According to publicity materials, the new institution was meeting a real need: "It is evident that this attempt at technical instruction has excited much public sympathy and that there is a widespread feeling that such instruction is wanted by manufacturers. The students who attended the four lectures that were given represented many of the leading firms of the district" (Yorkshire College, AR, 1874–1875). A year later, in 1875–1876, the university received the following testimonial: "At the close of the session, the Evening Class presented Mr. Beaumont with a testimonial expression of their appreciations of his method of teaching and his willingness at all times to impart information to his students. Their spokesman said that the fee had been a most profitable investment to himself, and whilst he was unable before entering the class to design any kind of cloth, yet he had now produced eighty designs of his own, which had received Mr Beaumont's approval, as had the cloth made from them" (ibid.).

Placing the applied arts on par with traditional academic subjects, the new universities and colleges drew on local industries for their curricula. Referring to Firth College, Sheffield, it was stated that "The first object of a college in the center of a great industrial population was that it should lay hold of the life of the industrial part of the people; that its education should start from the midst of their daily occupations, teaching them things which would help them in these occupations" (Sanderson 1972: 81). By the late 1880s, the new colleges had expanded their activities. In 1886–1887, Yorkshire College offered the following subjects: textile industries and dyeing, mathematics, physics, chemistry, geology, coal mining, biology, engineering, classics, modern literature and history, French, German, and Oriental languages. The college enrolled 370 registered students, 168 occasional students, 103 trained teachers, and 331 evening-class students. Clearly, the institution was thriving.

Links with business and industry went much deeper than curricular subjects. The students were studying courses intended to meet the needs of the local employers, and most of them were also drawn from the families of these same business owners. At Leeds, it was noted that "generally the students attending the day classes are the sons of manufacturers, managers and designers, but the evening classes are chiefly attended by artisans." In textiles, most of the day students were the sons of masters and entered their fathers' works on leaving college (Sanderson 1972: 98). Of the 270 students registered at Birmingham in the 1880s, parent backgrounds were listed as follows:

(i) *Professional (99)*
3 accountants, 2 army, 4 auctioneers, 1 almoner, 1 bailiff, 1 factor, 6 agents, 1 art director, 1 town clerk, 1 bank manager, 1 consulting brewer, 8 clergy, 5 government inspectors, 7 civil engineers, 3 doctors, 1 dentist, 15 managers, 1 organist, 4 professors, 1 physician, 9 solicitors, 16 schoolmasters, 3 surveyors, 4 surgeons.

(ii) *Manufacturers and merchants in large or expensive trades (45)*
1 basket manufacturer, 1 cycle manufacturer, 11 builders, 2 chandelier makers, 4 manufacturing chemists, 1 contractor, 3 paper makers, 1 flour merchant, 1 diamond merchant, 1 farmer, 1 hat manufacturer, 1 iron founder, 3 iron masters, 1 iron merchant, 10 manufacturers, 2 safety pin manufacturers, 1 wire merchant.

(iii) *Trades and special skills (56)*
1 butcher, 2 booksellers, 3 blacksmiths, 3 bakers, 1 cabinet maker, 2 confectioners, 7 grocers, 2 clothiers, 2 china gilders, 7 drapers, 1 decorator, 1 engineer, 1 goldsmith, 1 goldbeater, 7 jewellers, 1 mountmaker, 2 millers, 1 pawnbroker, 1 photographer, 1 silversmith, 1 tea dealer, 2 tailors, 1 tobacconist, 1 toolmaker, 2 watch makers, 1 beer dealer, 1 boiler inspector.

(iv) *Semi-professional white collar literacy-using occupations (35)*
3 bookkeepers, 16 clerks, 8 commercial travellers, 3 cashiers, 1 journalist, 1 printer's reader, 2 secretaries, 1 verger.

(v) *Artisans (35)*
1 engine driver, 14 engineers, 3 foremen, 1 gardener, 1 grazier, 2 gas engineers, 2 wire drawers, 2 joiners, 1 mechanic, 1 machinist, 1 miner, 1 metal worker, 1 packer, 1 quarryman, 2 turners, 1 weigher. (Sanderson 1972: 98–99)

This evidence demonstrates that the college drew the overwhelming majority of its students from families based in business and industry.

The local roots of the universities were strong. These roots were further strengthened by regular and well-attended public lectures. The professors from Yorkshire College regularly gave lectures across the West Riding, especially in Wakefield, Bradford, and Halifax. Lectures in the Leeds Philosophical Hall were commonly attended by 300 to 400 individuals (Yorkshire College, AR 1886–1887).

Close local links were apparent across all industrial activities in the West Riding, and Yorkshire College was able to make a real impact. In 1911–1912, for example, the teaching delivered by the Yorkshire College department of mining was revised to cover the key issues facing local mines. Responding to a demand for information about different forms of power transmission, the department developed a series of new programs covering the use of compressed air, gas engines, steam engines, and electrical power. The changes were successful, the college reported: "as a result of these changes, it is found that the students take a far keener interest in their work than was previously the case." The department also responded to other demands from industry. Following the Coal Mines Act of 1911, public lectures were given across the West Riding; very rapidly, over 30 teachers were trained by the university and were acting as instructors in the mines.

The textiles industries of Leeds also clearly valued their links with Yorkshire College. A number of graduates went on to leadership positions in local mills. As the *Yorkshire Post* reported, "When one compares the character of the trade of Leeds and the district of two decades ago with what it is at the present day and considers that many of the most important mills in the locality are supervised by Yorkshire College men, it becomes evident that the instruction imparted in that institution has in no small degree benefited the weaving industries of the city and neighbourhood. There has been a complete change in the classes and style of fabrics made in the district since the textile departments of the college commenced work. Some years ago Leeds was noted for its production of plain textures: now fancy fabrics both of woollen and worsted materials in very extensive varieties are made in the neighbourhood" (*Yorkshire Daily Post* September 19, 1894, quoted in Sanderson 1972: 86). Lists of registered students demonstrated the dominance of local links in student recruitment. At the same time, these lists show that "the local" could also have a global reach, as students came to the university not only from Yorkshire but from across the European continent, from Britain's colonial periphery, and from around the world. The localities of registered students in the University of Leeds in 1911–1912 are shown in table 9.1. Similarly, in 1904–1905, a register of 517 evening students in the University of Leeds showed 426 students from Leeds and the West Riding of Yorkshire; of these 517 students, 447 were men and 70 were women.

Clearly, links with business and industry, especially from the immediate region, were central to the development of universities in the period from 1870 to 1914. By 1914, colleges were well established

Table 9.1 Localities of registered students in the University of Leeds

	Arts, Science, Technology	Medicine
Leeds*	189	70
Bradford*	41	20
Halifax*	9	12
Huddersfield*	10	1
Hull	2	2
York	25	4
West Riding*	353	44
East Riding	30	3
North Riding	23	3
Other England	70	2
Scotland	1	–
Ireland	6	–
Egypt	8	–
India	8	4
Africa	1	–
Australia	3	–
China	6	–
France	5	–
Germany	4	1
Russia	3	–
USA	1	–
Sweden	2	–
Bulgaria	1	–
Italy	2	–
Austria	2	–

* Leeds and its immediate region.
Source: University of Leeds Annual Report, 1911–1912. Archives of the University of Leeds.

in Manchester, Birmingham, Leeds, Liverpool, Newcastle, Bristol, Nottingham, Sheffield, Reading, and Southampton. In various ways, these colleges played a significant role in meeting the needs of business and industry for skilled workers. In most cases, the need for technical education and training had been a primary motive behind the establishment of each university. Yet, by the end of the period, the value of research and knowledge creation began to grow in prominence. In Sheffield, the department of metallurgy contributed directly to the competitive advantage of local industry; for example, the results of research on high-speed steels were shared with Sheffield companies. Meanwhile, in the department of leather industries at the University of Leeds, work on sodium thiosulphate and the chemistry of the two-bath chrome process applied "the most modern chemical ideas to the practical and successful solution of problems which have long troubled the leather manufacturer, and some of the suggestions have already found profitable application in the industry" (University of Leeds, AR, 1911–1912). Between 1870 and 1914, higher education in the industrial cities of the United Kingdom, and especially in England, was transformed. At the heart of this expansion was the bond between universities, business, and industry. What, therefore, if anything, can higher education today learn from experiences a century or more ago?

SOME REFLECTIONS

It is clearly difficult to draw any direct comparisons between the world of higher education and business and industry in the late nineteenth and early twentieth centuries and the world of the early twenty-first century. Globalization, technological change, population growth, and massive social, economic, and political changes have all transformed the context within which the relationship between universities and business and industry exists. Nevertheless, some interesting observations arise based upon the experience of universities in the period 1870–1914. This concluding section offers eight observations that may hold lessons for higher-education leaders today.

First, the new universities that emerged in England in the late nineteenth century maintained a wide portfolio of courses, including part-time classes, evening classes, and weekend classes, as well as degree programs. Moreover, academic staff were often expected to offer public lectures and occasional classes. Such courses obviously met a need among local employers. While some universities today run similar programs, they are less common in leading research-led universities. The question might be raised: have leading research-oriented institutions become too fixed on the needs of the residential, full-time student, at the expense of other, more flexible, and accessible forms of educational delivery? How might today's research universities reach out to broader constituencies in diverse ways, thus expanding their range of stakeholders?

Second, universities before the end of the nineteenth century were, in effect, heavily engaged in continuing professional development. While there were exceptions, both by institution and by discipline, continuing professional development was an important component of universities' work. Yet, these activities diminished in UK universities during the 1980s and 1990s, often seen as "low level" work and/or uneconomic. Interestingly, there are signs that many major research-led universities are now returning to continuing professional development as both a form of high-level knowledge exchange and as a valuable source of increased income. Continuing professional development is not only worthwhile for staff but can also provide the basis for long-term relationships with partners in business and industry, similar in principle to some of the links forged by universities a century ago.

Third, new universities developing in the major industrial cities at the end of the nineteenth century were deeply rooted in their communities. They were funded by local people—not only by large donations, but also by ongoing subscriptions. Local authorities were influential in the establishment and development of universities in their cities and also funded scholarships for local people to attend courses. Most students were drawn from the immediate region; local business leaders were heavily involved in the governance and leadership of institutions; and universities were a source of civic pride (and civic competition). Today, many universities are strongly committed to working in their regions; the economic importance of universities in terms of local and regional income generation is often emphasized. Yet, at the same time, many universities have a "love-hate" relationship with their local authorities, sometimes complicated by planning issues or difficulties over numbers of students distorting the balance of local communities. Universities, sensitive to their autonomy, are also wary of any sense of "external" control or even influence. If universities are to respond more effectively to the needs of local employers and local industry and business, local connections may need to be strengthened in the modern university. It must be stressed that universities are often at the heart of regional economic success or are central to economic regeneration. It is less clear that involvement in their local communities is central to the day-to-day life of all academic staff and professors, as would have been the case in the late nineteenth century, or that the local university is the obvious choice for local people seeking personal advancement or local employers looking for enhancement of skills and knowledge. Local funding, local governance, and local student recruitment cemented the relationships between universities and business and industry before World War I. For some universities today, and for some academic staff, the emphasis is on global links and prestige, sometimes at the expense of local roots. Yet, if links with business are to flourish, local, regional, national, and international priorities need to be fused together.

Fourth, the relationship between universities and business and industry at the end of the nineteenth century was broadly based, embracing teaching (both basic and advanced), research (especially applied), professional development, and consulting. What would now be referred to as technology transfer was just one of the touchpoints of university-business partnerships and not necessarily the most important for either universities or businesses. By contrast, it can be argued that, in the 1990s and into the twenty-first century, universities became preoccupied with technology transfer, along with patents and licensing and the search for spin-out companies—possibly at the expense of wider, more deeply integrated relationships. The report of the Council for Industry and Higher Education and the Center for Business Research (2008), which called for a broadly based approach to links between universities and local businesses, may almost be seen as a call for a return to a practice that was commonplace a century ago.

Fifth, with close working relationships went a professional intimacy that enabled universities in the late nineteenth century to respond quickly to the needs of industry. Contacts were personal and based on mutual understanding; many academic staff, especially in science and technology, had worked in business and industry. These nineteenth-century universities would have been unfamiliar with many of the problems of communications that beset links between higher education and industry today; a century ago, there simply was no need for the "first point of contact" or the industrial liaison offices that now encourage and filter links between institutions and business.

Sixth, the scale of academic work in the late nineteenth century fostered local connections. Of course, the world of higher education today has changed hugely from a century ago. One area of change has been the rapid intensification of national and international competition and marketization, both in business and in higher education, and a related preoccupation with university comparisons and rankings. While the idea of competition in itself would not have been unfamiliar in the late nineteenth century, formal rankings and league tables—and the grossly distorting impact they have on the management and delivery of teaching and research—were not yet a feature of higher education. In the late nineteenth century, universities and their staff could focus on meeting the needs of their students and wider stakeholders. Yet, at the same time, the questions of status that are familiar today were certainly present in the late nineteenth century. Many new universities struggled initially to carve out and accept a different identity from the classical universities, and the teaching of the arts and humanities alongside science, technology, and medicine often created tensions. Owens College initially offered a broad range of subjects while Leeds and Sheffield, by contrast, were proud of their emphasis on technology. In Leeds, one of the founders of Yorkshire College, Sir Andrew Fairburn, believed the college should confine itself to industrial science both because the arts were of no practical use and because he thought greater attention to the arts might deter manual workers from attending (Sanderson 1972: 10). However, it soon became clear that a balanced range of subjects was essential to "university" status, and from 1889 this balance was a precondition for the receipt of public funding. Universities or university colleges were expected to be more than technical colleges. Questions of status were real, as illustrated by the comment of an Oxford academic who reflected on the qualifications of a graduate of one of the new universities in 1914: "He gets degrees in making jam, at Liverpool and Birmingham" (95). Here, perhaps, is an area of continuity over the intervening century. As today, some would have been proud to be the target of this comment; others would have been horrified.

Seventh, the changes in higher education in the period 1870–1914 throw some light on today's theories concerning the links between universities and business and industry. The idea of the Triple Helix involving not only universities and industry but also government was very remote in the late nineteenth century. National government is noticeable by its absence from the relationship between universities and business; there was no use of incentive schemes or national steering and regulation. One might ask whether, on balance, the steady growth of government involvement has helped or hindered links between universities and business. Along similar lines, the shift from Mode 1 to Mode 2 research, with an emphasis on applied research delivered by the needs of "customers" and often undertaken in association with business and industry, is often presented as a recent change in higher education. However, it is apparent that Mode 2 research is nothing new; on the contrary, it was central to the new universities emerging in the late nineteenth century. Thus, recent trends in higher education, often promoted by government or government agencies, may be seen as a *return* to Mode 2, not as a radical new development.

Finally, at a time when there is much debate on the funding of higher education and the role of the public university, it is important to note that the universities that developed in the years before World War I were almost wholly privately funded, from donations, subscriptions, "contracts" for particular purposes, and student fees.

Government grants for higher education began in 1889 and were allocated by a formula that reflected levels of local support, but these grants remained a small element within higher-education resource management. Universities in the late nineteenth and early twentieth centuries were continuously engaged in fundraising. For example, when Firth College opened in Sheffield in 1880, the first principal, A. T. Bentley, warned the city: "I can assure the people of Sheffield that they have not heard the last of our requisitions for money by a very long way.... We propose to charge [modest] fees which shall bring our instruction within the reach of all, and it is impossible with such fees that an institution like this should be self-supporting" (Chapman 1955: 25). The search for private funding for universities in the United Kingdom is nothing new. At the end of the nineteenth century, in the absence of large-scale government support from taxation, fiscal necessity was one factor that ensured a close working relationship between universities and business and industry. While the context of higher education has evolved, especially in terms of mass participation and ideas of individual self-fulfilment, the needs of the economy for an educated workforce continue to underpin public funding of higher education. With such funding increasingly under pressure, both higher education *and* business interests today have much to learn from the financial models of a century ago based on fundraising and fees. Links between universities and business and industry were at the heart of these financial models.

Here, therefore, are some reflections on how universities today, in tackling their problems and challenges, and, in particular, in looking to build their links with business and industry, can learn from their predecessors of a century ago. The history of higher education in the United Kingdom remains underresearched. We have much to learn.

Bibliography

Chapman, A. W. (1955) *The Story of a Modern University. A History of the University of Sheffield*. Oxford: Oxford University Press.

CIHE (Council for Industry and Higher Education) (2008) *Universities, Business and Knowledge Exchange*. London.

DTI (1999) *U.K. Competitiveness Indicators, 1999*. London: DTI.

Etzkowitz, H. (2008) *The Triple Helix: University-Industry-Government Innovation in Action*. London: Routledge.

Gibbons, M., C. Limoges, H. Nowotny, S. Schwartzman, P. Scott, M. and Trow (1994) *The New Production of Knowledge: The Dynamics of Science and Research in Contemporary Societies*. London: Sage.

Gosden, P. H. J. H. and A. J. Taylor (1975) *Studies in the History of a University 1874–1974*. Leeds: E. J. Arnold.

HEFCE (2008) *Industry-Academic Links in the UK, HEFCE Ref 98/70, Higher Education Funding Council for England*. Bristol: HEFCE.

—— (2010a) *Higher Education—Business and Community Interaction Survey: 2008–09*. Bristol: HEFCE, No. 14.

—— (2010b) www.hefce.ac.uk/news/hefce/2010/hebci.htm (accessed July 3, 2010).

Sanderson M. (1972) *The Universities and British Industry 1850–1970*. London: Routledge and Kegan Paul.

Shattock, M. (2003) *Managing Successful Universities*. Maidenhead: Open University Press.

UK Government (2008) *Higher Education at Work—High Skills: High Value, Department of Business, Innovation and Skills*.

University of Birmingham (2010) www.industry.bham.ac.uk (accessed July 12, 2010).

University of Exeter (2007) *Strategic Plan 2007–11*. Exeter: University of Exeter, UoL University of Leeds Archives.

CHAPTER 10

Universities and the Effects of External Funding: Sub-Saharan Africa and the Nordic Countries

Peter Maassen

INTRODUCTION

There has been a growing policy focus in OECD countries on the university's contributions to innovation and economic development. The main assumption underlying this focus, in simplified form, is that more complex and competitive economic and technological global environments require rapid adaptation to shifting opportunities and constraints. The university is expected to play a central role in this adaptation, since, as the main knowledge institution in any society, it is assumed to link research and education effectively to innovation. This expectation has been the underlying rationale for reforms aimed at stimulating universities to develop more determined institutional strategies and a strong, unitary, and professional leadership and management capacity that matches those of modern private enterprises. At the same time, higher-education policies have increasingly become coordinated with other policy areas, such as innovation and technology, as part of national (and supranational) knowledge and innovation policies (Braun, 2008: 234). In addition, other public and private actors have entered the higher-education policy arena, demanding to have influence in university policy matters. The underlying vision is to create a university that is dynamic and responsive to socioeconomic agendas and that gives priority to innovation, entrepreneurship, and competitiveness.

In developing countries, and especially in sub-Saharan Africa, there are different forces and policy arguments driving university dynamics. Here, the university is positioned in an international development policy arena, where the dominant actors are operating in policy frameworks codetermined by ministries of foreign affairs and development cooperation agencies. The development mission of the university is linked to poverty reduction and community support more than economic competitiveness, entrepreneurship, and innovation. What are the consequences of these different policy frameworks for African universities? How do they shape the ways in which African universities are expected to contribute to economic development?

One of the aims of the Higher Education Research and Advocacy Network in Africa (HERANA) is to foster a better understanding of the factors that influence the development of African universities, especially in relation to the long-term economic development of their countries. Traditionally, the productivity of African universities is presumed to have been hampered by a number of factors, such as lack of funding, lack of research infrastructure, and lack of qualified staff. The HERANA project has not taken these presumptions as given but has, instead, conducted detailed empirical analyses of the dynamics of a number of African flagship universities and their socioeconomic and political contexts. This chapter focuses on one of the factors identified in the HERANA project as possibly affecting the development of research functions in African flagship universities, namely, the external, or noninstitutional, funding of projects coordinated and implemented by university staff.

BACKGROUND

While in many developing countries—and in many emerging economies such as those of the so-called BRIC nations (Brazil, Russia, India, and China)—universities and university systems have gone through far-reaching quantitative and qualitative changes in the past 10–15 years, universities in sub-Saharan Africa seem to be lagging behind. The rapid transformation of universities is, for example, discussed in Altbach and Balán's work, *World-Class Worldwide* (2007), which focuses on the transformation of research universities in Asia and Latin America. Altbach and Balán have not included Africa in their analysis, because, they write, "We believe that Africa's academic challenges are sufficiently different from those of the nations represented here that comparison would not be appropriate" (Altbach and

Balán 2007: vii). Strikingly, the authors do not provide any arguments or data for this claim.

To get a better conceptual understanding of the challenges facing African universities we turn to Manuel Castells (2001), who has distinguished four major functions of universities, the specific nature and importance of which differs from society to society and over time. According to Castells (206–212), universities are core institutions (1) in the formation and diffusion of ideology, (2) in the selection of dominant elites, (3) in the generation of new knowledge, and (4) in the training of the bureaucracy. In discussing how these functions are performed by universities in developing countries, Castells points first to the fact that nearly all "Third World universities" are "rooted in a colonial past" (212). After the colonial period these universities were focused mainly on Castell's first two functions, that is, the formation of ideology and the selection of (national) elites. Recently, the fourth function—training—has become more important, with especially Asian universities increasing enrollment at an unprecedented rate. African universities have also grown, but much more moderately than their counterparts in the rest of the world, and mainly at the lower degree or diploma level. The participation rate in sub-Saharan African higher education is still much lower than in the rest of the world, averaging around 5 percent, with only two countries having participation rates over 10 percent (i.e., Mauritius and South Africa).[1] According to Castells (214), much of the growth in student numbers in Africa has taken place in traditional fields such as law, humanities, and social sciences rather than in science and technology (see also Kapur and Crowley 2008).

In most of sub-Saharan Africa, Castell's third category, the "generation of new knowledge," is argued to be the major area of underperformance in the sense that the research function of universities is weakly developed. Sub-Saharan Africa contributes around 0.7 percent to world scientific output, and this figure has *decreased* over the past 15–20 years (French Academy of Sciences 2006). Castells (215–217) presents a number of structural and institutional reasons that might explain this lack of progress in research. The structural reasons include low funding levels and "the cumulative character of the process of uneven scientific development," leading, among other things, to a lack of centers of excellence that are at the cutting edge of a specific area of specialization. Consequently, the academic environment in African universities is not attractive for talented national scholars, who move to overseas universities, especially in North America and Europe, where they find more appealing academic environments. Yet, the main institutional reason for a lack of progress in research is said to be the difficulties that African universities have in managing contradictory functions, that is, managing academic activities alongside political and ideological functions.

This chapter reviews the conditions under which modern universities are assumed to contribute to economic development. To do so, it compares some important elements of the "African university" with analogous elements of the "Nordic university." The Nordic region consists of Denmark, Finland, Norway, Sweden, Iceland, and the autonomous territories of Greenland, the Faroe Islands, and Åland. In size a large region (1.35 million square kilometres, excluding Greenland), in population a small region (around 25 million inhabitants), it scores well on all kinds of global (country-based) indices in the areas of knowledge economy and innovation.[2] Economically, the region's combined GDP ranks among the ten largest economies in the world. From a social and health perspective, the region has (together with Japan) the highest life-expectancy rates for females and males, as well as the highest levels of social and economic equality. From a higher-education and basic research perspective, the Nordic countries' higher-education participation rates are among the highest in the world (ranging from 50 to 70 percent), while (together with Switzerland) the region produces the highest number of scientific articles per capita. The impact of the region's scientific output is also among the highest in the world.[3] Additional higher-education indicators include the number of Nordic universities in the 2009 top 100 (7) and top 500 (24, or around 50 percent of all Nordic universities) of the Academic Ranking of World Universities,[4] as well as the success of Nordic researchers in applying for EU research funding in the seventh Framework Program (FP7).[5] In general, one can say that it is one of the most effective and successful regions in the world, with a high level of regional integration, sociopolitically, economically (including one labor market), culturally, and also academically, in the sense that the region has an open higher-education system agreed upon *before* the signing in 1999 of the Bologna Declaration and its aim of creating a European Higher Education Area (EHEA).

By comparing the Nordic university with the African university, this chapter reveals some of the structural elements that either help or hinder universities' ability to contribute to economic development, both nationally and regionally. This comparison involves three dimensions. First, the chapter compares the nature of the "pact" between higher education and society in the Nordic region and sub-Saharan Africa. Second, it compares the "academic core" of universities in both regions. Third, it compares the nature and impact of external research funding in both Nordic and African flagship universities. Comparisons are based on a study of university developments in the four main Nordic countries (Denmark, Finland, Norway, and Sweden) and in the flagship universities of six African countries (Botswana, Ghana, Kenya, Mauritius, Tanzania, and Uganda). It is important to emphasize that this chapter does not analyze the contributions of universities to economic development as such; rather, it explores the structural conditions under which such contributions can be expected to be made.

ANALYTICAL FRAMEWORK

This chapter begins with the premise that three interrelated factors shape the conditions under which a university might be expected to contribute to economic development. These three factors are: (1) the nature of the pact between universities, political authorities, and society at large; (2) the nature, size, and continuity of the university's academic core; and (3) the nature, management, and institutionalization of externally funded research projects at universities. These three factors are, in turn, influenced by local circumstances, for example, the nature of a country's economy, its political and governance traditions, its institutional characteristics (e.g., the "loosely coupled" nature of its higher-education institutions), and the external relations of its universities, especially with national authorities, foreign agencies, and industry.

The Nature and Role of the Pact between the University and Society

A pact can be defined as a long-term cultural, socioeconomic, and political understanding of the purpose or mission of universities; it lays out what is expected of universities and what the rules and values of the universities are (Gornitzka et al. 2007: 184). A pact is different from a contract based on continuous strategic calculation of expected value by public authorities, organized external groups, university employees, and students—all regularly monitoring and assessing the university on the basis of its usefulness for their self-interest. Rather, a pact is more stable, more implicit, and more fluid. In this chapter, the key actors involved in the pact between universities and society include national stakeholders (ministries, government agencies, and employer organizations), higher-education leaders (vice-chancellors, deans, and senior administrators), and external partners (especially funders, employers' organizations, interest organizations and unions). The relationships between each of these groups can affect the degree of consensus around a pact and the nature of the pact itself.

A key aspect of the maintenance of the pact—and the renegotiation of the pact when necessary—is the governance and coordination of relationships between various actors. At the broadest level, in a strong pact one will find effective communication, cooperation, consultation, and consensus between national authorities, institutional leaders, and external actors. This cooperation represents a coherent link between national authorities and institutional leaders. A strong pact will also show horizontal coordination between various policy areas, for example, science, technology, and higher education. In the European context, the role of research councils is important in maintaining this coordination, as are relationships between universities and the private sector. In the African context, by contrast, the role and influence of foreign donors is of particular importance. In terms of governance and coordination, the question is: to what extent do external actors contribute to the creation of a stable and institutionalized environment for the university, and in particular for the university's academic core? (Cossa 2008).[6]

The Nature and Role of the Academic Knowledge Core

The strength of the pact between the university and society influences the nature, strength, size, composition, and stability of the university's academic core, which, in turn, forms the basis for all the university's educational and research activities. The stronger and more extensive its academic core, the easier it will be for a university to defend its service to society, its institutional identity, and thus its own integrity against external or internal threats. The academic core is in the first place linked to academic degree programs and basic research activities. Clark (1983) has argued that

> Knowledge is the basic substance upon which and with which people work in academic systems; teaching and research are the basic activities for fashioning and manipulating this material; these tasks divide into autonomous specialties within which they are closely linked; the task divisions encourage a flat and loosely linked arrangement of work units; this structure promotes a diffusion of control; and, finally, purpose is necessarily ambiguous, with broadly worked goals

serving as legitimating doctrine for the specific goals of operating parts. (25)

In short, the academic core contains the institutional essence of and provides the organizational building blocks for the university. As such it represents the foundation for the university's status, continuity, and stability. Consequently, when it comes to externally funded academic activities, it is important to examine whether these activities contribute to maintaining, enlarging, and strengthening, or to weakening, the university's academic core.

The Nature and Role of Externally Funded Projects in Universities

We turn our attention now to the effects of external funders on university dynamics. By "funders" we mean a range of public agencies and private foundations that contribute directly to the functioning of higher-education institutions by funding projects implemented by university academic staff (Cossa 2008). These funders include national and supranational research councils, international agencies such as the World Bank, national development agencies, not-for-profit foundations, and private enterprises that fund research and consultancy activities. To understand the role of external funders in the management and governance of modern universities, we will start by discussing the well-known concept of loose coupling in university organization.

Traditionally, university staff have enjoyed a much higher degree of discretion than is enjoyed by staff in other public organizations that are subject to direct lines of command, such as the military, tax authorities, or national social-security services (Kogan and Hanney 2000: 22–24). As a result, the means of control over university activities are less directly hierarchical and more based on competition and mutuality than in many other public policy areas (Hood et al. 2004). In the 1970s, Weick (1976) noted that people in universities generally do not work through organized procedures passed down from leadership/management or technical experts. Even when things do occur through hierarchical leadership and planning, those inside the university do not feel that these rational practices explain much of what goes on inside their institution (1). In universities, Weick found, the administration was not the main source of expertise or decision making; rather, administrators and academic staff tended to have different roles, independent authority, low levels of standardization, and even different agendas. The name he assigned to the operational links within such a structure was *loose coupling*.

Loose coupling has positive and negative dimensions. Whether aspects of loose coupling are regarded as positive or negative depends on context. In general, as Bleiklie notes in his chapter in this volume, one can argue that many of the characteristics of the university as a loosely coupled organization have been seen (until recently) as positive in OECD countries. The university as a loosely coupled organization has functioned well in these countries because of the strength of the pact between university and society. Operating in a strongly institutionalized environment, OECD universities have been able to depend on (relatively) stable public funding streams.[7] University leaders, therefore, had—at least in theory—both the capacity and the time for "luxury" activities, such as strategic vision development, since they did not have to spend all their time on securing their institution's survival. As long as the public budget and allocation mechanisms were relatively stable and student demand was at least as large as institutional capacity, and as long as the legal framework surrounding the institution adapted to incremental changes in a piecemeal way, then it was presumed that a university would function optimally as a loosely coupled organization. Only recently, as Bleiklie notes, has this organizational arrangement begun to shift.

By contrast, universities in societies with a weak pact between the university and society have to operate in weakly institutionalized environments, without stable public funding arrangements. A large part of the leadership capacity has to be used for budget negotiations, and substantial annual budgetary swings are common.[8] In such circumstances, academic staff can be expected to turn to other sources of funding without the central university leadership being able to influence the details of these alternative funding relationships. In the case of universities in developing countries, these alternative funding relationships come from the relationships of individual academics (and their units) with external donor agencies. While loose coupling in the context of consistent and structural interconnectedness can make universities very effective and responsive organizations, loose coupling *without* coordination or integration can make universities vulnerable to fragmentation, insulated silos, and organizational paralysis.

Propositions and Assumptions

The influence of the abovementioned factors on universities' contributions to development can be expressed in terms of three propositions and assumptions.

Proposition 1: The stronger and more stable the pact between universities, university leadership, national authorities, and society at large, the better the universities will be able to make a significant, sustained contribution to economic development.

Assumption 1a: The development and maintenance of the pact between universities and society relies on effective governance, effective leadership, and coordination between key actors, as well as an understanding about the role of the university in development.

Proposition 2: The weaker the institutionalization of externally funded projects, the weaker the contribution of these projects to strengthening the academic core of the university.

Assumption 2a: With weakly institutionalized externally funded projects, the institution has a limited capacity to make a sustainable impact on development.

Assumption 2b: Universities make a more significant and sustained contribution to development when their development-related activities contribute to strengthening the academic core of the institution.

Proposition 3: All universities are loosely coupled organizations, implying that academic activities are driven internally.

Assumption 3a: Under ideal circumstances, loose coupling is a strength of the university, but in cases of a weak pact and a small and weakly institutionalized academic core, loose coupling can lead to institutional fragmentation.

4. DISCUSSION[9]

The Pact between the University and Society

In discussing the nature of the pact between the university and society in the Nordic and African countries, we will address the following indicators: (1) the nature of the national development framework in both regions; (2) the role of national ministries of education; and (3) the consistency of university funding.

National Development Frameworks

With respect to the clarity, consistency, and relevance of national frameworks for development, there is a clear intercountry variety both *within* the Nordic region and *between* the Nordic countries and the six African countries examined in the HERANA study. In the Nordic region, the most explicit national framework has been developed by Denmark in the form of its globalization strategy. The strong focus of this strategy on the importance of knowledge as a foundation for economic development has put Denmark's universities (and colleges) in a more central position in the economic policy arena. The main consequences of this strong framework are, first, a reform process aimed at changing the Danish university landscape drastically, including expectations of clearer strategic profiling of the universities and a more direct relationship between universities and the private sector, and second, a sharp increase in public funding invested in university research.

Finland, too, in the 1990s instituted a national development framework called the national information society program. It aimed to make Finland one of the world's leading Information and Communications Technology countries (Hölttä and Malkki 2000). This program has played a very important role as a framework for the Finnish national knowledge and innovation policy. Unlike the Danish globalization strategy, however, Finland's national information society program lacked an earmarked budget for university research, though it did have an effect on the funding decisions and programs of the government (and the national academy of sciences) in the areas of science and technology, as well as the life sciences.

Sweden and Norway do not have specific national development frameworks as do Denmark or Finland. In Sweden there is a political agreement on the importance of investing a relatively large part of the public GDP in academic research. As a consequence, Sweden is among the top three countries worldwide in terms of public GDP invested in research. Of the four Nordic countries Norway is the one with the least explicit knowledge-policy framework. A recent national commission on higher education even concluded that Norwegian politics had abdicated its role in higher education and research policy (NOU 2008). In practice, this implies that the national research council plays a more important role than government in determining national development frameworks, at least when it comes to investments in research. (Also important in understanding the Norwegian case is the role of regional policies in the country's development.)

Two of the six African countries in our study, Botswana and Mauritius, have begun to discuss the role of universities in developing a knowledge economy. In Botswana, the government's emerging focus on a new role for universities in national development is evident in the flagship university's strategic plan, the gradual increase in research funding, the goal of establishing innovation hubs, and the creation of the new Botswana University of Science and Technology. The other four countries are lagging behind when it comes to addressing the notion of a knowledge economy in their society.

The Role of the Ministry of Education

In the four Nordic countries the ministries responsible for the university sector have the capacity to make predictable allocations to universities. The relationships between the ministries and the universities are characterized by a high level of mutual trust, at least compared with the situation in other OECD countries. Nonetheless, differences exist among the Nordic countries. On the one hand we find the Danish tradition in which the minister "sits on top of the universities," steering the university system from a close distance. On the other hand, the Swedish higher-education system is governed in many areas by a separate agency (*Högskoleverket*), which has its own legal status and is a reflection of the Swedish "mutual consultation" society model. In Sweden, the minister rarely interferes directly with the governance of the universities. These differences are further reflected in the roles of the ministerial bureaucracy, the parliament, the representative agencies, and the university representatives.

The Finnish and Norwegian traditions lie somewhere in between the Danish and Swedish "extremes," but all four of the main Nordic countries have good relations between their universities and ministries of education when it comes to consistent and predictable funding—even if the *form* of university funding differs from country to country. One important funding difference concerns the use of formal, multiyear contracts between ministries and individual universities. Norway is the only Nordic country where no such contracts are used; instead, the Norwegian ministry of education uses annual goal-oriented reports as a major element in its governance relationship with universities.

Funding patterns, in turn, reflect national policies related to knowledge and innovation (Braun 2008). Here too Denmark and Finland show the clearest signs of a "knowledge triangle" of research, innovation, and higher education. Denmark has even gone so far as to integrate the responsibilities for these core areas—science policy, university policy, technology policy, and innovation policy—into one ministry. Finland has created other ways to coordinate knowledge and innovation areas, leaving higher-education and research policy as the responsibility of a separate ministry. The effectiveness of the Finnish way shows that Denmark's "superministry" for coordinating knowledge and innovation policy is not necessarily the best way (ibid.).

In the African countries, by contrast, ministries of education are, in general, weak, with limited capacity to make predictable financial allocations to universities. In sub-Saharan Africa, ministries of education or higher education are positioned at the margins of their respective national governments. In the national policy arena, a number of other ministries, notably health and agriculture, have direct bilateral relationships with specific faculties of the national universities, even though these ministries invest only limited resources in university activities. Other actors involved in higher-education policymaking are national representative bodies of the universities and development agencies from the North. Moreover, in these countries, there are no multiyear contracts that link the ministry to the university. In general, the financial and governance relationship between the ministry and the university is organized around the responsibility for charging and administering tuition fees. The exception is Mauritius, which seems to have more executive administrative capacity for governing its university.

Funding Consistency

In the Nordic countries, the main characteristics of the funding relationship between universities and government are the consistently high level of public funding, the rejection of the introduction of tuition fees (at least for Nordic/EU students), and the use of basic grants to cover a large part of the government's aid to universities.

When it comes to funding consistency, there are important differences between Nordic and sub-Saharan African countries. While Mauritius has a relatively stable and consistent funding mechanism for its university, the situation in four of the other five countries in our study is the opposite (Botswana being somewhere in between the two "extremes"). This inconsistency in external funding relationships is translated internally: for most African universities, there is no long-term funding horizon whatsoever.

The indicators discussed above and the other indicators identified in the underlying study show a strong pact between society and university in the Nordic countries and a weak pact in most of the African countries. Mauritius and to some extent Botswana show signs of a pact that is stronger than in other African countries, but even Mauritius and Botswana have relatively high levels of funding inconsistency and lack an effective national development program for "guiding" the governance of universities (the fact that Norway and Sweden also operate without a clear national development program shows that the notion of "a pact between university and society" is highly complex and has to be examined carefully). We turn now to an analysis of the ways in which the three factors discussed in this section—the role of a national development framework, the role of the ministry of education, and the role of consistent funding—shape the university's academic core.

The Academic Core

The HERANA study has provided us with a wealth of data on the African universities involved. Much of this data concerns the academic core of the selected African universities. Here the discussion of the academic core will be limited to the balance between undergraduate and graduate students, the distribution of students among disciplinary areas, and the research output of academic staff. The academic core indicators discussed in this section suggest a number of major differences between Nordic and African flagship research universities. These differences give a clear indication of the limitations of the academic core in African universities. At the same time, we can also see changes in African universities that reflect their efforts to strengthen their academic core.

Tables 10. 1 and 10. 2 show that the balance between undergraduate and graduate students is more equal in the Nordic universities than in the African universities, but in the period 2000–2007, with the exception of the University of Ghana, all the African universities showed an increase in postgraduate over undergraduate students, so the degree of balance is increasing.

A second indicator concerning the academic core is the number of MA and PhD level graduates. Tables 10.3 and 10.4 show, with respect to the African universities, a rapid growth in MA students in most universities, as well as an overall increase in the number of (formally enrolled) PhD students. However, the number of graduates has in general not increased proportionally. While one would expect a time lag in the growth of graduates, still, at the PhD level, the number of graduates remains low. Each of the four Nordic universities has a larger number of PhD students and produces more PhD graduates as a percentage of the total population and as a percentage of citizens with bachelor's degrees. This is all the more striking when one considers that, in the Nordic countries, PhD students are members of

Table 10.1 Enrollments according to level, 1999/2000 and 2006/2007, selected African universities

University	Degree level	1999/2000	2006/2007	Average annual growth rate for the period from 1999/2000 to 2006/2007
Makerere University	Undergraduate	20,638	31,390	+ 6.4%
	Postgraduate	1,337	3,026	+ 12.4%
University of Mauritius	Undergraduate	4,828	6,448	+ 4.9%
	Postgraduate	464	1,052	+ 14.6%
University of Ghana	Undergraduate	10,156	24,780	+ 13.6%
	Postgraduate	1,298	1,682	+ 3.8%
University of Dar es Salaam	Undergraduate	7,389	17,569	+ 13.2%
	Postgraduate	702	3,125	+ 23.8%
University of Botswana	Undergraduate	10,896	14,039	+ 3.7%
	Postgraduate	840	1,445	+ 8.1%
University of Nairobi	Undergraduate	13,955	33,019	+ 13.1%
	Postgraduate	2,028	6,367	+ 17.8%

Source: HERANA project/CHET.

Table 10.2 Enrollments according to level, 2007, selected Nordic universities[1]

University	Degree level	2007
University of Copenhagen	BA/MA/PhD	21,152 18,638
University of Helsinki	BA/MA/PhD	13,048 24,486
University of Oslo	BA/MA/PhD	13,797 16,236
University of Stockholm	BA/MA/PhD	22,422 1,543

[1]The overview of student numbers in the Nordic universities includes only the data for 2007. The introduction of Bologna Process–related reforms makes it difficult to compare the 2000 data with 2007 data. In addition, the Swedish government had not yet joined the Bologna Process in 2007. Therefore, it was not possible to present separate data for bachelor and master's students for the University of Stockholm.

Source: HERANA project/CHET.

Table 10.3 Masters and doctoral degree enrollments and outputs; 1999/2000 and 2006/2007, selected African universities

University	Degree level	Year 1999/2000	Year 2006/2007
University of Botswana	MA enrollment/graduation	493/124	977/166
	PhD enrollment/graduation	8/3	51/3
University of Ghana	MA enrollment/graduation	1,198/207	1,580/576
	PhD enrollment/graduation	67/2	102/11
University of Mauritius	MPhil/PhD enrollment/graduation	114/7	193/10
Makerere University	MA enrollment/graduation	1,059/337	2,767/744
	PhD enrollment/graduation	23/10	32/23
University of Nairobi	MA enrollment/graduation	1,746/303	6,145/988
	PhD enrollment/graduation	42/26	62/32
University of Dar es Salaam	MA enrollment/graduation	552/158	2,165/392
	PhD enrollment/graduation	54/10	190/20

Source: HERANA project/CHET.

Table 10.4 Masters and doctoral degree enrollments and outputs; 1999/2000 and 2006/2007, selected Nordic universities

University	Degree level	1999/2000	2006/2007
University of Copenhagen	PhD enrollment/graduation	1,339/299 (in 2005)	2,168/347
University of Helsinki	PhD enrollment/graduation	N/A	2,203/445
University of Oslo	PhD enrollment/graduation	1,169/229	2,277/344
University of Stockholm	PhD enrollment/graduation	1,815/195	1,543/233

Source: HERANA project/CHET.

Table 10.5 Number of articles in refereed academic journals (2007) in selected African and Nordic universities

University	Total number of articles (2007)
University of Botswana	126
University of Dar es Salaam	70
University of Nairobi	136
University of Ghana	101
University of Mauritius	26
Makerere University	233
University of Oslo	3,483
University of Helsinki	4,001
University of Copenhagen	3,894 (in 2005)
University of Stockholm	N/A

Source: HERANA project/CHET.

staff and are paid a salary at a level higher than in any other OECD countries where PhD students have staff status.

Finally, we note the academic output of university staff. Table 10. 5 offers an overview of the number of academic publications produced by the staff of the universities in our study. Tables 10.6 and 10.7 summarize the research output and research impact of scientists in selected countries based on their number of publications and their relative citation index rankings. These data show that, based on their rate of publication and their relative rankings in world citation indices, universities in the Nordic region have a much stronger research profile—and thus, it would seem, a much stronger academic core—than universities in sub-Saharan Africa.

The Role of External Funders

To understand the challenges African universities face in strengthening their academic core, we discuss in this section one of the most important factors that causes continuous "underperformance" in the area of research in African universities, namely, the role of external funders. Our initial analyses of the African universities suggest that there is a very weak level of institutionalization of externally funded projects. The first reason for this weak institutionalization of externally funded research is that the main actors involved in university governance—the internal university leaders, the national ministry of education, and the external donor agencies—all have different visions of the university's role in development. Donor agencies in general rely upon an instrumental vision

Table 10.6 Scientific publication in 2006–2008 in selected countries

Country	Number of articles 2006	% of world production		Number of articles per 1,000 inhabitants	Average annual change in number of articles 02–06 (2006–2008). In %
		2006	2008		
United States	293,254	25.8	24.3	0.99	3.8
United Kingdom	77,056	6.8	6.5	1.28	3.4
Germany	72,236	6.4	6.1	0.88	3.0
Japan	71,143	6.3	5.8	0.56	0.8
China	69,664	6.1	7.3	0.05	19.9
France	51,591	4.5	4.4	0.83	3.1
Canada	44,119	3.9	3.7	1.37	7.2
Italy	39,522	3.5	3.5	0.68	5.4
Spain	30,785	2.7	2.8	0.71	7.1
Australia	27,515	2.4	2.4	1.35	6.3
India	25,672	2.3	2.4	0.02	10.1
The Netherlands	23,417	2.1	2.0	1.44	5.4
Switzerland	16,947	1.5	1.5	2.26	6.2
Sweden	16,572	1.5	1.4	1.84	2.7 (2.1)
Denmark	8,866	0.8	0.8	1.64	4.1 (4.6)
Austria	8,357	0.7	0.7	1.02	3.6
Finland	8,321	0.7	0.7	1.59	3.4 (3.9)
Norway	6,751	0.6	0.6	1.46	7.9 (9.2)

Source: National Science Indicators/Thomson Scientific/NIFU STEP.

in which the university is seen as one of the tools for reducing poverty and improving living conditions (medical and food-wise), especially in rural communities. Meanwhile, the national ministries of education as well as other national political agencies (especially other ministries and representatives of the private sector) see the university in the first place as instrumental in the implementation of national agendas and specific agency programs. There is an underlying expectation that the university should play a role in general economic development and in assisting national agencies to improve health care and agricultural policies. University leaders, by contrast, place far less emphasis on an instrumental vision; instead, they emphasize a more traditional academic vision related to a Republic of Science/Humboldtian view.

In practice, these different perceptions of the university's role in development result in donors funding projects that contribute to the realization of their main policy aims (poverty reduction through

Table 10.7 Relative citation index for selected countries, total numbers for five-year period 2002–2006 (world average = 100)

Country	Index	Country	Index
Switzerland	145	Japan	91
United States	135	China	73
Denmark	135	Brazil	67
The Netherlands	132	India	60
United Kingdom	125		
Sweden	123	World average	100
Belgium	122	OECD average	109
Finland	120	EU average	106
Germany	119		
Norway	118		
Austria	117		
Canada	116		
France	110		
Australia	108		
Italy	107		
Spain	101		

Source: National Science Indicators/Thomson Scientific/NIFU STEP.

Note: Based on publications in the period 2002–2006 and citations of these publications in the same period. Index for each country is weighed on the basis of the country's relative field distribution of articles.

agricultural improvement and community outreach) while the national ministry of education and other national agencies expect the university to contribute to the implementation of competing policy and development agendas (typically without making the necessary funds available for these activities). The main governance actors for African universities—internal leaders, ministers of education, and donor agencies—consult and talk with each other, but in the end, they all act independently with respect to the university. University leaders invest their meager and relatively unstable funding in the maintenance of the academic core. The ministry of education is in general weak and does not have sufficient regulatory or funding power to direct universities' contributions to economic development. Other ministries and national agencies (e.g., agriculture) are more powerful and include the university as an important actor in their policy arenas, but this relationship is rarely accompanied by satisfactory levels of funding. And external donors invest in their own specific projects with very few efforts to coordinate their mutual activities and link their investments directly to national development agendas. As a consequence, universities in sub-Saharan Africa are highly fragmented, operating in a weakly institutionalized environment.

This system (or nonsystem) has major consequences for the internal structure and administrative operations of African universities. For example, the University of Dar es Salaam has a central administrative department for planning and funding with over 125 staff members. A large part of its capacity is used for handling the initial phase of donor projects, that is, contract preparation, negotiations, checking/controlling project intentions, and monitoring intended outcomes, as well as reporting on each individual project to the donor in question. In all of this, the university's own strategic plan plays a marginal role as a consequence of donors' preference for their own programs. Moreover, nearly all externally funded projects have a limited time span, usually three–five years. Donors expect sustainability but do not usually offer any guarantees of continued funding or project (area) support.

A Ghanaian study by Manuh et al. (2007) illustrated this point. The authors argued that the economic decline and the introduction of Structural Adjustment Programs (SAPs) in the 1980s dealt a heavy blow to university funding for basic research by drying up the internal funds for universities. This was in part related to the downplaying of higher education by international agencies, such as the World Bank, and more recently UNESCO. SAPs undermined both the autonomy of academics and the capability of many universities to support basic research. Manuh and his colleagues (2007) showed that consultancy took the place of basic research in African universities. The picture the authors painted of the status and conditions of academic research in the 1980s has not changed much in Ghana or in other African countries, as evidenced in the authors' argument that inadequate funding levels led academic staff to rely on external sources to fund their projects. In many cases, university research committees allocated most of their (limited) research funding to conference travel rather than actual research projects.

In the Nordic countries the situation is very different. The main external funders of research projects (national research councils and the EU's FP7) have an agenda that is developed in close consultation between all the main actors involved, including university representatives, in the framework of the pact between university and society (a pact not unlike the one Taylor identified in British universities at the turn of the twentieth century). Funds are distributed on the basis of competition between applicants, and in judging proposals, the quality of the applicants and their proposals are (among) the main criteria for selection. The use of these criteria has direct, major effects on the maintenance of the academic core of the applicants' universities. It confirms the importance of investing in academic activities (first and foremost high-quality research) and in building academic teams and training the next generation of academic researchers. As Ivar Bleiklie notes in this volume, the whole process of external research funding is deeply rooted in the academic core of the university and contributes to continuously investing in academic capacity (used, among other things, in the supervision of MA and PhD students as well as postdoctoral candidates). Another effect concerns the requirement of these external funding agencies to produce academic output in the form of articles in refereed journals, or other publications whose quality has been screened according to traditional (and increasingly inter-/transnational) academic review procedures. Thus, an important part of the large academic research output of Nordic universities is produced in the framework of externally funded projects, implying that, in principle, there is a mutually strengthening relationship between basic government funding for universities and external research council funding. These activities are in the end expected to provide important contributions to economic development in the Nordic countries.

As indicated, the role of external funders (mainly donor agencies) differs in African and Nordic universities. In African universities, external funders usually have an agenda in which poverty reduction is a core aim. The agenda is usually developed without direct contributions from university representatives, and as our HERANA project indicates, the funding available for realizing the agenda is not distributed on the basis of academic quality per se, but on the basis of bilateral contacts, donor preferences, and competition between donors (not between academics). In selecting projects to fund, donors to African universities are not focused in the first place on academic quality but rather on the extent to which a project might contribute to the implementation of a donor agenda. When it comes to higher-education projects, there is practically no coordination between donors, implying that there are no common donor aims. Most projects, therefore, take place in isolation, without any indication of how a project is expected to contribute to overall national development. In addition, donors rarely require that a project should lead to academic publications. In general, the only output required is a report to the funder.

This relationship between African universities and external funders has serious effects. While for individual faculty the projects are an important source of income, the effects on African flagship universities as knowledge institutions are typically negative. Contrary to the effects of external funders in the Nordic countries, external funders of African universities do not in general contribute to strengthening the academic core of the institutions by investing in improving quality or building capacity; instead, the projects they fund often *diminish* capacity in core academic activities. In practice, while most externally funded projects in an African university are led by senior academics, the knowledge basis of the project is typically only indirectly related to the academic area of the project leader. Many involve consultancies rather than actual academic research. The consequences, as expressed in the interviews undertaken in the HERANA project, are often that senior academic staff spend most of their time leading one or more externally funded projects. These projects rarely produce academic publications in the framework of the externally funded projects, and there are no incentives to use the projects in educational degree programs.

CONCLUSIONS

This chapter has discussed the conditions under which African universities attempt to contribute to the economic development of their countries. African universities are not "standing still," and in a number of respects they are moving in the same direction as their Nordic counterparts. Nonetheless, African universities face a number of barriers in their efforts to respond to the challenges of the global economy and the development needs of their own societies. Two barriers stand out. First, African universities in general operate in a development vacuum, without compelling frameworks that coordinate the role of universities in national development. Of the six selected countries, only Mauritius and to some extent Botswana have started to discuss the challenges of the global economy and the role that higher-education funding and policy might play in developing a local version of the "knowledge economy." The other African countries are caught in a development vision that focuses mainly on poverty reduction, community development, and training central state bureaucrats. In these countries, a weak pact between university and society leads to a very limited vision of university research. Second, the main external funders for universities in Africa, that is, development aid (or donor) agencies, actually *reduce* capacity in universities' academic core. As such, donors seem caught in a vicious cycle of implementing their own nation's development aid agenda, operating in countries that do not have a clear development vision of their own, and interacting with academic staff of universities who depend on external funding to supplement their meager university salaries. While various projects get limited funds each year (e.g., the total amount invested by donor agencies in university projects in Africa amounts to less than US$1.5 billion in the period 2000–2005 (Maassen et al. 2007)), this money does little to improve African universities. If donors wish to promote capacity-*building* rather than capacity-*reducing* investments in African universities, they might examine the ways in which the relationship between universities and external funders in their own countries leads to positive outcomes. It can be argued, for example, that if donors were willing to reserve 10 percent of their joint annual investments in African university projects for establishing an Africa-wide research council, they would make a major contribution to strengthening the conditions under which African universities are expected to contribute to the (economic) development of their respective countries and their continent.

Notes

I want to thank the colleagues in the HERANA project, especially NicoCloete, Joe Muller, Tracy Baily, Pundy Pillay, and Romulo Pinheiro, for their input in this chapter. I also want to thank Anthony Welch for his valuable comments on a previous draft.

1. See UNESCO's tertiary education statistics: http://stats.uis.unesco.org/unesco/TableViewer/tableView.aspx?ReportId=167
2. For example, in the 2009 Knowledge Economy Index (KEI) published by the World Bank, the four main Nordic countries are all positioned in the top five (see http://info.worldbank.org/etools/kam2/KAM_page5.asp).
3. See National Science Indicators, Thompson Reuters Research Analytics Group, Philadelphia, PA, United States (http://thomsonreuters.com/products_services/science/science_products/a-z/national_science_indicators/).
4. The so-called Shanghai Ranking; see http://www.arwu.org/ARWU2009.jsp. After the United States and United Kingdom, the Nordic region has the most universities in the Shanghai Ranking Top 100.
5. This includes the new European Research Council (ERC), where around 10 percent of all grants to date have been awarded to Nordic researchers.

6. A full overview of all indicators used in the HERANA study can be found at www.chet.org.za. This chapter discusses only a few of these indicators.)
7. This includes income from tuition fees and research council funding.
8. By a swing we mean a difference in real terms in the public budget level for the universities of more than 15 percent from one year to the next.
9. The nature and size of this chapter does not allow for a full discussion of all indicators identified in the framework of the project. In addition, the structuring and analysis of the empirical data for the HERANA project is still not finished (see www.chet.org.za). Therefore, at this stage the discussion will be limited to a few indicators per area.

Bibliography

Altbach, Ph. G. and J. Balán (2007) (eds.) *World Class Worldwide. Transforming Research Universities in Asia and Latin America.* Baltimore: Johns Hopkins University Press.

Birnbaum, R. (1988) *How Colleges Work.* San Francisco: Jossey Bass.

Braun, D. (2008) Organising the Political Coordination of Knowledge and Innovation Policies. *Science and Public Policy,* 35 (4) (May): 227–239.

Castells, M. (2001) Universities as Dynamic Systems of Contradictory Functions. In J. Muller, N. Cloete, and S. Badat (eds.) *Challenges of Globalization. South African Debates with Manuel Castells.* Cape Town: Maskew Miller Longman, pp. 206–224.

Clark, B. R. (1983) *The Higher Education System. Academic Organization in Cross-National Perspective.* Berkeley: University of California Press.

——— (1998) *Creating Entrepreneurial Universities: Organizational Pathways of Transformation.* Oxford: Pergamon.

Cossa, J. (2008) *Power, Politics and Higher Education in Southern Africa. International Regimes, Local Governments and Educational Autonomy.* Amherst, NY: Cambria Press.

Dinham, S. and C. Scott (2000) *Enhancing Teacher Professionalism: The Need to Engage with the Third Domain.* ACEA Conference, Hobart, Australia.

Duignan, P. (1988) Reflective Management: The Key to Quality Leadership. *International Journal of Educational Management,* 2 (2): 3–12.

French Academie of Sciences (2006) *Sciences et pays en développement Afrique subsaharienne francophone.* Paris: L'académie des sciences.

Glassman, R. (1973) Persistence and Loose Couple in Living Systems. *Behavioural Science,* 18: 83–98.

Gornitzka, Å., P. Maassen, J. P. Olsen, and B. Stensaker (2007) Europe of Knowledge. Search for a New Pact. In P. Maassen and J. P. Olsen (eds.) *University Dynamics and European Integration.* Dordrecht: Springer, pp. 181–214.

Höltta, S. And P. Malkki (2000) Response of Finnish Higher Education Institutions to the National Information Society Program. *Higher Education Policy*, 13: 231–243.

Hood, C., O. James, B. G. Peters, and C. Scott (eds.) (2004) *Controlling Modern Government. Variety, Commonality and Change.* Cheltenham: Edward Elgar.

Kapur, D. and M. Crowley (2008) *Beyond the ABCs: Higher Education and Developing Countries.* Working paper number 139. February 2008. Center for Global Development. (www.cgdev.org/content/publications /detail/15310)

Kerr, C. (2001) *The Gold and the Blue. A Personal Memoir of the University of California 1949–1960.* Berkeley: California University Press.

Kogan, M. and S. Hanney (2000) *Reforming Higher Education.* London: Jessica Kingsley.

Maassen, P. and J. P. Olsen (2007) *University Dynamics and European Integration.* Dordrecht: Springer.

Maassen, P., R. Pinheiro, and N. Cloete (2007) *Bilateral Country Investments and Foundations Partnership Projects to Support Higher Education across Africa.* Cape Town: CHET. (http://www.chet.org.za/papers/bilateral -country-investments-and-foundations-partnership-projects-support -higher-education-a)

Manuh, T., S. Gariba, and J. Budu (2007) *Change and Transformation in Ghana's Public Funded Universities: A Study of Experiences, Lessons and Opportunities.* Oxford: James Curry; Accra: Woeli.

March, J. G. and J. P. Olsen (1975) *Choice Situations in Loosely Coupled Worlds.* Unpublished manuscript. Stanford University.

NOU (2008) *Sett under ett. Ny struktur I høyere utdanning.* Norges offent- lige utredninger, 2008: 3. Oslo: Akademika A.S.

Oliver, C. (1991) Strategic Responses to Institutional Processes. *Academic Management Review*, 16 (1): 145–179.

Olsen, J. P. (2001) Organizing European Institutions of Governance—A Prelude to an Institutional Account of Political Integration. In H. Wallace (ed.) *Interlocking Dimensions of European Integration.* Houndmills: Palgrave, pp. 323–353.

——— (2007) The Institutional Dynamics of the European University. In P. Maassen and J. P. Olsen (eds.) *University Dynamics and European Integration.* Dordrecht: Springer, pp. 25–54.

Scott, W. R. (2001) *Institutions and Organizations* (second edition). Thousand Oaks, CA: Sage.

Selznick, P. (1949) *TVA and the Grass Roots.* Berkeley: University of California Press.

Weick, K. (1976) Educational Organizations as Loosely Coupled Systems. *Administrative Science Quarterly*, 21: 1–19.

——— (1982) Administering Education in Loosely Coupled Schools. *Phi Delta Kappan* (June): 673–676.

Conclusion: Lessons from the Past, Considerations for the Future

Adam R. Nelson and Ian P. Wei

Though the contributors to this volume offer different perspectives on "the global university," taken collectively they present a distinctive critique of existing work on this much-debated phenomenon. Some higher-education scholars tend to accept the rhetoric of "globalization" at face value; they try to fit nearly anything they observe into a model that oversimplifies. This volume takes a different approach. It stresses complexity over simplicity, divergences over convergences, local and national variations over global or international conformity. As the chapters in this volume show, greater account must be taken of the remarkable diversity that exists among universities pursuing "world-class" status—as well as those *not* pursuing this status. Indeed, the contributors to this volume contend that diversity should be considered a strength, not a weakness, in global higher education, both from a strategic and from a systemic perspective. Universities, they note, do not—and should not—follow the same path.

The contributors to this volume also note that, as social organizations, universities are multifaceted and should not be interpreted as mere businesses. While the scholarship on globalization and higher education understandably stresses the relationship between universities and today's "global knowledge economy," too much of the literature on this subject characterizes the "commercialization" or "commodification" of higher education as inexorable, even inevitable. This volume takes a different approach. Without denying that universities, in both their public and private forms, must provide "value for money" (and must, perhaps, "make research pay"), the contributions to this volume adopt a much broader view of the purposes of universities, stressing their social, cultural, intellectual, and even "spiritual" dimensions. Universities, after all, are not (only) profit centers, and to view them chiefly in this way is to mistake their deeper historical raison d'etre.

Together, the chapters in this volume seek to bring a deeper historical perspective to the study of "the global university." Each chapter engages an interpretive framework rooted in a broad appreciation of history—both historical contextualization and historical explanation. While scholars of the global university sometimes look back a decade or two (perhaps three or four), to understand their subject, the chapters in this volume place current debates in a far more expansive historical context, reaching back not just decades but centuries to identify the long-term influences that have shaped the form (and reform) of universities over time. As every student of history knows, some "reforms" are transient or shallow while others are deeper and more enduring. This volume focuses on the latter, hoping to capture the ways in which globalization—itself a phenomenon with a very long history—is affecting the operation as well as the core mission of universities.

The contributors to this volume share the conviction that higher-education policymakers gain much from a broad historical perspective. University leaders and managers responding to a rapidly changing global higher-education environment often confront the fundamental questions raised in this volume: What sort of organization *is* the university? Whose interests does it serve, and how? What have been, or should be, its guiding ideals? What institutional arrangements, strategies, and investments are most likely to facilitate cross-national collaboration—or fruitful competition—between universities, not just universities in the highest echelons of global prestige but across the whole spectrum of postsecondary education? How can university leaders ensure that their institutions foster the sort of teaching and research that advance not only economic interests but also basic values such as equal opportunity, peace and security, prosperity and sustainability, and the health and well-being of people in an interdependent global community? To answer these questions in a way that is useful to both scholars and policymakers, this volume draws on the lessons of history.

While each chapter offers its own unique contribution to higher-education policy debates, several cross-cutting themes emerge. The section headings point to a number of these themes: the importance of regional variations; the evolving structure of university governance;

the competing demands of academic work; the enduring struggle to improve undergraduate and postgraduate education; and the ever-present conflicts over "external" funding in the university. Each of these themes figures prominently in the literature on "the global university," and this volume makes a valuable contribution to each of these areas of scholarship. In addition to these core themes, however, a few others emerge in these essays. Among these, four stand out: first, the importance of national particularities and the role of the state in higher-education policy; second, the importance of clarifying the differences between universities and businesses; third, the importance of recognizing (and mitigating) the deleterious effects of global competition in higher education; fourth and finally, the importance of historical perspective in higher-education leadership. These four themes are elaborated below.

National Particularities and the Role of the State

Many of the contributors to this volume point to the significance of national and regional particularities in higher-education policymaking. Ka Ho Mok shows how, in their efforts to build world-class universities that contribute to economic prosperity, East Asian states have developed their own distinctive strategies that combine regulation and deregulation and prioritize interregional partnerships. Citing parallels with European higher-education integration under the Bologna Process, he notes that university planning in East Asia is nonetheless carving out its own unique path. Far from succumbing to an isomorphism derived from American cultural hegemony, Mok argues, Mainland China is rapidly coming to play a major coordinating role in both East Asian and Southeast Asian higher-education policy. Anthony Welch observes, however, that China is not alone in its bid for influence in this region. Australian offshore campuses in Malaysia and Vietnam demonstrate that strategic initiatives attributed to globalization can be highly diverse. Moreover, when the policies that Glen Jones and Bryan Gopaul describe are brought into the picture—in this case, Canadian funding policies intended to respond to international student mobility—it becomes clear that different states develop very different approaches to higher-education management in the context of globalization. National and regional particularities remain vital and must not be overlooked.

Other chapters reinforce this point. Ivar Bleiklie reminds us that policies similar in their rhetoric and goals may not be similar in effect;

national peculiarities and "path dependencies" ensure that national differences persist. Along the same lines, Chen, Shen, and Cai accept that China's shift toward general education is part of a global trend—a trend that has been shaped by American models—but, as they see it, China's "return" to general education has not been interpreted as a form of neocolonialism precisely because the Chinese have viewed it, in part, as a link to Confucian traditions. In other words, an ostensibly "global" trend has taken on distinctive meanings in China. Similar dynamics appear in other chapters. Peter Maassen explains that, since African universities operate under very different conditions than universities in OECD countries, external funding has different effects on African universities' academic core and their capacity to contribute to economic development. To ensure that external funding has the desired impact in African countries, Maassen offers the specific policy suggestion that donors should put 10 percent of their joint annual investments in African university projects toward an African research council. With such a council, African universities could direct financial resources toward priorities set by themselves, not by external (so-called international) donors. Even—perhaps especially—in an era of globalization, academics at a national and regional level have a key role to play in higher-education policymaking.

The state serves as the crucial link between national and international, local and global, levels of institutional planning, management, and leadership. Surveying past ties between universities and industry, for example, John Taylor concludes that it was (and still is) essential for university leaders to build local and regional as well as national and international relationships. To neglect the former could have long-term negative effects. In a similar way, Rosemary Deem insists on the need to think of universities not as local, national, or international, but as operating at all three levels simultaneously. Indeed, each contributor to this volume agrees that "the global university" is not one thing but many, depending on diverse local, national, and regional circumstances. While universities in Asia, Australia, Africa, Europe, and North America undoubtedly share certain elements, their responses to global pressures differ. This point may seem obvious—perhaps even axiomatic—yet, in the context of proliferating global rankings and increasingly frantic efforts to achieve world-class status (a still-ambiguous phrase measured according to arbitrarily globalized rubrics), the diversity of national and institutional strategies is too often minimized in some quarters of the literature. To reemphasize, the global university is not one thing but many.

Obviously, this focus on diversity challenges the neoinstitution-alists' emphasis on convergence. It notes that, while in some ways universities may be conforming to common models, their paths are idiosyncratic. Moreover, it bears noting that, in neoinstitutionalist theory, final convergence never actually occurs; this goal constantly recedes on the horizon of institutional experience. Convergence remains an *historical* process, and, as such, it is open to contingency and change. For this reason, the end of this process remains a mat-ter of theoretical speculation and hypothesis rather than empirical observation or evidence. What *is* observable and verifiable is the extraordinary variety of national and institutional strategies that mark contemporary higher education around the world. Particularly when one looks beyond a "given" set of institutions (typically elite research universities), one sees many different ways of being or becoming global. These differences complicate neoinstitutionalist theory, but they also offer hope to higher-education leaders who do not follow the herd—those who seek *alternate* paths into the future and realize that one size does not, and cannot, fit all. In the twenty-first century, "the global university" will continue to assume many forms.

Universities Are Not (Only) Businesses

Just as the contributors to this volume agree that global universities will take a variety of forms, they also agree that universities are not (only) businesses. Universities may feel the same pressures as busi-nesses to position themselves in competitive markets and operate strategically and efficiently to advance stakeholder interests, but "aca-demic capitalism" remains an oxymoron. Anthony Welch notes that, even when states design higher-education policies to develop knowl-edge-based industries, other issues come into play: higher-education systems function as "important repositories of national cultures and treasured national status symbols." Rosemary Deem—who interro-gates the adverse consequences of viewing universities as financial engines rather than as institutions with deeper social aims—reveals that top-down policies stressing academic competition and "entrepre-neurialism" often fail to achieve desired results. "Although in theory academics can be told what and how to teach," she observes, "line management does not make them teach well, nor does it fit the cul-ture of academic research, which rarely leads to straight-forward or predictable results." The so-called new managerialism in the United Kingdom, which applies business-like administrative principles to uni-versity governance, may yield short-term efficiencies at the expense of long-term effectiveness. The question is: where does the real "value" of universities lie? How are universities *different* from businesses?

Few would contend that universities—at least modern universities—do not have a role to play in economic development. The disagreement arises over what the university's role should be and how it should be managed. Much of the debate concerns expectations about short- and long-term economic contributions and how these "contributions" can or should be directly measured. Take the case of students and "learning outcomes." Unlike some, the contributors to this volume maintain that students are not (only) commodities, teaching and learning are not (only) commerce, and knowledge is not (only) pursued so that it can be bought or sold. John Taylor's chapter on university-business partnerships stresses that civic institutions founded in the United Kingdom in the nineteenth century supplemented courses in the applied sciences with lectures in literature. Similarly, in their chapter on the shift from specialized to general education in Chinese universities, Chen, Shen, and Cai explain that elite students—future "knowledge workers"—are presumed to benefit from broad cultivation as they prepare for leadership positions in a postindustrial society. Xu Xiaozhou and Xue Shan make this point most forcefully in their chapter. If universities are to seek larger truths and solve long-term social problems, they argue, then universities must be different from other types of social organizations; they must protect the unfettered freedom to pursue knowledge, wherever that pursuit may lead. They must encourage and reward high-quality teaching and research, even if the immediate practical results of this work cannot be measured. To accept the commodification of the university under the guise of globalization, Xu and Xue contend, is to betray the university's core value: the value of teaching, research, and service that is (at least partly) detached from the pursuit of profit. Should this ideal perish, they warn, all of society, *including* business interests, will regret its loss.

No contributor to this volume is so naive as to assume that modern universities can separate themselves entirely from the forces of economic globalization, nor would any of them claim that teaching, research, and service have no economic value. Rather, following the lead of Max Weber (who is cited in two chapters and lurks in others), they maintain that universities must distinguish clearly between the pursuit of knowledge for profit and the pursuit of knowledge "for its own sake." To neoliberals who see private enterprise as the key driver of public well-being, this volume responds that the modern university has long been "entrepreneurial," but it has also been at its best (and recognized as such) when it has guarded the ideal of "pure" research and teaching, apart from narrow utilitarian demands. Similarly, to postmodernists who argue that no modern institution—least of all universities—can escape the vortex of structural and symbolic power in which learning is a consumer good (or credential), research is another saleable product, students and faculty are forms of human capital (which, *not* who, generate "intellectual property"), and the value of knowledge is determined solely by the market, this volume responds that universities around the world (not merely in the West) have stood for such ideals as free and open inquiry, rational judgment, independent criticism, and cooperative deliberation. Without these ideals, the very *idea* of the modern university would die (some, of course, think it already has). The university would then indeed become a mere business, and such a change, once it occurred, would be irreversible.

Admittedly, such a perspective comes to light only if one takes a broad historical view of the purposes of universities. Those who see higher education through a lens that encompasses only the recent past are likely to miss these other aims of the university, or at best to consider the noninstrumental aims of the university to be primarily rhetorical. Yet, to study the long history of the university is to appreciate its contributions not only to commerce but also to values that make commercial success *possible* in a well-ordered society: civil discourse, equal opportunity, legal transparency, access to information, and so on. The university's special value lies not (only) in bringing ideas to market—as it has done for centuries—but in encouraging and protecting intellectual risk. The university is historically a conservative institution, but its conservatism has a progressive side in that it eschews any and all constraints on human thought. Accepting "reason" as its only limit, the university must not restrict itself to "ideas that pay." To serve human society in all its dimensions, the university must be more than a business.

MITIGATING THE EFFECTS OF COMPETITION

Universities must be open to the broadest possible range of ideas, but they do not exist in a vacuum. Nearly every chapter in this volume begins with a statement about the competitive pressures facing universities in the context of globalization. Implicit in these statements is an acknowledgment that competition, especially for the top spots in global rankings, produces both "winners" and "losers." Ka Ho Mok stresses the ways in which East Asian governments have directed unprecedented resources to elite universities while exposing others to competition in privatized markets. Anthony Welch, likewise, points to inequalities between nations (especially between nations in the North and South) as well as inequalities *within* nations caused by the unequal provision of higher education. In the case of cross-border trade in educational services, including the establishment of foreign branch campuses, Welch stresses the moral responsibility that wealthier countries have to attend to these inequalities—a responsibility that some have begun to tackle through new quality-assurance systems. Along similar lines, Peter Maassen investigates why African universities are not in a position to compete with universities from OECD countries. He shows that, often, the policies of European and North American development agencies do little to strengthen African universities' research infrastructure; rather, they *weaken* these universities' "academic core" and thereby perpetuate imbalances of power. Maassen's suggestion for a donor-funded African research council, mentioned above, is designed to remedy these imbalances, at least in part.

Some say that global competition improves universities by pushing them to offer better "outcomes" in terms of both teaching and research. Many chapters in this volume, however, note that, while competition may have led to improvement in some institutions (see, for example, John Taylor on the "civic" universities of the late nineteenth century), it has also led to growing inequalities—not only in funding but also in the teaching and research missions of many universities. Xu Xiaozhou and Xue Shan note that economic pressures have led over time to a *neglect* of teaching, with students losing out. Rosemary Deem adds that the rapid "massification" of higher education in the twentieth century led to "significant concerns about institutional missions and structural differentiation within higher-education systems." In other words, massification may have increased access, but it also increased stratification. Along these lines, Glen Jones and Bryan Gopaul point to the ways in which mobility in an ever-more-globalized academic labor market clusters talent in specific regions and careers, thereby reinforcing historic inequalities. Canadian scholarship policies, for example, have led the best and brightest to selected universities, thus creating hierarchies in a higher-education system originally predicated on the idea of institutional equality. Do universities that regard themselves as world-class have a duty to mitigate the effects of a competition in which they are the chief beneficiaries? Perhaps so. Their aim should not be to dampen competition (or aid weak institutions) but rather to strengthen the *overall* benefits of higher-education systems globally. The reason to do so is obvious: competition is most productive over the long run when it alleviates, *not* when it perpetuates or exacerbates, inequality.

It would be impossible, of course, to list all the ways in which the university has been transformed by global competition, but numerous examples surface in this volume. Ivar Bleiklie, for instance, charts the rise of a new academic elite defined by its role in national and supranational governance structures—particularly the editorial boards of international journals, the prestige of which can influence everything from grant funding to university rankings based on citation indexes. New forms of "network governance," Bleiklie shows, have profound effects on both inter- and intrainstitutional administrative hierarchies. Ka Ho Mok alludes to similar inter- and intrainstitutional dynamics in his analysis of East Asian attempts to create world-class universities—the phrase itself a recognition (perhaps a celebration) of inequality. Mok subtly unpacks the ways in which East Asian states have sought to balance, on the one hand, a neoliberal perspective that sees inequality as a spur to competitive action with, on the other hand, a commitment to equity in which higher education provides access to genuine social opportunity. In China, as elsewhere, this balancing act has been—and likely will continue to be—very delicate indeed.

Too often in the literature on global higher education, the "value" of competition is in the eye of the beholder. Those in the university rankings business generally assume that competition between institutions produces endlessly creative approaches to meeting social needs. Others, however, worry that a blind pursuit of rankings leads to dangerous conformity and leaves basic needs unmet. Current rankings, for example, provide little incentive to focus on undergraduate instruction or, for that matter, research areas that do not register in specific citation indexes (one thinks of social work, urban architecture, or rural planning). A field like history, though it enjoys broad public support, emphasizes books rather than articles and thus fares poorly in most indexes; it, therefore, struggles to justify its value in the ubiquitous cost-benefit analysis. When the criteria that structure competition (and, in turn, evaluation) narrow, *any* institution is in jeopardy of appearing useless; likewise, as the criteria used to judge higher-education contract, the university becomes more and more vulnerable to criticism for being uncompetitive. Paradoxically, however, if universities give in to such criticism too readily, they may in the end achieve more "competitive" rankings even as they becomes more "useless" to society. Certainly, this is a fate that higher-education policymakers should hope to avoid.

THE VALUE OF HISTORICAL PERSPECTIVE

It is clear from these chapters that a deeper and more accurate understanding of higher education in the past can aid higher-education policymakers in the present. This statement is more than a truism about the benefits of "historical perspective." Too often, scholars of the global university, like scholars of globalization more generally, give the impression that everything is happening for the first time simply because similar trends, practices, or strategies in the past were described in different terms. This volume seeks to correct that impression. Nearly every chapter stresses the importance of history. Anthony Welch, for example, finds the origins of private universities and foreign branch campuses in Malaysia and Vietnam in the lingering effects of structural adjustment programs in the 1980s and the Asian financial crisis of the 1990s. Maassen similarly identifies structural adjustment programs—together with international donor policies—as an enduring cause of dependency in African universities. Glen Jones and Bryan Gopaul show that Canadian government policies concerning doctoral education can be understood only in light of the interaction between federal and provincial governments since the early twentieth century. And John Taylor notes that today's links between universities and industry are pursued as if this were a new development, but such links were foundational in the new universities created in the United Kingdom between 1870 and 1914. Comparing university-industry relations then and now, Taylor notes specific ways in which today's partnerships could be enhanced by learning from the past.

Learning from the past is the central theme of this volume. Ian Wei uses the past as a heuristic device to help interpret the present, chiefly to identify "absences" in current policy discourses that might be remedied. Describing a medieval discourse that expressed ideals genuinely held or at least respected by all members of the university—a discourse that was useful in negotiations with external stakeholders—he calls on today's academics to look for points of common interest and to use these commonalities to steer the rhetoric of globalization in ways that bring various university constituents together rather than driving them into postures of unrelenting and perhaps unhelpful competition. In a similar way, Ivar Bleiklie helps readers see that a balance between "collegiality" and "hierarchy" in university governance has a long history—a history that can help institutional leaders think creatively to maximize universities' productivity today. The past is a vast repository of alternative conceptions that can be mined usefully (albeit carefully and cautiously) by today's higher-education leaders. Using the past to inform policy choices in the present is the aim of Chen, Shen, and Cai in their chapter on China's "return" to general education. They argue that China's acceptance of a trend based on an American model can be explained only if we see the earlier rise of specialized training—in both China and the West—as a product of industrialization and the subsequent return to general education as a sign of the emergence of a *post*industrial, knowledge-based society.

Each chapter in this volume is borne of the conviction that historians and social scientists have a duty to use analysis of the past to generate clearer understandings of the present, to identify a wider range of policy options, and to help higher-education policymakers anticipate the consequences of their decisions. It does not offer specific roadmaps or recipes for universities to "win" the race for world-class status, nor does it give advice to universities hoping to *become* global. Rather, taken as a whole, it demonstrates that, in the current environment of "the global university," policy ideas are often fragmented, and power is concealed, even from those who wield it. Thus everyone—higher-education leaders, policymakers, stakeholders—adopts the rhetoric of globalization, referring to universities as autonomous businesses, but states still seek to control higher education to serve national interests. Administrators trumpet top-down management structures, with efficiency gains supposedly compensating for the loss of democratic legitimacy, but new forms of "network governance" are undermining those very structures. The organizations that construct global rankings have great influence, but few know what (or where) these rankings organizations are. Power is exercised without reference to formal governance structures and, thus, without explicit claims to legitimacy; claims to academic authority mean less than ever before. Upon inspection, "the global university" seems increasingly rudderless, operating amid chaos and illusion. Only with a broader historical perspective can we hope to achieve clarity of understanding—and then construct more coherent ways forward.

CONTRIBUTORS

Ivar Bleiklie is Professor of Political Science at the Department of Administration and Organization Theory, University of Bergen. He currently directs the ESF-funded project Transformation of Universities in Europe. He has published numerous books and articles on higher education policy and organizational change in the higher education sector. Among his publications are *University Governance: Western European Comparative Perspectives*, Dordrecht: Springer 2009 (ed. with C. Paradeise, E. Reale, and E. Ferlie); *From Governance to Identity*. Dordrecht: Springer 2008 (ed. with Alberto Amaral and Christine Musselin); *Transforming Higher Education. A Comparative Study* (2nd edition), Dordrecht: Springer 2006. (ed. with M. Kogan, M. Bauer, and M. Henkel); *Governing Knowledge: A Study of Continuity and Change in Higher Education*, Dordrecht: Springer 2005 (ed. with Mary Henkel); and *Policy and Practice in Higher Education: Reforming Norwegian Universities*, London and Philadelphia: Jessica Kingsley 2000 (with R. Høstaker and A. Vabø).

Rosemary Deem is currently Dean of History and Social Sciences at Royal Holloway, University of London, Visiting Professor of Education at Bristol University, and Visiting Professor of Management at Leicester University. Until January 2009 she was Professor of Education and Research Director for Faculty of Social Sciences and Law at the University of Bristol. An Academician of the UK Academy of Social Sciences, Rosemary is a sociologist who has also worked at Loughborough, York, the Open and Lancaster Universities, and the former North Staffordshire Polytechnic. At Lancaster University she was Head of the Department of Educational Research (1992–1994), Dean of Social Sciences (1994–1997), and Founding Director of the University Graduate School (1998–2000). She was director of the UK Learning and Teaching Support Network Education Subject Centre ESCalate from 2001 to 2004, a UK Education Research Assessment Exercise panelist in 1996, 2001, and 2008, has twice chaired the British Sociological Association and was Vice-Chair of the Society for Research into Higher Education from 2007 to 2009. From 2001 to 2005 she was joint editor of the Blackwells international journal the *Sociological Review* and is currently on the Editorial Board of *Studies in Higher Education, Equal Opportunities International, Higher Education,* and *Higher Education Quarterly.* She has just completed codirecting (with colleagues from Cardiff Business School) a UK Economic and Social Research Council–funded project on change agents and leadership development in UK public services. Recent publications include (with S. Hillyard and M. Reed, 2007) *Knowledge, Higher Education and the New Managerialism: The Changing Management of UK Universities,* Oxford: Oxford University Press, 2007 (ed. with D. Epstein, R. Boden, F. Rizvi, and S. Wright), *Geographies of Knowledge, Geometries of Power: Higher Education in the 21st Century; World Year Book of Education 2007,* New York: RoutledgeFalmer, 2007.

Bryan Gopaul is a doctoral candidate in the Higher Education program at the Ontario Institute for Studies in Education of the University of Toronto. His doctoral research focuses on the socialization of doctoral students in Engineering and Philosophy. In addition to doctoral education, Gopaul has research interests in the academic profession, critical pedagogy, and the public good of higher education. His authored and co-authored publications can be found in *The Handbook of Engaged Scholarship, Equity and Excellence in Education, Journal of Higher Education Outreach and Engagement, Canadian Journal of Higher Education* and *Academic Matters.* For three years, as a TA Trainer with the Teaching Assistants' Training Program (TATP) at the University of Toronto, he provided workshops about inclusive teaching practices to TAs across the university. Gopaul was a member of numerous departmental and institutional committees and was a graduate student representative for the American Educational Research Association (AERA) as well as for the Graduate Education Council (GEC) of the University of Toronto.

Chen Hongjie is Professor of Higher Education at the Graduate School of Education and Director of the Institute of Higher Education Research at Peking University, P. R. China. He is the Editor-in-Chief of the *Peking University Education Review.* His research concerns the history of higher education, knowledge production and higher education, and quality in graduate education. His publications in these areas include *The Classical German Idea of the university and Its Impact on Chinese Universities* (Chinese version, 2002, second edition 2006), *Between China and Germany: Universities, Scholars, and Communication* (Chinese version, 2010), *A National Report on the Quality of Chinese Doctoral Education* (Chinese version, 2010), *The Quality of the PhD: Concepts, Evaluation, and Trends* (Chinese version, 2010), and *Ideas, Knowledge, and Higher education* (Chinese version, 2011).

Glen A. Jones is the Ontario Research Chair in Postsecondary Education Policy and Measurement and professor of Higher Education at the Ontario Institute for Studies in Education of the University of Toronto. His research focuses on higher education policy, systems, and governance. His publications include *Higher Education in Canada: Different Systems, Different Perspectives* (Garland, New York, 1997, an updated Chinese translation by Professor Rongri Lin was published in 2008); *Governing Higher Education: National Perspectiveson Institutional Governance* (with Alberto Amaral and Beret Karseth, Kluwer, 2002) *Creating Knowledge, Strengthening Nations* (with Patricia McCarney and Michael Skolnik, University of Toronto Press, 2005), and *Canada's Universities Go Global* (with Adrian Shubert and Roopa Desai Trilokekar, Lorimer, 2009). He received the Distinguished Research Award from the Canadian Society for the Study of Higher Education in 2001. Further information on his research and publications can be found at www.glenjones.ca.

Cai Leiluo is Assistant Professor of Higher Education at the Graduate School of Education, Peking University, P. R. China. Her research concerns the history of Chinese higher education between 1917 and 1949 as well as higher education governance.

Peter Maassen is Professor of Higher Education at the University of Oslo. Previously he was director of the Center for Higher Education Policy Studies (CHEPS), University of Twente, the Netherlands. He is the editor of the series Higher Education Dynamics (Springer), and has written and (co)edited more than 100 international publications. His latest work includes a book edited with J. P. Olsen entitled *University Dynamics and European Integration*. Among his main current functions are academic coordinator of the HEEM Erasmus Mundus Master programme in Higher Education; member of the Board of the *Centrum für Hochschulentwicklung* (CHE), Gütersloh, Germany; and member of the Executive Board of the University College Oslo (*Høyskole i Oslo*).

Ka Ho Mok is Chair Professor of Comparative Policy and Associate Vice President, External Relations, of the Hong Kong Institute of Education. He is concurrently Dean of Faculty of Arts and Sciences and Co-Director of Centre of Governance and Citizenship at the Hong Kong Institute of Education (HKIEd). Before joining the HKIEd in 2010, Professor Mok was Associate Dean of Faculty of Social Sciences at the University of Hong Kong and Founding Director and Chair Professor of Centre for East Asian Studies, University of Bristol, UK. Professor Mok is no narrow disciplinary specialist but has worked creatively across the academic worlds of sociology, political science, and public and social policy while building up his wide knowledge of China and the region. He has published extensively in the fields of comparative education policy, comparative development and policy studies, and social development in contemporary China and East Asia. In particular, he has contributed to the field of social change and education in a variety of additional ways, not the least of which has been his leadership and entrepreneurial approach to the organization of the field. His membership on numerous editorial boards, commissions, in key scholarly societies all contribute to the recognition that he is among the best in his field. In the past few years, Professor Mok has also worked closely with the World Bank and UNICEF as International Consultant for comparative development and policy studies projects.

Adam R. Nelson is Professor of Educational Policy Studies and History at the University of Wisconsin-Madison. He received his PhD from the Department of History at Brown University. His chief publications include *Education and Democracy: The Meaning of Alexander Meiklejohn, 1872–1964* (University of Wisconsin Press, 2001); *The Elusive Ideal: Equal Educational Opportunity and the Federal Role in Boston's Public Schools* (University of Chicago Press, 2005); and *Education and the Culture of Print in Modern America*, coedited with John L. Rudolph (forthcoming, University of Wisconsin Press, 2009). He is currently working on a book entitled *Empire of Knowledge: Nationalism, Internationalism, and Scholarship in the Early American Republic*. His research has been funded by grants from the Charles Warren Center for the Study of American History at Harvard, the National Endowment for the Humanities (NEH), the National Academy of Education/Spencer Postdoctoral Fellowship Program, the Advanced Studies Fellowship Program at Brown, and the Vilas Associate Program at the University of Wisconsin-Madison.

Xue Shan is a doctoral candidate in the College of Education at Zhejiang University, P. R. China. Her research interests include educational policy, the internationalization of higher education, and the management of universities. Her doctoral research focuses on the internationalization strategy of the universities from the perspective of the Resource-based View.

John Taylor has over 20 years of experience as a senior manager in higher education, working at the Universities of Leeds, Sheffield, and Southampton before moving into an academic career. As Director of Planning at the University of Southampton he was responsible for all aspects of strategic and operational planning, as well as management information and resource allocation. He played a central role in the analysis of national and international trends in higher education and in developing university strategy in key policy areas such as selectivity in research, broadening access, lifelong learning and diversification of funding. He is particularly known for the development of research strategy that helped to elevate the University of Southampton to its present position among the leading research universities in the UK. As Director of Planning, he was involved with all the main policy developments in UK higher education. At the University of Southampton, John is Director of the Centre for Higher Education Management and Policy at Southampton (CHEMPaS). Professor Taylor has a wide range of international experience having worked in Australia, South Africa, Croatia, Sweden, Romania, Serbia, Hungary, Portugal, Finland, China, Cyprus, Pakistan, Jamaica, Canada, Uruguay, and the United States.

Ian P. Wei is Senior Lecturer in Medieval European History at the University of Bristol. He works on intellectual culture and the social history of ideas in Western Europe in the twelfth and thirteenth centuries. His published work chiefly explores the role of intellectuals in medieval society, especially the authority and status of the masters of theology at the University of Paris in the late thirteenth century. He also writes about the different ways of knowing developed by learned men and women in various social contexts, and the political and social views that they put forward, especially with regard to money, sex, and politics. Since 2004 he has co-coordinated the "Ideas and Universities" project for the Worldwide Universities Network. In 2009–2010 he was a member of the Institute for Advanced Study at Princeton University.

Anthony R. Welch is Professor of Education, University of Sydney, specializing in education policy, with particular interests in Australia,

East Asia, and Southeast Asia. His current work focuses largely on higher education reforms, an area where he has consulted regional governments and international agencies. A recent Fulbright *New Century* Scholar, he has also been Visiting Professor in Germany, United States, Japan, United Kingdom, Hong Kong, and France. Recent books include *The Professoriate* (2005), *Education, Change and Society* (2007), and *The Dragon and the Tiger Cubs* (on China-ASEAN relations) (2010). His next book is on Southeast Asian higher Education. Professor Welch also directs the nationally funded research project: *The Chinese Knowledge Diaspora*.

Shen Wenqin is Assistant Professor of Higher Education at the Graduate School of Education, Peking University, P. R. China. His research concerns the ideas and institutions of higher education from historical and comparative perspectives, as well as the development of graduate education. He has published many papers in these fields. He has also published the book *The Origin, Development and Modern Transformation of the Western Idea of Liberal Education: A Conceptual History* (2011).

Xu Xiaozhou is Dean and Professor, College of Education, Zhejiang University. He is also Director of the Institute of Innovation Education and Entrepreneurship, the national innovative research base of "Innovation Management and Sustainable Competitiveness." His research focuses on Comparative Education, Education Policy, Higher Education, and Educational Innovation and Entrepreneurship Education. His many books include *Idea and Reality in Higher Education* (China Ocean University Press, 2009); Ka Ho Mok and Xu Xiaozhou: "When China Opens to the World: A Study of Transnational Higher Education in Zhejiang, China," *Asia Pacific Education Review* (2008); *Autonomy and Restriction: Comparative Studies on Policies of Universities* (Zhejiang Education Press, 2007); *Excellence and Efficiency: Studies on Prior Development Strategies of University* (Zhejiang Education Press, 2007); *Changes in Higher Education Policy Series* (which includes six books, ed. with Xu Hui, Zhejiang Education Press, 2007); *Modern Korean Higher Education* (Zhejiang University Press, 2007); *Educational Innovation: Perspectives of internationalization* (ed. with Roberto Giannatelli, Zhejiang University Press, 2006); *History of Foreign Educational Thought (7)* (Hunan Education Press, 2002); and *Studies in the Recent Reforms of Higher Education Structure in the Europe and the United States* (Neimenggu University Press, 1997).